SUSTAINABILITY LEADERSHIP

THEORIES, PARADIGMS, AND PRACTICES FOR EMERGING VALUE-LEADERS

Marco Tavanti, Ph.D.

PLANET
HEALING
PRESS

Chapter 2: CONSCIOUSNESS PARADIGMS: For New Sustainability Mindsets 47

Chapter 3: WELL-BEING DIMENSIONS: For Happiness, Thriving and Prosperity 73

FOREWORD

Sustainable Development is the main engine to enhance human welfare on this planet, today and in the future. It is not just one out of many options. It is the only path to a shared collective future for humanity.

Let me say that:

This book is an extraordinary guide to understanding the various sustainability and leadership-related paradigms, which will enable such sustainability to bear abundant fruit.

This book gives us an efficient road map to learn and reflect about possible options and priorities for both, developed and developing countries.

This book is an urgent call for action, which may require deep reforms of today's global and local governance systems, including power structures and political systems, as the Achilles Heel of humanity's future.

This book asserts the importance of human consciousness in setting a path to transform existing mindsets and forms of leadership; with leadership as the most important decision variables in shaping our future. (Sustainable Development demands a specific state of collective consciousness so that leaders guide us to a mutually beneficial horizon).

This book demands a major revolution in values, beliefs, habits and attitudes because our societies are very socially fragmented, within an international community often guided by the self-interest of a hand full of powerful countries.

This book embodies an incredible act of generosity in presentation and guidance; this way of sharing will greatly benefit the youth and the new generations to come.

This book is mandatory, not only for high school and university students, but also for governments and community leaders and corporate managers as well.

My first encounter with the theme of Sustainable Development was in the mid 1970s, when I was doing my doctorate degree on resource economics, with a great emphasis on 'institutional economics' (i.e., the relationship among economic and social actors beyond markets). At that time, the substance of our debates on sustainable development was mainly related to: *"the capacity a given economy had to maintain a well-defined level of expected net future benefits, surging from a set of investments and policy interventions"*. In essence, the debate was on *policy design* as much as it was on the *ex-post evaluation* of the real net impacts of those interventions, both over space and time. Sustainability was defined and established in relationship to these inseparable economic effects over space and time. Thus, the supremacy in decision-making was located at the center of the economic reasoning and rational. This is what we call now "economic sustainability", given that social and environmental sustainability came much later, at least, in the way we understand these issues today.

One example, which captured most of my professional attention was the important 'paradox of time frames', where variable "time" was a key determinant of sustainability. Specifically, this paradox showed a situation in which a country, or an international development agency, designed and arranged financing (ex-ante) for a water reservoir project (a big dam), to last for 100 years, while the empirical evidence (ex-post) showed that such projects were only capable to last for 30 years, or less. Parenthetically, these were investments which demanded huge amounts of financial resources (country's foreign debt), while their actual net benefits were far below expectations (i.e., they had a negative rate of return). As a result, many countries ended up with a great deal of foreign debt accumulated! At that time, we stated that *"these investments were not economically sustainable"*.

As an environmental economist, I knew that, in many development interventions, the situation had a lot to do with ecological and environmental causes and conditions (e.g., the demise of a natural forest around the dam, resulting in very high rates of sedimentation, which diminished its capacity and longevity). But, the core of the debate was not directly related to ecology or environment per-se, but to the fundamental issue of how to appropriately optimize the corresponding inter-temporal benefits and costs. The same situation arose in every sector of the economy (e.g., infrastructure, education, health, community development…); naturally, the way to argue the case for sustainability was different, but, with a common concern: the economic return of the investment or policy involved.

I remember the slogan that was put in front of those of us demanding a different approach to sustainable development: i.e., *"a good economic analysis would take care of all aspects of sustainable development"*, mostly understood as addressing negative externalities of all sorts. Thus, attaining sustainability depended mainly on the quality of the economic analysis (and still does!).

Within such a context, a number of fundamental economic considerations became very relevant. For example: (i) the debate around *"the value of the discount rate"* in project evaluation because, at a certain time in the future, higher levels of a discount rates meant that any net benefit became practically irrelevant for decision making; (ii) the definition of proper economic prices, or so-called "shadow prices", to value the benefits and costs of investments and policies to be implemented (several books were written about this, including, for example, the UNIDO Guidelines on Benefit Cost Analysis); (iii) the quantification and valuation of the benefits and costs of projects or policies, which embodied very large amounts of goods and services that were not traded in markets; (iv) the relative "weights" needed to maximize the equity and social impacts of development interventions (i.e., so that the poor people accrue most of the net benefits), and thus, the distinction of financial, economic, and social rate of return (the evaluation and approval of projects based on a social rate of return was short lived); and (v) the creation of surrogate methods for the appraisal of environmental goods and services not traded in the market; i.e., the Travel Cost Method, The Option Demand Method, The Least Cost Method, and the like.

This first bend of sustainable development, with a strong economic intake, branched out into a series of fundamental policy questions that are still relevant today. A prominent one was about the true impact of 'Development Assistance" ("Foreign Aid") into developing countries—whether it was productive or wasted. For example, we debated why development assistance worked well when donors' expatriates were involved directly into the development implementation process, while it did not work well when they left the country. This is, once again, an issue related to the level and the distribution of net benefits over space and time. In this case, sustainable development was linked directly to the role human capital in developing countries.

In spite of the ingrained economic bias, the literature of the 1960s-1980s was very rich in content and scope. To me, it nourished the discussions and philosophical underpinnings of, for example, rural development, basic needs, and some important environmental issues such as desertification and renewable energy; i.e., an extraordinary branch of local and regional economics. Unfortunately, the debate shifted too much and this part of the literature on sustainable development was lost (including the debate on globalization). In my experience, the economic analysis and the underpinnings of sustainability were and are rather poor.

As a result of the pressure exercised by NGOs in the late 1970s and 1980s, most international organizations accepted to add to the economic analysis an Environmental Impact Statement (EIS) and a Social Impact Statement (SIE), subjugated to the economic analysis. This was an attempt to expand the definition of sustainability, recognizing the relative importance of several forms of capital: physical and financial capital, human and social capital, and natural capital.

Following the emphasis on economics, sustainable development became a composite of many forms of capital and their intricate inter-relations. Thus, we witnessed the results of many studies and research, which surfaced at the time, regarding the nature of these inter-relationships (e.g., physical capital and natural capital), and more powerful arguments were developed on environmental sustainability and social sustainability.

During that period, very few investment projects were stopped or rejected as a result of a negative environmental or social impact statement; because, these statements were carried out more ex-post to the economic analysis than ex-ante. In the end, those impact statements did not modify the premises (factor composition) of the initial economic analysis. And, thus, maintaining the 'supremacy' of economic issues, reasoning, and concerns, with respect to the social and environmental ones, which remained as residuals "to be corrected" in some form in the future.

This book demonstrates several decades later, the need for a different form of reasoning and thus, for a different form of leadership and mindset, in order to tip the balance towards a more comprehensive and encompassing way to see the essence of sustainable development. This becomes an essential dimension to knit sustainability with leadership in one single paradigm. The book convinces all of us of their inseparable nature.

Finally, the relative importance of each side of The Sustainability Triangle--*with its three corners: economics, nature and social*--has significantly changed over time. This is very relevant consideration in the selection of (i) a given sustainability and/or leadership paradigm and (ii) an investment or a policy package. It has evolved from a single concentration on the 'economic vertex', to two sides of the triangle: first, to the side of 'economic' and 'social capital'—i.e., *social-capitalism*; and two, to the side of 'economic' and 'natural capital'—i.e., *eco-capitalism*. In the past, lots of good work has surfaced from these two sides of the triangle, with some of the wisdom accumulated being lost.

In the future, all the attention should be concentrated on those paradigms on sustainability and leadership, which focus on the side of 'social capital' and 'natural capital'—i.e., *eco-citizen-rism*. This change in relative importance is not trivial, as behind each side of the sustainability triangle there are people, institutions, communities, incentives, values, power structures, consciousness, etc.; all, establishing a support system to a given choice of paradigm.

Now, the key question becomes: *What paradigm are we going to choose in order to attain our next level of inner and outer development and transformation?*

Alfredo Sfeir-Younis, Ph.D.
Chancellor, Chile
International Association of Educators for World Peace **1**

INTRODUCTION

NEW THINKING FOR NEW LEADERSHIP

The world stands on a precipice, and many of our current leaders need to be equipped or more confident to marshal the resources needed to safeguard both present and future generations. As we journey into an epoch characterized by escalating environmental crises, there's an urgent need to redefine leadership, ensuring it's equipped to navigate these turbulent times. The mounting crises, fueled by climate change and human oversight, serve not just as a grim testament to our planet's vulnerability but also as pressing calls for leadership transformation and renewed frameworks. Leadership can no longer be anchored in dated norms and mere responsive measures; this critical juncture necessitates visionaries who foresee challenges and proactively craft solutions.

Sustainability Leadership: Theories, Paradigms, and Practices for Emerging Value-Leaders presents an immersive exploration into the paradigm shifts needed in our leadership ethos. At its crux, it emphasizes the essentiality of understanding and internalizing the mindset imperative for initiating and executing decisions prioritizing sustainability, resilience, and collective well-being. As the boundaries between man and nature blur and the repercussions of our actions become increasingly evident, the dimensions of leadership must expand to encapsulate holistic thinking, foresight, and an unwavering commitment to planetary stewardship. **1**

This book transcends being a mere template for novel paradigms. Instead, it underscores the urgency for a holistic, systemic, value-anchored, and future-centric decision-making approach surpassing narrow corporate or individual gains. It asks readers to respond to a profound and multi-dimensional call to care. Care for each other, the environment, ethical businesses, and our connected destinies. This is an invitation to rekindle our shared humanity and inherent bond with nature while reigniting our commitment to craft a brighter future for every inhabitant of this world and the generations to come. Within these pages, you'll find theoretical frameworks coupled with pragmatic examples, illustrating leadership shaped by sustainability imperatives and driven by the ideals it advocates. The paradigms explored are more than just theoretical musings; they are actionable blueprints already transforming global organizations. These practices, illustrated here, extend beyond mere financial gains to emphasize a balanced coexistence with the world around us. **2**

As you immerse yourself in these pages, you'll see that this book is more than a rallying cry— it is an invitation to grow, change, and lead with intention and foresight. Whether you're an aspiring leader, an experienced executive, or an aware citizen, this book provides the knowledge and tools to navigate sustainability leadership's complex yet hopeful terrain. Here, you're encouraged to adopt fresh perspectives, innovative paradigms, and revitalized practices.

New Thinking for New Leadership

Our era's unique and unparalleled global challenges demand fresh mindsets, welcoming innovative paradigms, and evolved thinking. Traditional models, typically marked by linear perspectives, short-lived goals, and a human-centric outlook, need reevaluation to address our complex predicaments. As a guiding principle, sustainability urges us to adopt renewed cognitive structures for leadership. These emerging paradigms blend systems thinking, eco-consciousness, and forward-thinking principles—each vital in charting our way forward.

1. Systems Thinking

The Interconnected Web of Reality.

Systems thinking demands an understanding of the interconnected nature of the world. Rather than isolating issues into silos, it encourages leaders to recognize the intricate relationships between various system elements. As we will explore later in the analysis of sustainability leadership mindsets, this holistic perspective is crucial in identifying leverage points, anticipating unintended consequences, and implementing solutions that resonate across the system. For instance, addressing economic inequalities is not just about wealth redistribution; it involves understanding its ties to education, healthcare, access to technology, and even climate change. Systems thinking, therefore, fosters a leadership style that is intricate, adaptable, and comprehensive in its approach. **3**

2. Complex Thinking

A leadership mindset unafraid to face difficulties.

Complex thinking, as a leadership mindset, is an evolution of systems thinking and eco-systems thinking, tailored to confront and resolve the multifaceted, often daunting challenges in sustainability. This approach is characterized by a fearless willingness to face difficulties head-on, particularly those categorized as "wicked problems" – issues that are complex, unpredictable, and resistant to straightforward solutions. Rooted in systems thinking, complex thinking demands an acute awareness of the intricate interconnections within and between systems, whether ecological, economic, or social. It extends the principles of eco-systems thinking by not just recognizing the delicate balance of the natural world but also by understanding the dynamic interplay between human activities and environmental health. Leaders who embrace complex thinking are distinguished by their capacity to integrate diverse perspectives, think strategically over the long term, and innovate within the framework of these vast, interconnected systems. They are adept at navigating the uncertainties and ambiguities inherent in environmental challenges, using adaptive and resilient approaches to devise solutions that are both effective in the present and sustainable for the future.

In essence, complex thinking in sustainability leadership combines the depth of systems and ecosystem thinking with a courageous, proactive stance towards solving the most challenging and intricate issues facing our planet. Unlike linear methods, complex thinking embraces non-linear dynamics, feedback loops, and the co-evolution of human and natural systems. It underscores the importance of long-term planning and the development of learning organizations that are capable of evolving and responding effectively to the ever-changing landscape of sustainability challenges. In essence, complex thinking equips sustainability leaders with the tools to develop comprehensive, innovative solutions that are both environmentally responsible and sustainable for the long haul. **4**

3. Eco Thinking

Harmony with the Nature's Wisdom of Interdependence.

At the core of eco and ecosystems thinking is the profound understanding of the ecological systems' intricate and delicate balances, emphasizing the interdependence and mutual nourishment of all life forms. This mindset encourages leaders to learn from and align with the complex yet harmonious energy transformations and relationships in nature. It's a significant shift from exerting control over the natural world to forming a symbiotic relationship with it. By viewing humanity as an integral part of the larger ecosystem, eco-thinking underscores the importance of every organism and their collective contribution to the planet's equilibrium.

Leaders who adopt this approach prioritize conservation, engage in regenerative practices, and seek inspiration from biomimicry, a design principle that finds innovative solutions by mirroring the wisdom found in nature's time-tested patterns. This perspective is crucial in ensuring that economic growth and technological development are pursued responsibly, not compromising the delicate ecological balances that sustain life on Earth. In essence, ecosystems thinking fosters a leadership approach that deeply respects and works in unison with the Earth's natural rhythms and cycles. **5**

4. Future Thinking

Envisioning Tomorrow's Possibilities Today.

Future thinking in sustainability leadership entails a visionary approach, where leaders are tasked with looking beyond the immediate horizon to the long-term future, pondering the kind of legacy they wish to leave for the coming generations. It's a commitment to the long-term well-being of both the planet and its inhabitants, ensuring that the decisions and actions of today do not compromise the ability of future generations to meet their own needs. By incorporating future scenarios, simulations, and forecasting into their strategic planning, leaders can anticipate changes and potential challenges, adopting a forward-thinking mindset that allows for adaptation and growth.

This methodical approach to envisioning tomorrow's possibilities today ensures that decisions are made with a comprehensive understanding of their long-term impact, promoting sustainability as a core value. Through this lens, leaders evaluate the sustainability of resources, the resilience of ecosystems, and the well-being of future societies. By doing so, they aim to create an enduring foundation for prosperity that respects environmental limits and social equity, ensuring that future generations inherit a world that is not just survivable but one in which they can flourish and continue to innovate for a better future. **6**

5. Executive Thinking

Translating Ambitious Visions into Possible Realities.

Executive thinking within the context of sustainability leadership is a dynamic and pragmatic mindset that extends beyond mere adherence to principles and values in theory; it's about the tangible translation of visionary ideas into concrete actions. Executive capacity is a critical facet of effective leadership, especially for those championing sustainability solutions. It's not just about acknowledging the importance of sustainable practices; it's about cultivating the necessary executive competencies to actualize these practices within an organization and extend their influence outward. This level of thinking involves a deep understanding of how to operationalize principles into strategic actions, ensuring that the ideals of sustainability are embedded in the very fabric of organizational operations and culture. Leaders with this capacity are adept at translating sustainability goals into tangible outcomes, leveraging their leadership skills to drive systemic change and inspire collective action that resonates beyond the confines of their immediate environment.

This executive approach is intricately connected to visionary competencies. It requires foresight to identify sustainable opportunities and threats long before they become obvious to others. Such leaders are proficient in interpreting global trends and local demands, translating them into strategic imperatives that align with the overarching vision of sustainability. **7**

5

The ability to move seamlessly between innovation, agility, negotiation, and stakeholder engagement is critical. It allows leaders to turn sustainability visions into reality by fostering a culture of continuous improvement and innovation. **8** Their agility ensures that the organization remains resilient despite environmental and market fluctuations. Through negotiation, they balance competing interests, integrating sustainability into the core of business practices and public policy. Finally, stakeholder engagement is what turns a vision into a collective mission, galvanizing action across different sectors and communities.

An executive thinker in sustainability leadership sees the bigger picture—a vision transcending individual and organizational ambitions. This vision encompasses a sustainable future for the planet and all its inhabitants, recognizing that the well-being of the environment is inextricably linked to the prosperity of humanity. Through a blend of strategic action, collaborative effort, and a commitment to continuous learning and adaptation, executive thinking in sustainability leadership is about making that grand vision a reality.

The intricate dance of these five cognitive frameworks—systems thinking, complex thinking, eco-thinking, future thinking, and executive thinking—offer a promising blueprint to value leaders who strive for a better world for this and future generations. They show the need for discovering new mindsets in business leadership across sectors and renewed practices for corporations and organizations at various levels for multiple stakeholders. **9**

Sustainability Leadership in a New Era

The emerging complex, systemic priorities of the 21st century are no longer "business as usual." Climatic anomalies, depletion of resources, and social disparities have reached critical levels, and sustainability has become paramount. Gone are the days when businesses could operate in silos, ignoring the ripples they create in the wider environment.

The "Friedman Doctrine," which emphasized maximizing shareholder profits as a business's primary responsibility, is now facing scrutiny in the 21st century. As today's intricate sustainability challenges converge with a heightened global stakeholder awareness, here is a growing demand for businesses to adopt a more integrated approach. This approach must balance profit-making with broader ethical, environmental, and social considerations, recognizing the interconnectedness of economic success, societal well-being, and environmental health.

Today, as global citizens, we are more interconnected and interdependent than ever. The pressing challenges of our time, underscored by the worsening climate crisis and widening social gaps, demand changes in actions and shifts in our thinking. This book on Sustainability Leadership delves deep into this change in thinking, stressing the need for new thinking and urging leaders to embrace novel business practices.

New Thinking for New Mindsets

Traditional business mindsets, primarily centered on profit-making, need to evolve. As the world grapples with the consequences of unchecked growth and over-consumption, the call for a sustainable mindset has never been louder. This is not about incremental adjustments or superficial corporate social responsibility (CSR) initiatives but a fundamental re-evaluation of how businesses perceive their role in the larger societal and ecological context. Sustainability leadership requires understanding that businesses are not merely economic entities but integral parts of a more extensive socio-ecological system.

The next step in this evolution is the adoption of a regenerative mindset. This approach goes beyond resilience and sustainability, focusing on creating systems that restore and rejuvenate rather than merely maintaining the status quo. Regenerative business practices aim to positively impact the environment, society, and the economy, recognizing that these elements are interconnected and dependent on each other. Leaders embracing this mindset are committed to innovation and practices that contribute to healing the planet and fostering societal well-being. This requires a paradigm shift from extraction and exploitation to restoration and renewal. It's a transformative approach where the success of a business is measured not just by its financial performance but by its contribution to the regenerative capacity of our world. **10**

New Practices Beyond Profit to Purpose

As stakeholders from around the globe demand transparency, responsibility, and meaningful impact, there is a burgeoning need for novel business and organizational practices that transcend mere profit. Embracing a "Beyond Profit to Purpose" paradigm is not just altruistic but imperative. This new era calls for organizations to embed purpose into their core, fostering an environment where profits are harmoniously intertwined with broader societal and environmental well-being. Here are three of these prominent dynamics that make a case for new "purpose-driven" business and organizational practices:

1. **Global Social Responsibility:** No longer can businesses ignore the broader social impacts of their operations. Leaders must acknowledge and address social inequalities, ensure fair wages, promote diversity and inclusion, and contribute to improving communities. The age of responsible capitalism is here, and businesses are being evaluated not just by their financial health but by their commitment to social upliftment.

2. **Eco-environmental Circularity:** The linear "take, make, dispose" model is neither viable nor responsible. Companies must transition to circular models where resources are continually reused, recycled, and regenerated. This does not just minimize environmental harm but also uncovers new opportunities for innovation and growth in the realm of sustainable solutions.

3. **Prosperity and Well-being Purposes:** The final measure of a business's success is no longer limited to its balance sheet. Increasingly, companies are being assessed based on their contribution to the holistic well-being of society. This includes creating jobs, offering products or services that enhance the quality of life, and operating in a manner that prioritizes all stakeholder's mental and physical health.

This book makes the case for embracing these new paradigms and articulates the implication of "sustainability leadership" in theories and practices. This is not just another book on green practices or corporate social responsibility. It is a clarion call for business leaders to step up and spearhead the change the world so desperately needs. It is an invitation to lay the foundation for a future where businesses do not just thrive but also enable the planet and its people to flourish.

Furthermore, "Sustainability Leadership" transcends beyond just conceptual frameworks; it invites readers into a transformative journey of leadership development and personal and professional evolution. As we transition into an era of heightened global challenges, the ability to adapt, learn, and listen becomes invaluable. This book emphasizes the importance of embracing fresh perspectives and diverse contexts, not just as a response to immediate crises but as a continuous process of growth and understanding. Readers are encouraged to leave the world better than they found it and equip future generations with the knowledge, empathy, and tools they need to tackle their unique challenges. This work underscores the convergence of sustainability with leadership, urging every reader to become an agent of impactful change within their spheres and in the broader global community.

Organization of the Book

This book, structured in two comprehensive parts, provides readers with a profound grasp of the subject, charting a course through its theoretical underpinnings and practical manifestations.

Part I: Theories and Paradigms delves deep into the conceptual bedrock of sustainability leadership. Here, the conversation initiates with "Shared Values," exploring how "sustainability leadership" relates to the many existing leadership theories. As we progress, the "Consciousness Paradigms" chapter unravels the cognitive and mindset shifts required to embrace sustainability. With "Well-being Dimensions," we scrutinize the symbiotic relationship between leadership, society, and holistic health. "Resilient Adaptations" then steers the discussion towards the malleability and adaptability inherent to visionary leadership in turbulent times. The section culminates with "Stewardship as Care," emphasizing the intrinsic responsibility of leaders to guard and nurture the resources and communities under their guidance.

Transitioning to Part II: Practices and Applications, the book shifts its lens to the tangible aspects of sustainability leadership, echoing the 5Ps model of the SDGs. Each chapter in this section is dedicated to an element vital to sustainability: "Purpose: Caring for Principles" underscores the essence of a moral foundation in guiding sustainable actions. "People: Caring for Community" emphasizes the imperative of placing societal well-being at the core of leadership decisions. "Planet: Caring for Our Environment" articulates the intricacies of eco-centric leadership, advocating for harmonious coexistence. In "Peace: Caring for Human Rights," the narrative pivots to the promotion of justice, equity, and the safeguarding of rights as central tenets of sustainable leadership. "Prosperity: Caring for Good Business" champions the cause of businesses that thrive and contribute positively to the world. The book's narrative arc concludes with a holistic look at the need to work across sectors and collaborate in trans-disciplinary perspectives to create effective and impactful "Partnerships". This concluding section emphasizes the power of collaboration and collective action, underscoring the belief that sustainable leadership is not a solitary journey but a collaborative endeavor to face the "wicked (complex) problems" of our time.

As you journey through this book, you'll encounter a mix of established theories, evolving paradigms, and practical takeaways, each playing a pivotal role in guiding you toward a deeper grasp of sustainability leadership. The extensive citations from seminal works in the field provide avenues for further exploration and understanding of these dynamics. The different examples of pioneering companies and leaders championing the tenets of sustainability leadership underscore that this is not a fleeting trend but an indispensable trajectory toward a shared and brighter future for everyone.

PART I

THEORIES
AND
PARADIGMS

CHAPTER I

SHARED VALUES

ACROSS LEADERSHIP THEORIES

Overview

The chapter reviews the main leadership theories by analyzing their value contributions, how they reflect the values of the sustainability leadership paradigm, and the complexity and challenges of sustainability practice. We delve into the heart and spotlight the contributions of twenty main leadership theories and their foundational values and contributions to the emerging sustainability leadership paradigm. This chapter delves into the intrinsic role of values in leadership. Leadership is presented by directing, influencing, and cultivating a strong foundation built on ethics, morals, and beliefs. By placing "values" at the heart of leadership, one can inspire, guide, and nurture teams and organizations toward an ethically sound and socially responsible common vision.

Leadership Theories & Sustainability Values

In the quest to address sustainability challenges, various leadership theories offer distinct values and implications that can enrich and guide sustainability practices. With its vast scope encompassing environmental, social, and economic dimensions, sustainability requires a nuanced and diverse approach that multiple leadership paradigms can inform. For instance, while transactional leadership may provide clarity and structure through its reward-penalty mechanism, driving immediate action toward sustainability goals, transformational leadership can inspire and mobilize individuals to look beyond immediate tasks and envision a sustainable future. Similarly, with its adaptive nature, situational leadership can guide leaders to respond flexibly to the diverse and evolving challenges of sustainability initiatives.

The multifaceted nature of sustainability demands a broad toolkit of leadership strategies. Using one strategy is not enough. Instead, using a composite approach, drawing from the strengths and values of various leadership theories, provides a richer, more holistic framework for driving sustainability initiatives effectively. Here, we consider the contributions to sustainability practices as values. **1** By recognizing and integrating each theory's value contributions, leaders can navigate the intricate landscape of sustainability with greater agility, vision, and effectiveness. We, therefore, use the term "shared values" to signify the values contributed by various leadership theories, styles, and perspectives. **2**

Here is why:

1. The Multifaceted Nature of Sustainability Challenges: Sustainability challenges range from climate change and loss of biodiversity to social inequalities and economic disparities. Each challenge requires a unique set of skills, approaches, and perspectives to address effectively. For instance, while an autocratic style may effectively implement urgent climate mitigation strategies, inclusive or democratic leadership might better address social inequalities by ensuring diverse voices are heard.

2. Historical Contexts and Evolutions: Though they might not have been crafted considering sustainability, past leadership theories contain valuable insights. For instance, the authoritative nature of the Great Man Theory might resonate with the need for visionary sustainability leaders who can drive and inspire change. Similarly, the adaptive leadership model offers tools for navigating the ever-changing terrain of sustainability challenges.

3. Diverse Cultural and Geopolitical Contexts: Sustainability issues manifest differently across various cultures and regions. What is a pressing concern in one area might be less urgent in another. Thus, the leadership approach must be tailored based on cultural values, regional priorities, and local challenges. While a participative leadership style might work in one cultural context, a more directive approach might be needed in another.

4. Need for Collective and Collaborative Action: The shared and post-heroic leadership models emphasize the importance of collective wisdom and action. Given the global nature of many sustainability challenges, collaboration across borders, sectors, and disciplines is essential. No single leader or paradigm can drive this; it requires a collective effort, emphasizing the importance of multiple leadership styles working in tandem.

5. The Interplay of Macro and Micro Perspectives: While macro leadership theories, like systems thinking or quantum leadership, provide a broad overview and approach to sustainability challenges, the micro perspectives, like trait theory or situational leadership, offer insights into individual motivations, behaviors, and actions. Both levels are crucial for holistic sustainability leadership.

In essence, while there are core characteristics that define sustainability leadership – like long-term thinking, ethical grounding, inclusivity, and a systems perspective – the richness of leadership theories, both past and current, offers a repository of tools, strategies, and perspectives. **3** Effective sustainability leaders can fluidly navigate these paradigms, choosing the most relevant aspects to suit the diverse contexts within which they operate. This adaptive and integrative approach ensures a more comprehensive, sensitive, and effective route toward sustainable futures.

The Studies on Leadership for Sustainability

The study of leadership is vast and ever-evolving, with thousands of books on the topic being published each year. This abundance of literature underscores the diversity and depth of thought surrounding leadership. **4** From this expansive library of knowledge emerges many theories and approaches, each presenting its unique perspective and nuances. Given such a vast repository, it is a formidable task to sift through every leadership approach. However, a deeper look into the primary leadership theories can provide invaluable insights into how they intersect with and inform the idea of sustainability leadership.

Sustainability, encompassing various environmental, social, and economic considerations, demands an intricate understanding and a versatile approach. This is where the various leadership theories come into play. For instance, while transactional leadership, with its clear reward-penalty mechanisms, can instill a sense of discipline and immediate accountability in sustainability practices, transformational leadership can galvanize entire organizations, inspiring them to transcend individual or short-term gains in favor of a broader, sustainable vision. Then there is situational leadership, which emphasizes adaptability, enabling leaders to respond to the challenges effectively and evolving scenarios that sustainability initiatives often present.

The essence of this discussion is to highlight that sustainability, given its multifaceted nature, requires an integrative leadership approach. No singular leadership model can capture the comprehensive demands of sustainable practices. Rather, by synthesizing insights from various leadership theories, leaders can construct a robust framework for navigating the complexities of sustainability. The richness of the leadership discourse, reflected in the thousands of books and studies available, offers a treasure trove of strategies, perspectives, and tools that can be harnessed to drive impactful sustainability leadership.

Let us delve into what the main leadership theories bring to sustainability leadership.

Trait (Great Man) Leadership and Sustainability

The Trait Leadership Theory posits that specific inherent qualities predispose certain individuals to be effective leaders. They come from Thomas Carlyle's "great man" theory **5**, which suggested that the inherent characteristics of notable figures shaped history; this approach emphasizes the innate attributes of leaders. Within sustainability leadership, there's value in recognizing that certain traits—like foresight, empathy, and resilience—can bolster sustainable initiatives. Leaders naturally inclined towards these traits might more readily envision long-term environmental consequences, connect deeply with impacted communities, or remain undeterred when sustainable endeavors meet obstacles. Specifically, as highlighted by the great man theory, the charisma inherent in some individuals could be a potent tool for rallying and motivating teams or entire organizations toward sustainable initiatives. When applied to modern sustainability challenges, this theory suggests that while leadership traits can be cultivated, some leaders might possess an intrinsic advantage in championing sustainability causes due to their innate characteristics.

Skills (Development) Leadership and Sustainability

The Skills Approach to leadership shifts the focus from innate traits to cultivating and developing specific leadership skills. Rooted in Robert Katz's **6** three-skill framework—comprising technical, human, and conceptual skills—this perspective underscores that these abilities can be nurtured over time, allowing leaders to evolve and adapt. In the realm of sustainability leadership:

- **Technical skills** empower leaders to understand, evaluate, and implement advanced sustainable technologies and practices. This hands-on skill set ensures leaders can effectively introduce and oversee green initiatives, understanding their intricacies and requirements.

- **Human skills** emphasize interpersonal relationships, which are essential for rallying teams and stakeholders behind sustainability goals. Effective communication, empathy, and conflict resolution all play a pivotal role in achieving consensus and fostering a culture of sustainability within organizations.

- **Conceptual skills** allow leaders to visualize the broader picture, integrating sustainability into the very fabric of organizational strategy. Leaders with strong conceptual abilities can identify long-term sustainability trends, forecast potential challenges, and weave sustainable thinking into the organization's strategic blueprint.

Given the multifaceted challenges of sustainability, leaders across all tiers of an organization—from top-level executives to middle managers and supervisors—benefit from honing these three skill sets. By emphasizing their development, organizations ensure a robust, comprehensive approach to sustainability leadership rooted in vision and actionable skills.

Behavioral (Style) Leadership and Sustainability

Behavioral theories of leadership revolve around the premise that effective leadership results from learned behaviors rather than innate traits. Such theories accentuate that individuals can drive sustainable outcomes by adopting specific leadership behaviors. The foundational styles posited by Blake and McCanse—paternalistic and opportunistic—highlight diverse ways leaders can nurture or exploit sustainability objectives, respectively. [7]

- **Autocratic leaders** with their command-centric approach can swiftly institute and enforce sustainable protocols, ensuring rapid alignment with sustainability goals.

- **Democratic leaders** value participation, fostering a culture of collective decision-making. This inclusive approach can be invaluable in sustainability initiatives, as it harnesses diverse insights to shape robust, well-rounded green strategies.

- **Laissez-faire leaders**, through their hands-off approach, empower teams to innovate and drive sustainable solutions organically, drawing from grassroots insights and enthusiasm.

- **People-oriented leaders** focus on fostering strong interpersonal relationships, which is essential in building a unified team passionate about sustainability.

- **Task-oriented leaders** prioritize goal accomplishment, aligning tasks and objectives directly with sustainability milestones, ensuring tangible progress.

Pioneering research from the Michigan and Ohio State Leadership Studies further dissected leadership behaviors, deepening our understanding of how leaders act and interact. [8] These insights are particularly critical in sustainability, where diverse challenges require a spectrum of leadership behaviors.

Leadership styles, rooted in the behavioral approach, represent a leader's distinct methods to guide, motivate, and inspire their teams. Each style's essence, molded by factors like experiences, values, and skills, brings unique value to sustainability leadership:

- **Directive leadership** offers clear guidance, essential in navigating the complexities of sustainability initiatives.

- **Supportive leadership** nurtures a culture of trust and empathy, fostering commitment to sustainability objectives.

- **Participative leadership** champions collective decision-making, integrating diverse perspectives to shape comprehensive sustainability strategies.

- **Achievement-oriented leadership** drives teams towards sustainability excellence, continually raising the bar and inspiring innovation.

In the broader business context, the salient leadership styles—Autocratic, Democratic, Laissez-faire, and Transformational (see below)—offer distinct contributions to sustainability. [9] Whether through decisive action, collective creativity, empowering autonomy, or visionary inspiration, these styles reflect the diverse facets of effective sustainability leadership.

Contextual (Situational & Contingency) Leadership and Sustainability

Contextual perspectives, including situational and contingency leadership theories, highlight the dynamic interplay between leaders and their surrounding environment. At its core, this perspective underscores that leadership effectiveness hinges on aptly responding to the nuances of a given context.

- **Situational Leadership Theory:** Rooted in the Hersey-Blanchard Situational Leadership model, **10** this approach posits that leaders need to fluidly adapt their style based on the specific demands of a situation, especially considering the competency and commitment of their team members. This agility is paramount in sustainability as sustainability challenges range from regulatory intricacies and technological advancements to community engagement and shifting cultural paradigms; more than a one-size-fits-all leadership approach is needed. Situational leaders with this adaptive mindset are adept at recalibrating their strategies to address diverse sustainability challenges. Their proactive nature ensures that sustainability endeavors are responsive to current demands and geared toward future needs, making a blend of reactivity and visionary foresight.

- **Contingency Leadership Theory:** This approach delves deeper into the alignment between leadership styles and situational difficulties. While situational leaders modify their style per context, there might be situations that necessitate entirely different leaders. **11** This is particularly resonant in sustainability contexts, given the multifaceted nature of sustainable challenges. For instance, navigating stringent environmental regulations might require a leader well-versed in legal frameworks, while championing a company-wide cultural shift towards sustainability might be best helmed by a leader with profound interpersonal and motivational skills. By endorsing a tailored leadership approach, the Contingency Theory bolsters the prospect of achieving sustainable milestones. It advocates for organizations to strategically align their leadership placements with the specific sustainability challenge, ensuring that leadership resources are optimized for maximum impact.

Overall, contextual (situational and contingency) leadership theories bring forth the compelling argument that sustainability leadership necessitates both adaptability in style and strategic alignment with context. These theories provide a framework for navigating sustainability challenges by emphasizing the importance of context-aware leadership practices.

Leader-Follower (Path-Goal & LMX) Leadership and Sustainability

Path-goal leadership theory and Leader-Member Exchange (LMX) theory are both leadership theories that focus on the relationship between a leader and their subordinates.

- **Path-Goal Theory in Sustainability**: Rooted in aligning leadership with a follower's needs, the Path-Goal Theory accentuates the leader's adaptability in clearing barriers and furnishing the requisite direction. Navigating the multifaceted terrains of sustainability, from evolving tech solutions and financial intricacies to regulatory shifts and cultural dynamics, leaders embodying this theory proactively equips their teams with tools, insights, and morale to conquer these challenges. While addressing the immediate hurdles, leaders prioritize empowerment and acknowledgment, linking sustainability deep within the organization's core values. It is about meeting sustainable targets and crafting a workspace where sustainability breathes into every action, decision, and triumph. **12**

- **Leader–Member Exchange (LMX) Theory and Sustainability**: The LMX Theory delves deep into the intricate relationships between leaders and their team members, emphasizing that each bond is distinct, bearing its weight of trust, loyalty, and understanding. LMX emphasizes differential relationships, which can lead to the categorization of "in-groups" (members with whom leaders share a high-quality relationship) and "out-groups" (members with whom the relationship is more distant or formal). **13** However, this theory illuminates a path of personalized leadership and innovation within sustainability. As leaders comprehend each member's unique passions, skills, and concerns, they tailor sustainability roles to align perfectly with individual proficiencies. Whether it is spearheading a green tech initiative or championing ethical supply chains, the personalized approach ensures sustainability efforts resonate on a deeper, more personal level. This heightened rapport cultivated through LMX means that when a leader introduces sustainable objectives or green transitions, the buy-in from the team is profound and genuine. It is a constructive interaction between leader and follower, where sustainability initiatives emerge from a bedrock of trust, collaboration, and mutual aspiration. Instead of a unilateral mandate, sustainability, through the lens of LMX, becomes a collective ambition built on individual strengths and shared visions. **14**

Power-Influence Leadership and Sustainability

The Power-Influence leadership theory delves into how leaders use power and influence to drive their teams toward goals. While power signifies the authority to enforce decisions, influence subtly shapes behaviors and beliefs without overt force. Different leadership styles emerge from the varied interplay of power and influence, each deeply rooted in hierarchical structures or interpersonal relationships.

French and Raven's seminal study in 1959 forms the bedrock of this theory, **15** highlighting five pivotal power sources:

- **Coercive Power**: Rooted in force, this power type nudges individuals into action by threatening negative consequences. In the sustainability context, this power is invoked to ensure adherence to environmental protocols. For instance, potential penalties for not meeting sustainability standards might motivate teams. However, overdependence on this power might stifle true innovation and commitment.

- **Reward Power**: Leaders utilize this power by acknowledging and rewarding sustainable endeavors. Financial incentives or public recognition create a proactive environment where eco-friendly behaviors are consistently celebrated and replicated.

- **Legitimate Power**: This power emerges from an official position or role. Such leaders can mandate sustainability targets, introduce eco-friendly policies, or channel resources to green projects, structurally guiding the organization's sustainability vision.

- **Referent Power**: Drawing from personal charisma and respect, leaders with this power inspire through their actions. By personifying sustainable values, they encourage others not by directives but by forging genuine relationships founded on shared environmental ideals.

- **Expert Power**: Leaders who bring specialized knowledge in sustainability wield this power. Their in-depth understanding of eco-practices, from innovative green technologies to sustainable business models, positions them as invaluable assets, guiding the team through informed decisions.

These power-influence dynamics are further explained by the **Strategic Contingencies Theory (SCT),** which proposes that power often resides with specific organizational subunits or individuals who address pressing challenges or bring distinct skills to the table. **16** In a sustainability lens, a team pioneers waste-reducing technology, for instance, becomes influential. Their expertise becomes central to shaping the organization's green strategy. Such a dynamic emphasizes recognizing diverse strengths within an organization and championing a collaborative, decentralized approach to sustainability leadership.

Transactional (Management) Leadership and Sustainability

Transactional Leadership Theory, emphasizing structured agreements and mutual expectations, is deeply ingrained in the management approach to organizational and societal dynamics. This leadership style offers clarity and direction by setting clear expectations and employing a reward-penalty mechanism. Especially in sustainability, this methodology is invaluable. Clear targets for carbon emissions reduction, waste recycling, or green procurement are set. With the strategic use of rewards, ranging from financial incentives to professional opportunities, organizations foster an environment where eco-friendly practices become second nature to teams.

Conversely, the transactional approach underscores the importance of accountability. Penalties for breaches, such as non-compliance with green standards, emphasize an organization's dedication to its sustainability goals. Feedback is a cornerstone of this leadership style, with regular sessions highlighting accomplishments or guiding recalibrations in the sustainability journey, promoting a culture of ongoing improvement.

While systematic and rigid, transactional leadership offers a pragmatic roadmap for organizations. The clear reward-penalty structure propels short-term sustainability achievements, which, when viewed collectively, contribute to realizing broader environmental visions.

Transformational (Relational) Leadership and Sustainability

Transformational leadership, deeply rooted in relational dynamics, redefines traditional leadership paradigms by emphasizing inspiration, personal growth, and the cultivation of shared visions. Unlike other leadership styles, it transcends routine transactions and tasks to push individuals towards greater collective aspirations. Within the sustainability framework, transformational leaders utilize this inherent charisma to emphasize the interconnectedness of organizational goals with broader societal and environmental aspirations. They do not view sustainability as merely a checklist or an operational goal; for them, it is a shared journey, a collective responsibility that binds every team member to the organization's green mission. **17**

These leaders are agents of change; their enthusiasm and commitment to sustainable practices become compelling within the organization. By painting an evocative picture of a sustainable future, they articulate the broader societal advantages of green initiatives, going beyond immediate organizational gains. The unique strength of transformational leaders lies in their ability to link individual values with overarching sustainability objectives, fostering a sense of personal stake and deep commitment. Their approach ensures every employee sees their role as functional and crucial to the broader environmental mission, making sustainability personal and purpose driven.

Feedback, dialogue, and a culture of continuous learning further bolster the transformational leader's approach to sustainability. They maintain open communication channels, valuing insights from diverse organizational tiers. This inclusivity ensures adaptability in sustainability strategies, addressing real-world challenges and capturing emergent opportunities. By creating an environment where innovative solutions are encouraged and valued, they advance organizational green initiatives and contribute to wider societal shifts toward sustainable practices and values.

Transformational leadership is similar but different from 'transformative" leadership. Transformative leadership is a concept that focuses on driving societal change and addressing systemic issues at a broader level. Unlike transformational leadership, which is centered on inspiring and motivating individuals within an organization to improve performance and achieve extraordinary outcomes, transformative leadership goes beyond organizational boundaries to influence and reshape societal norms and structures. Transformative leaders seek to address root causes of societal issues, such as inequality, injustice, or environmental degradation, aiming for long-term, sustainable changes that benefit the wider community. They use their position and influence to challenge existing paradigms and encourage collective action towards a more equitable and sustainable society. This approach is often associated with social movements, policy changes, and community organizing, as opposed to the more organization-centric focus of transformational leadership. **18**

25

Transformative leadership is highly relevant to sustainabilit leadership because it encompasses a visionary and change-oriented approach that is essential for addressing the complex challenges o sustainability. Transformative leaders inspire and empower others to innovate and pursue new solutions, fostering a culture o collaboration and continuous learning. This leadership style is particularly effective in the context of sustainability, where addressing environmental, social, and economic issues requires systemic change and the ability to navigate uncertainty. By encouraging forward-thinking, adaptability, and a long-term perspective, transformative leaders are crucial in guiding organizations and communities towards sustainable practices and goals. Their ability to drive significant change aligns well with the fundamental principles of sustainability, which include stewardship, responsible resource management, and a commitment to future generations. **19**

Servant (Stewardship) Leadership and Sustainability

Central to the ethos of servant leadership is the concept of "stewardship." Stewardship, the careful and responsible management of something entrusted to one's care, is an essential component of servant leadership and naturally aligns with sustainability principles (we explore this idea later in this book). Servant leaders view their role not merely as managers but as stewards entrusted with the welfare of their teams, the organization, and, by extension, the larger community and environment. This deep sense of responsibility extends beyond immediate needs, considering the long-term impact of decisions and actions. **20**

In the context of sustainability, stewardship means managing resources, both human and environmental, in a manner that ensures their viability and well-being for future generations. With their inherent steward-like approach, servant leaders are attuned to the balance needed between immediate organizational goals and broader, long-term societal and ecological impacts. Their commitment to listening and empathy ensures a holistic perspective, considering the needs of the environment, communities, and future generations. Servant leaders prioritize environmentally responsible, socially equitable, and economically viable practices through this stewardship lens. [21]

The stewardship dimension of servant leadership provides a robust foundation for sustainability. Servant leaders champion sustainable practices by seeing themselves as caretakers of the present and future, ensuring today's decisions do not compromise tomorrow's potential.

Servant leadership is similar to but different from "service leadership," which shares some societal concerns with the notion of stewardship. Service leadership extends its focus beyond organizational confines to societal welfare and the common good, embodying a responsibility toward ethical, social, and environmental concerns. This approach, common in public service and corporate social responsibility, seeks to impact the broader community positively. This extends beyond servant leadership, which focuses on internal dynamics, fostering a culture of trust, empowerment, and empathy, and is particularly effective in human resources and organizational development. Both styles, though distinct, reflect a commitment to serving and stewarding, either on a societal or organizational level and beyond the service economy. [22]

Service leadership and sustainability leadership, while appearing different, converge on a shared goal of creating a more sustainable future. Both leadership styles are centered around considering long-term impacts and prioritizing the welfare of stakeholders. Service leadership, with its focus on societal welfare and the common good, is highly relevant to sustainability leadership due to its alignment with the core principles of sustainability. This leadership style emphasizes ethical decision-making, community engagement, and a long-term perspective, all of which are essential for addressing the complex challenges of sustainability. Service leaders prioritize the broader societal impact, engaging in innovative solutions and empowering communities, which mirrors the sustainability goal of balancing economic, social, and environmental well-being. Their commitment to ethical responsibility and collaborative approaches aids in developing inclusive, effective sustainability strategies, thus ensuring that actions taken today do not compromise the ability of future generations to meet their needs. **23**

Authentic Leadership and Sustainability

Authentic leadership is intrinsically tied to the principles that underpin sustainability. Both concepts emphasize a deep-rooted authenticity, a commitment to the greater good, and the recognition of long-term impacts over short-lived gains. Leaders who embody authentic leadership principles prioritize transparency, integrity, and ethical decision-making, aligning seamlessly with sustainability's core demands. By being self-aware, these leaders understand the profound implications of their choices on the environment, society, and organizational culture. They recognize that for sustainability to be effective, it cannot merely be a tick-box exercise but must be woven deeply into the ethos of an organization.

In his pioneering book on authentic leadership, Bill George, former CEO of Medtronic, proposed a value framework encompassing self-awareness, relational transparency, balanced processing, and a robust moral code, which translates effectively to sustainable practices. Authentic leaders, through relational transparency, can articulate the importance of sustainability goals clearly and honestly, fostering trust. Their commitment to balanced processing ensures that diverse viewpoints, especially those related to environmental and social impacts, are considered in decision-making. Additionally, their unwavering moral foundation aligns perfectly with the ethical considerations vital to sustainability, ensuring decisions that benefit the organization, society, and the environment. **24**

Overall, authentic leadership, emphasizing empathy, effective listening, and emotional intelligence, help make genuine and lasting sustainable change. When leaders are genuine in their commitment, their teams and stakeholders can sense the authenticity, resulting in increased commitment and effort toward achieving sustainability objectives. This integrated approach ensures sustainability becomes more than just a strategy; it becomes a lived value and practice.

Ethical (Virtuous) Leadership and Sustainability

Virtuous or character leadership operates at the intersection of personal integrity and ethical conduct. [25] Central to this leadership style is the unwavering commitment to virtues like honesty, courage, humility, and integrity. In an age where authenticity and transparency are highly prized, these virtues become the bedrock of trusted leadership. While the term 'virtue' is often housed within the broader context of 'ethics,' it merits its distinctive exploration in leadership theories. Virtue leadership emphasizes the importance of character and moral excellence in leaders, advocating for actions and decisions rooted in courage, temperance, and wisdom. It suggests that for organizations to truly thrive, especially in sustainability, their leaders must go beyond ethical considerations and embody virtues that shape their vision, decisions, and interactions. [26]

When applied to sustainability, ethical leadership transforms environmental responsibility from a mere operational task to a moral obligation. Leaders championing this approach not only advocate for sustainable practices but do so with a deep-seated conviction that it is the right thing to do. They view sustainability through a lens of ethical imperatives, positioning it as a core value rather than a peripheral endeavor.

In practical terms, an ethical leader's approach to sustainability is characterized by genuine transparency and a commitment to truth. Such a leader would be forthright about the organization's environmental footprint, transparently communicating achievements and areas needing improvement. There is no room for superficiality or greenwashing; instead, they prioritize genuine efforts, even if they face short-term challenges. Their honesty ensures that stakeholders understand the organization's sustainability journey, whether they are employees, consumers, or investors.

Beyond transparency, the virtues inherent in ethical leadership, such as courage and humility, drive proactive action and continuous improvement. Courageous leaders would tackle significant sustainability challenges head-on, even if solutions require substantial resources or radical shifts in business models. Meanwhile, humility allows them to acknowledge when strategies fall short, learn from mistakes, and seek external expertise or collaboration when needed. This blend of virtues ensures that ethical leadership does not just promote sustainability. Still, it embeds it deeply within organizational culture and ethos, making it an integral aspect of business and societal value creation. **27**

Psychodynamic Leadership and Sustainability

At the heart of the psychodynamic approach to leadership is an intricate understanding of human behavior and the underlying forces that drive it. This leadership style delves deep into an individual's past experiences to uncover the foundational elements that influence their present actions and decisions. **28** Within sustainability, this translates into recognizing and addressing deep-seated beliefs, biases, or patterns that might support or hinder sustainable practices. For instance, a leader with a deep understanding of the psychodynamic approach might recognize that an employee's resistance to new sustainable initiatives could be rooted in past experiences where such changes led to job losses. By acknowledging and addressing these underlying fears, the leader can better facilitate recognizing and accepting sustainability initiatives.

The psychodynamic leadership approach emphasizes personal introspection and the development of self-awareness, both for leaders and followers. This mutual understanding of individual personality types and the historical contexts from which they emerge is pivotal for effective collaboration. The field of leadership development is indeed influenced by psychodynamic theory, which emphasizes the unconscious processes and motivations that shape a leader's behavior. Leaders gain heightened self-awareness by exploring these deep-rooted influences, often stemming from past experiences and inner conflicts. This understanding, in turn, allows for more authentic, effective leadership and improved decision-making. Consequently, many leadership development programs integrate elements of the psychodynamic approach to enhance a leaders' introspection and overall effectiveness. **29**

In sustainability practices, this could mean identifying team members who, due to their past experiences, might be more passionate about certain aspects of sustainability, like water conservation or renewable energy. Leaders can then channel this passion into dedicated project teams or task forces. Conversely, understanding the backgrounds and experiences of those more resistant to sustainable changes can guide leaders in tailoring more effective, personalized communication or training sessions, addressing the root of the hesitation.

Furthermore, sustainability is inherently about long-term thinking and acknowledging the interconnectedness of systems. The psychodynamic approach, which acknowledges the complex web of past experiences influencing current behaviors, parallels this mindset. Leaders employing this method might draw connections between past organizational decisions and their long-term impacts on sustainability, using these insights to inform future strategies. For example, understanding a past decision's detrimental environmental impact might shape a more informed, integrated approach to future projects. Thus, psychodynamic leadership, emphasizing depth, reflection, and understanding the complexities of human behavior, offers invaluable tools for driving sustainability practices rooted in empathy, understanding, and forward-thinking.

Post-Heroic Leadership and Sustainability

The traditional hierarchical leadership models may respond poorly to sustainability complexities in an increasingly interconnected and rapidly changing world. Post-heroic leadership, by its very design, counters this limitation. **30** By emphasizing a distributed and collective leadership structure, it facilitates the pooling of diverse expertise, perspectives, and skills essential for navigating the multifaceted challenges of sustainability. In an organization employing a post-heroic approach, the value of shared knowledge becomes palpable. For instance, insights from ground-level employees, middle management, external partners, and consumers can be invaluable when considering a shift to more sustainable production methods. This collective intelligence approach ensures that sustainability initiatives are well-rounded, feasible, and consider a broad spectrum of potential impacts.

31

Moreover, post-heroic leadership inherently fosters a culture o empowerment, collaboration, and shared responsibility. At its core sustainability requires a collective effort, with each stakeholde playing a part. The post-heroic approach democratizes the leadership space, allowing more individuals to take ownership of sustainability initiatives. This sense of shared responsibility can invigorate teams leading to more proactive identification of sustainable opportunities and solutions. For instance, a distributed leadership model migh encourage different organizational departments to champion thei eco-friendly initiatives, creating positive change throughout the entity.

Lastly, the value of adaptability in post-heroic leadership cannot be overstated, especially in sustainability. The challenges associated with environmental conservation, social responsibility, and economic viability are dynamic and often unpredictable. A singular, top-down leadership approach can react slowly to these changing dynamics However, a post-heroic model can be more agile in decentralized decision-making. Decisions can be made closer to the ground allowing for real-time adjustments in sustainability strategies. This adaptability ensures that organizations remain resilient and responsive, capable of evolving with the ever-changing landscape o sustainability challenges and opportunities.

Adaptive Leadership and Sustainability

In an era marked by swift environmental, social, and economic changes, the essence of adaptive leadership becomes paramount especially when applied to sustainability. Sustainability challenges ranging from emerging ecological threats to evolving governmenta policies, necessitate a leadership style that can pivot with the ebb and flows of these challenges. Adaptive leadership, as conceptualized by Ronald Heifetz and Marty Linsky, emerges as a solution to this dynamic landscape. **31** Central to this leadership approach is acknowledging that while the overarching vision of sustainability remains unchanged, the strategies to achieve it might need continuous refinement. This agility ensures that organizations can swiftly respond to new sustainability data, research findings, or societal demands, ensuring their environmental strategies remain relevant and effective.

Emotional intelligence, organizational justice, development, and character – the four cornerstones of adaptive leadership – are pivotal in bolstering sustainability initiatives. For instance, emotional intelligence aids leaders in comprehending the diverse stakeholder sentiments tied to environmental endeavors, be it employee concerns about new eco-friendly protocols or a community's apprehension about renewable energy installations. By tapping into this emotional compass, adaptive leaders can craft sustainability solutions that resonate on a deeper, more human level. Furthermore, the dimension of leading with empathy enables leaders to prioritize community and stakeholder well-being, ensuring that sustainability actions foster inclusive benefits. Adaptive leaders leverage their penchant for self-correction and reflection when facing challenges like transitioning to sustainable technologies. They anticipate potential roadblocks, such as resistance to new systems or methodologies, and proactively devise mitigation strategies. Their focus on creating win-win solutions ensures smooth sustainability transitions with minimal friction and maximum stakeholder buy-in.

An example of adaptive leadership is a company's transition to renewable energy solutions. Recognizing the imperativeness of this shift for sustainability, adaptive leaders would not just mandate the change but anticipate potential technical and human challenges. They might foresee the need for employee retraining, or the concerns of local communities impacted by establishing a wind farm. Through empathy, reflection, and open dialogue, the leaders would navigate these challenges, ensuring the company's sustainability goals harmoniously with its people's and surrounding communities' well-being. Such an approach solidifies that true sustainability concerns ecological conservation and fostering harmonious stakeholder relationships.

Shared (Team) Leadership and Sustainability

Shared leadership is another paradigm that shifts from the traditional hierarchical model to a more egalitarian distribution of leadership roles. **32** In this construct, leadership is not the exclusive domain of a select few; instead, it is a shared responsibility that permeates the team or organization. This emphasis on collaborative decision-making is pivotal in addressing sustainability challenges. When multiple voices, each equipped with unique perspectives and insights, converge to deliberate on sustainability strategies, the resultant solutions tend to be more comprehensive, resilient, and attuned to diverse stakeholder needs.

Within the sphere of sustainability, shared leadership offers a myriad benefit. For one, decentralizing leadership responsibilities encourages a widespread culture of accountability. Instead of a singular sustainability department or officer driving eco-friendly initiatives, there is a collective force – comprising various departments, teams, and individuals – steering the organization towards its green objectives. This collective approach amplifies the sense of ownership. When team members feel they have a stake in crafting and actualizing sustainability goals, their commitment to these objectives intensifies. They are not merely executing top-down directives but are active participants in sculpting the organization's environmental journey. This heightened engagement can propel more proactive and innovative sustainability initiatives as individuals feel empowered to voice novel ideas and solutions.

Moreover, the essence of shared leadership mirrors sustainability's interdependent and interconnected nature. Just as shared leadership thrives on collaboration and mutual reliance, sustainability is an intricate web of environmental, social, and economic components, each influencing and depending on the other. Thus, organizations that embrace a shared leadership model inadvertently align their operational ethos with the foundational principles of sustainability. By fostering a culture where leadership is a shared journey, and every member's input is valued, organizations amplify their sustainability prowess and fortify their resilience to navigate the complex challenges that the future of sustainability might present.

Complexity (Systems) Leadership and Sustainability

At its core, complexity leadership is rooted in the understanding of systems theory and acknowledges that organizations and their environments are not static entities but dynamic, evolving systems. Such leaders do not merely react to challenges; they anticipate, adapt, and guide their organizations through the intricate dance of interconnected variables that define our modern socio-environmental landscape. 33

The sustainability agenda itself is emblematic of this complex system. Consider, for instance, the challenge of reducing carbon emissions. It is not just about technological innovation in renewable energy; it also involves understanding global economic markets, shifting societal values, regulatory landscapes, and geopolitical dynamics. A complexity leader, recognizing these interdependencies, will be adept at fostering collaboration across different sectors, leveraging the power of diverse stakeholders, and facilitating synergies to drive sustainable outcomes. Their unique perspective enables them to see the 'bigger picture,' ensuring that sustainability initiatives are not just tactical responses, but strategic maneuvers grounded in a deep understanding of systemic dynamics.

Furthermore, complexity leadership recognizes that traditional top-down mandates may fall short in a world of volatility, uncertainty, complexity, and ambiguity (VUCA). Instead, it emphasizes emergent leadership – where innovation and solutions can arise from any part of the organization or system. This means fostering an environment where everyone feels empowered to contribute to the organization's sustainability mission regardless of their role. Complexity leaders drive organizations towards sustainable practices and shape a harmonious future where businesses, societies, and the environment coexist by championing a holistic, systems-based approach.

Complexity and system-thinking leadership imply a strong commitment to collaboration and partnership across organizations, sectors, and disciplines. If we persist with our conventional "siloed" strategies and "competitive" stances, we risk curtailing the very potential for transformative progress we aspire to achieve. It also reflects that the "good company" paradigm is not enough unless embedded into sustainable, collaborative, and systemic approach for corporate global citizenship. **34**

In the quest for global sustainable development, SDG 17 stands out: Partnerships are paramount. As the 2030 Agenda unfolds, it's evident that no nation, developed or developing, can navigate this transformative and complex journey in isolation. This universality demands collaborative action, with sustainability leadership taking center stage. **35**

Inclusive (Diversity) Leadership and Sustainability

Inclusive leadership recognizes that our world's sustainability challenges are multifaceted, often transcending borders, cultures, and disciplines. As we face these global concerns, it is not enough to merely acknowledge the diversity of voices; it is paramount to include and value them in decision-making processes actively. An inclusive leader realizes that for solutions to be truly sustainable, they need to resonate with and be effective for a broad spectrum of stakeholders. These leaders are characterized by their deep-seated self-awareness, continuous curiosity, the courage to confront their biases, vulnerability in acknowledging what they do not know, and genuine empathy. They believe diverse experiences, knowledge, and perspectives bring about richer, more innovative, and comprehensive solutions to complex sustainability issues. **36**

The behaviors exhibited by inclusive leaders underscore their commitment to driving sustainable change. By visibly committing to diversity and inclusion, they set an organizational standard and influence their external ecosystems to adopt similar values. Humility ensures they remain open to learning and pivoting based on diverse inputs. Challenging the status quo, holding others accountable, and personally prioritizing diversity and inclusion are actions that spark systemic changes. In sustainability, such leaders recognize that solutions derived from diverse perspectives are more robust, adaptable, and reflective of the needs of various communities.

In the bigger picture, inclusive leadership is imperative for sustainability in today's interconnected world. Companies and organizations that embrace this style of leadership are more likely to develop sustainability strategies that are holistic, adaptable, and supported by a wide range of stakeholders. When people from diverse backgrounds, experiences, and perspectives come together under an inclusive leader, they can craft solutions that anticipate and address various challenges and opportunities. Such an approach promotes environmental, social, and economic sustainability and champions a more just and equitable world where every voice is valued.

Cross-Cultural (CQ) Leadership and Sustainability

Cross-cultural leadership is crucial in today's globalized world, where sustainability challenges often extend beyond national or regional boundaries. The essence of cross-cultural leadership is not merely about communicating effectively with people from diverse backgrounds but about deeply understanding and respecting diverse perspectives. This ensures that strategies for sustainable practices resonate across cultures, making them more universally effective and inclusive. For instance, while an American leader might prioritize swift decision-making, they can appreciate a Japanese team's emphasis on consensus-driven actions. Hence, cross-cultural leadership bridges these diverse methodologies, enabling more cohesive, adaptable, and effective sustainability initiatives. [37]

Central to effective cross-cultural leadership is Cultural Intelligence (CQ). It goes beyond acknowledging cultural differences and delves into adapting leadership styles based on those nuances. The four components of CQ – CQ Drive, CQ Knowledge, CQ Strategy, and CQ Action – provide a framework for leaders to approach multicultural scenarios with genuine interest, understand cultural influences, think critically about interactions, and adapt behavior to various cultural norms. For instance, a leader with high CQ Action can seamlessly adjust their verbal and non-verbal behaviors to resonate with diverse cultural norms, enhancing the effectiveness of sustainability communication and implementation in diverse settings.

In the broader context of sustainability, cross-cultural leadership armed with CQ is invaluable. Solutions must be universally applicable and adaptable as the world grapples with pressing environmental and societal challenges. Leaders with robust CQ can foster stronger international collaborations, ensuring that sustainability initiatives are not siloed but are comprehensive, drawing from a mosaic of cultural insights. By tailoring sustainability strategies to be culturally sensitive these leaders ensure the effectiveness of these initiatives and promote global unity in the face of shared challenges.

Eco Leadership and Sustainability

At the heart of eco leadership is recognizing the intricate web of connections that constitute our world. This leadership style profoundly anchors itself in the principle of ecological stewardship, placing the health and vitality of the ecosystem at the forefront of decision-making. Unlike conventional leadership approaches that often emphasize productivity and growth from a primarily human-centric viewpoint, eco leadership sees the broader ecological context as pivotal. This means viewing the environment not merely as a stakeholder but as an intrinsic part of the organizational ecosystem. Dr. Simon Western's conceptualization of eco-leadership serves as a call to challenge and redefine traditional organizational purposes. **38** In his vision, success is not solely about business metrics; it also encompasses ecological balance, conservation, and practices that rejuvenate rather than deplete our natural environment. **39**

Eco-leaders help facilitate this transformation in today's businesses. They view organizations as interdependent entities within a larger, interconnected global environment, encouraging the creation of ecosystems that consider both stakeholders and competitors. Their leadership style promotes collaboration, emphasizing networks and cooperative relationships that foster holistic growth. They are proactive, foreseeing challenges like climate change and the limitations of natural resources and steering their organizations toward sustainable solutions. Furthermore, these leaders champion distributed leadership, acknowledging that individual's and team's collective intelligence and potential can drive meaningful change. Empowering implies that their organizations are dynamic and responsive to immediate and future ecological challenges.

The Eco-Leadership Institute formed in 2022 by Dr. Simon Western is a good example of this effort. They offer training in eco-leadership formation and eco-coaching. The institute aims to equip leaders with the skills, mindset, and knowledge necessary to navigate the complexities of our times. As businesses grapple with the pressing need for sustainability, eco leadership emerges as an indispensable paradigm, reframing how we perceive success, value, and organizational purpose in the age of ecological consciousness.

Regenerative (Restorative) Leadership and Sustainability

The paradigm of regenerative sustainability leadership is crucial as it recognizes that preservation of our environment is no longer sufficient. We must shift our focus toward rejuvenating and revitalizing our ecosystems to ensure that our actions today foster a thriving future for all. This approach is characterized by a proactive stance that not only seeks to maintain but actively enhance the natural systems we depend upon, affirming that our choices today can forge a legacy of positive impact for future generations.

The concept of "generation's regeneration" is more than an aspiration; it is a commitment to a shared journey. It signals a transformative approach that every individual can adopt, regardless of their role in society. This ethos provides a framework for actionable solutions to the pressing global emergencies we face, underpinning a movement towards lasting, systemic change. **40**

Regenerative leadership, inspired by regenerative design principles, calls for a holistic approach that learns from nature's resilience. This leadership style transcends traditional "green" practices that focus solely on management or conservation. Instead, it seeks to create systems that are resilient, self-sustaining, and in sync with the natural world. As various sectors begin to embrace regenerative principles, leadership, too, must evolve. The aim is to cultivate systems that are not only sustainable but also capable of renewal and regeneration, mirroring the self-sustaining cycles found in nature. In doing so, we can aspire to a future where our social and environmental systems are not just sustained but invigorated and fortified for generations to come. **41**

Conscious (Quantum) Leadership and Sustainability

Conscious or quantum leadership takes inspiration from the principles of quantum physics, where the universe is understood not as a series of isolated components but as an intricately woven tapestry of interconnected systems and phenomena. This philosophy resonates with sustainability, which, at its core, rests on the understanding that our ecological, social, and economic systems are linked. Such a holistic view compels leaders to make decisions with a broader perspective, considering the ripple effects across various subsystems and recognizing that a shift in one area can have profound implications elsewhere. **42**

At the heart of conscious leadership lies an elevated awareness that transcends traditional managerial paradigms, emphasizing the profound interconnectedness of all systems. This deep consciousness is crucial for sustainability leadership. As conscious leaders are attuned to the delicate balance of our ecological, social, and economic ecosystems, they recognize that every decision has consequences, often in areas not immediately obvious. Their leadership approach is anchored in mindfulness, ensuring that sustainability is not just a box to be checked but is an integral part of the decision-making process, reflecting a genuine commitment to long-term planetary health.

The heightened consciousness in this leadership model makes leaders more receptive to the nuances and complexities inherent in sustainability challenges. They do not just see problems; they perceive the intricate web of causes, effects, and potential solutions. This perception helps them anticipate the cascading implications of their actions, ensuring more comprehensive and lasting solutions. Data or immediate outcomes do not just drive conscious leaders; they are motivated by a deeper sense of purpose, resonating with the ethos of sustainable practices. Their decisions stem from deep introspection and foresight, aiming to harmonize organizational objectives with broader societal and environmental well-being.

Conscious leadership transcends conventional paradigms and embraces a broader, more holistic worldview. It aligns seamlessly with sustainability leadership, which demands a big-picture approach, a keen understanding of interdependencies, and the agility to respond to an ever-shifting landscape. Their consciousness propels them to foster a culture of sustainability throughout the organization, ensuring that every stakeholder, from the boardroom to the grassroots, operates with a shared commitment to a sustainable and harmonious future.

Integrating Values for Leadership Sustainability Practices

Our exploration so far into the different leadership theories, while extended to these 20 theories, is just the beginning. Many current and emerging leadership theories and approaches could be added to this list. Emerging new leadership paradigms and styles need further investigation. Here is a list of additional and emerging leadership perspectives with sustainability value implications:

- **Charismatic Leadership:** Charismatic leaders inspire and energize their followers, which can be pivotal in rallying support for sustainability initiatives and instilling a shared vision for a greener future.

- **Women Leadership:** Women leaders often bring unique perspectives and inclusive approaches to decision-making, which can be instrumental in integrating sustainability values into organizational cultures and policies.

- **Human-centered Leadership:** This approach prioritizes the well-being of employees and stakeholders, aligning with sustainability values by fostering a workplace that values social responsibility and ethical practices.

- **Nature Leadership:** Nature leadership emphasizes learning from and integrating nature's principles, promoting sustainability by advocating for practices that respect and preserve the natural environment.

- **Pacesetting Leadership:** Pacesetters lead by example and set high-performance standards, which can effectively track sustainability goals and foster a culture of excellence in environmental stewardship.

- **Participative/Democratic Leadership:** This leadership style involves team members in decision-making, facilitating a collaborative approach to implementing and innovating sustainable practices.

- **Affiliative Leadership:** Affiliative leaders create emotional bonds and harmony, encouraging a collaborative and supportive workplace that can be conducive to achieving sustainability goals through teamwork.

- **Level 5 Leadership:** Characterized by a blend of humility and professional will, Level 5 leaders are effective in embedding sustainability into the core values and long-term strategies of their organizations.

- **Digital Leadership:** Digital leaders leverage technology to drive change, offering opportunities to use digital tools and platforms to advance sustainability initiatives and engage stakeholders.

- **Narcissistic Leadership:** Although often challenging, narcissistic leaders can sometimes bring a bold vision and drive that, if properly aligned, can advance sustainability agendas.

- **Toxic Leadership:** Typically counterproductive, toxic leadership can nevertheless serve as a cautionary example of practices and attitudes that sustainability-focused organizations should avoid.

- **Crisis Leadership:** Crisis leaders are adept at navigating through turbulent times, a skill crucial for steering organizations towards sustainable practices during environmental or social crises.

- **Change Leadership:** Change leaders are skilled in managing transitions, which is crucial for organizations looking to shift towards more sustainable business models and practices.

- **Appreciative Leadership:** This leadership style focuses on recognizing and building upon the organization's strengths, which can be pivotal in fostering a culture that values and pursues sustainability.

- **Humanistic Leadership:** Humanistic leaders prioritize ethical values and human welfare, aligning closely with sustainability by promoting socially responsible and environmentally sound practices.

- **Evolutionary Leadership:** Evolutionary leaders focus on long-term, systemic change, essential for driving the deep, transformative shifts required for true sustainability in organizations and societies.

With the complexities of sustainability and the rapid evolution of leadership studies, there will be many new areas of further research.

In subsequent sections, we will focus on the multifaceted dimensions of sustainability leadership. At its core, sustainability leadership is rooted in paradigms, principles, and practices. However, its true potency emerges not from the siloed application of a single theory but from a blend of values taken from a spectrum of leadership theories. Understanding a situation's unique challenges and intricacies, these values form the bedrock of impactful sustainability leadership. The 20 leadership models we have studied each offer a distinct lens through which we can view the foundational tenets of sustainability leadership: holistic thinking, all-encompassing decision-making, and the equilibrium of environmental, social, and economic aspirations. Inside real-world challenges, every leadership theory presents a repertoire of strategies, tools, and approaches tailor-made for sustainability initiatives.

Modern leaders, standing at a pivotal juncture, face the challenge of selecting values and leadership styles that will significantly impact communities, organizations, and the planet. Discernment and critical self-reflection are vital for effective sustainability leadership. Understanding various leadership paradigms and styles is crucial in fostering insightful self-reflection. Some additional questions for discernment and self-reflection in shaping a sustainable leadership approach may include:

- How can we ensure our leadership approach actively contributes to environmental stewardship and social responsibility?

- In what ways can our leadership style be a catalyst for sustainable innovation and change within our organization?

- How do we balance short-term organizational goals with the long-term sustainability vision?

- What measures can we take to make our leadership approach more inclusive, considering diverse perspectives in sustainability decisions?

- How can we effectively communicate and embody sustainability values to inspire and motivate our teams?

- In what ways can we leverage our leadership position to advocate for and implement sustainable practices both within and beyond our organization?

- How do we remain agile and responsive to the evolving challenges and opportunities in the sustainability field?

- What strategies can we employ to integrate ethical considerations and sustainability principles into everyday business decisions?

- How do we measure the impact of our leadership on both the organization's sustainability performance and broader societal and environmental well-being?

- In what ways can our personal values and beliefs align with, and enhance, our professional commitment to sustainability leadership?

Reflecting on these questions can guide leaders in integrating sustainability values into their strategic and operational decisions, addressing the complex challenges of our times, and paving the way for a more sustainable and prosperous future.

Key Takeaways: Shared values

1. **Depth of Leadership Theories:** This chapter extensively reviews 20 main leadership theories, illuminating their foundational values and alignment with the sustainability leadership paradigm. This showcases the depth and diversity of thought within leadership studies.

2. **Central Role of Values:** Leadership transcends mere direction and influence. The chapter underscores the importance of integrating ethics, morals, and beliefs as central tenets, implying that true leadership is value-driven at its core.

3. **Complex Challenges of Sustainability:** Leadership theories are not just theoretical constructs; they have practical implications, especially in navigating the multifaceted challenges of sustainability. This chapter highlights the interplay between these theories and real-world sustainability issues.

4. **Integration of Sustainability Values:** The chapter has provided an overview of the interconnection of leadership theories with sustainability values and explored how traditional and emerging leadership models can be reconciled and integrated with sustainability values, bridging conventional leadership principles with modern sustainability demands.

5. **Actionable Insights from Studies:** The review of leadership studies offers empirical sustainability leadership insights, drawing from various research efforts on the subject, to provide a grounded understanding of how leadership and sustainability intersect in the real world. This sets the stage for integrating these values into leadership sustainability practices, where theory meets practice, offering actionable guidelines for leaders to adopt and implement.

CHAPTER 2

CONSCIOUSNESS PARADIGMS

FOR NEW SUSTAINABILITY MINDSETS

Overview

This chapter focuses on the interplay between sustainability and consciousness, emphasizing that sustainable thinking transcends mere environmental actions to represent an elevated awareness of our long-term influence on the planet. Through sections ranging from the role of sustainability in leadership and the essence of conscious leadership for sustainability to real-world examples of leaders who epitomize these principles, we explore the consciousness paradigms of sustainability leadership. We investigate the nuances of leading with mindfulness, the intrinsic bond between consciousness and sustainability, and the evolution from sustainability mindsets to conscious leadership. We conclude with a forward-looking perspective, the chapter presents conscious sustainability leadership as the beacon for a brighter, more sustainable future.

Sustainability as a Leadership Mindset

Sustainability is a term that has increasingly entered the lexicon of businesses, governments, and societies at large. However, a prevailing misconception equates sustainability strictly with environmental conservation ("green") or long-term financial viability. Such narrowed interpretations can obscure the multi-faceted nature of sustainability, which goes well beyond these dimensions. To genuinely understand sustainability in leadership, it's important to recognize its holistic breadth and depth, encompassing diverse aspects from ecological responsibility to emotional and spiritual intelligence.

The concept of "The Sustainability Mindset" offers a comprehensive framework to elucidate this. As defined, it is "a way of thinking and being that comes from a broad understanding of the ecosystem's manifestations, from social sensitivity, as well as an introspective focus on one's personal values and higher self and finds its expression in actions for the greater good of the whole." **1**

Dr. Isabel Rimanoczy's sustainability mindset model is a comprehensive framework encompassing a multifaceted approach to understanding sustainability. This model combines cognitive, emotional, and spiritual dimensions into a comprehensive approach to sustainability. Instead of treating sustainability as a series of boxes to check or targets to achieve, it positions sustainability as a mindset—a deep-seated conviction rooted in a broader understanding of the world and our place. It combines various dimensions of thinking, feeling, and being in the world to create a holistic view of sustainable leadership. It includes four content areas and twelve principles distributed across these main content areas.

Ecological Worldview

This is not just about understanding the tangible state of our planet, but it also taps into our emotional, psychological, and spiritual responses to the environment. Individuals can foster a deeper connection to and responsibility for the environment by integrating emotions with ecological facts. This first area includes two principles:

> **1. Eco literacy:** This principle highlights the importance of understanding our planet's challenges, comprehending its interrelated complexities, and forming an emotional bond. It urges individuals to move beyond data and connect with our world's broader representation.

2. My Contribution: We can take proactive steps toward rectification by realizing and acknowledging our roles in contributing to environmental and social problems. This principle emphasizes personal responsibility and accountability.

Systems Perspective

Rooted in the idea that everything is interconnected, this approach challenges traditional linear thinking, often dominating our decision-making processes. By understanding the intricate web of relationships and causations in systems, leaders and organizations can make more holistic decisions, considering long-term impacts and wider repercussions. Here, the spotlight is on the impacts of decisions in the immediate future and the long run. Sustainable actions need foresight, considering implications that resonate across time and space. This area includes four principles:

3. Long-term Thinking: Here, the spotlight is on the impacts of decisions in the immediate future and the long run. Sustainable actions need foresight, considering implications that resonate across time and space.

4. Both and Thinking: This idea challenges binary thought processes. It promotes solutions that are inclusive of all stakeholders, valuing diversity and multiple perspectives. Such an approach is key to fostering harmonious societies and ecosystems.

5. Cyclical Flow: Mirroring the cyclical processes of nature, this principle stresses the importance of understanding and respecting natural cycles. It prompts individuals to see themselves as part of nature, governed by its inexorable laws.

6. Interconnectedness: Recognizing the innate interconnected nature of all things ensures more inclusive and holistic decisions. This principle asserts that while we are all distinct, we are part of a larger whole.

49

Emotional Intelligence

Beyond standard intelligence metrics, emotional intelligence emphasizes the importance of introspection, empathy, and understanding oneself and others. In the context of sustainability, i pushes individuals and organizations to consider the human element of every decision, ensuring that actions taken are compassionate, fair and just. This area includes three principles:

7. Creative Innovation: Encouraging the incorporation of non-rational wisdom alongside rational thought, this principle highlights the importance of intuition, creativity, and imagination in crafting sustainable solutions.

8. Reflection: In a world driven by speed and efficiency, pausing to reflect can be revolutionary. This principle promotes slowing down, taking a step back, and contemplating the broader implications of our actions.

9. Self-awareness: By deeply understanding our values, beliefs, and motivations, we gain the power to control and redirect our actions toward sustainability. This principle encourages introspection and self-scrutiny.

Spiritual Intelligence

This transcends religious connotations and dives into questions of existence, purpose, and interconnectedness. Sustainability reminds us that we are a part of a larger whole and that our actions have spiritual and existential implications, not just material ones. This content area grounds the individual in understanding the current state of our planet both intellectually and emotionally. It delves into profound existential inquiries about our place and purpose in the universe. This last area of the sustainability mindset includes three principles:

10. Oneness with Nature: Recognizing and feeling our intrinsic connection with nature can profoundly shape our behaviors. This principle promotes a harmonious relationship with all beings, fostering a spiritual bond with the universe.

11. Purpose: A clear, value-driven purpose can guide our actions and decisions. We contribute positively to the world by grounding our purpose in higher values. This principle emphasizes being fully present, compassion, and a deep connection with the universe.

12. Mindfulness: Cultivating mindfulness can significantly enhance awareness, compassion, and our predisposition toward positive environmental and social actions. This principle calls for an active connection with the greater good.

Dr. Rimanoczy's sustainability mindset model is a powerful tool for helping make a paradigm shift. It pushes individuals and organizations to transcend traditional boundaries by incorporating emotional, systemic, ecological, and spiritual perspectives into a unified worldview. This all-encompassing approach doesn't just deepen our understanding of sustainability; it reshapes our interaction and existence within the world.

Embracing this sustainability-focused mindset equips leaders with the tools and perspective to address broader societal challenges and effect lasting, positive change. Leadership actions and a foundational commitment to ecological harmony, social equity, and the holistic welfare of communities and ecosystems characterize such a mindset. This leadership approach necessitates a particular brand of stewardship that cultivates an organizational ethos of sustainability. Leaders with this mindset are attuned to global socio-environmental concerns and prioritize the greater good. They include moral responsibility and genuine care into their strategic choices. By fostering and championing this sustainability mindset, leaders create a way for a hopeful, equitable, and thriving future for all.

Conscious Leadership for Sustainability

Conscious leadership is a leadership paradigm that emphasizes the power of collective genius and individual energies. It also approaches leadership with a level of consciousness that pulls from the "inner elder" aspect of our being and less on the "outer ego."

Conscious leadership, firmly anchored in acknowledging, galvanizing, and leveraging individuals' collective talents and vigor, signifies a transformative departure from conventional leadership approaches. Unlike traditional methods that often revolve around top-down decision-making and hierarchical power dynamics, conscious leadership emphasizes collaboration, holistic understanding, and tapping into the innate potential of every team member. This approach fosters an environment where everyone feels valued, their insights are sought, and their energies are directed toward a unified purpose. By embracing such a leadership style, organizations nurture personal growth among their members and cultivate innovative ideas and solutions that emerge from diverse perspectives. In essence, conscious leadership transcends old paradigms, introducing a more inclusive, empowered, and interconnected way of leading.

Conscious Leadership: Elevating Humanity Through Business written by John Mackey and his coauthors explains what it means to lead with true consciousness. Having already written about *Conscious Capitalism,* where he transformed the food industry with Whole Foods. Mackey's journey has symbolized the power of principle and purpose-driven entrepreneurship. He illustrates "conscious" leadership examples describing visionary thinking, virtues, and mindset supporting this leadership style. **2**

Attributes of Conscious Leaders for Sustainability

In his award-winning book *Developing the Conscious Leadership Mindset for the 21st Century* Jeffrey Deckman explains this leadership approach. **3** In a *Forbes* article, he summarizes the need for this approach by tapping into the profound wisdom of the "inner elder" within us rather than being dominated by the "outer ego." **4** He further outlines five attributes that he believes are consistently evident in every conscious leader. These leaders manifest as a tribal elder, a steward, a navigator, a facilitator, and a healer.

1. **The Elder:** A conscious leader epitomizes the essence of a tribal elder. Such leaders transcend personal aspirations for power or riches, focusing instead on the collective well-being of their tribe. They operate from a heightened consciousness

by embracing attributes like wisdom, patience, and discipline. Their tools aren't coercion or dominance but fairness, integrity, and a genuine respect for others. The true markers of their success are the health, safety, happiness, and prosperity of every "tribe" member.

In the context of sustainability leadership, the Elder represents the timeless wisdom that respects and understands the value of natural resources, cultures, and traditions. Short-term gains or personal ambitions do not drive such a leader but are deeply committed to the environment's and society's long-term well-being. Their focus on collective well-being ensures that decisions prioritize ecological balance, societal growth, and future generations. By emphasizing fairness and respect, they can foster a culture of sustainable practices, ensuring every member of their community benefits from and contributes to a sustainable future.

2. **The Steward:** Serving as stewards, conscious leaders act as the protective caregivers of their tribe, tending to everyone's unique needs. Much like a master gardener who understands the distinct requirements of every plant, these leaders identify what nourishes and harms each member. Stewards vigilantly watch for threats, ready to intervene, whether the challenges arise internally or externally. They emphasize nurturing talent, pruning detrimental elements, and promoting growth.

   Like the protective elder, the Steward is the guardian of the environment and society. Recognizing the unique value and needs of different ecosystems and communities, they proactively protect, restore, and rejuvenate. Their protective stance ensures that resources are used judiciously, minimize waste, and involve communities in decision-making processes. Their vision extends to anticipating environmental and societal threats, positioning them to act before issues escalate, and ensuring a harmonious relationship with nature and people.

3. **The Navigator:** Positioned at the ship's helm, the navigator is the guiding visionary. They determine the course and foster

a collaborative environment where everyone's energies align with the objectives. However, their approach is distinct: they don't impose directions but inspire collective alignment through their elevated consciousness, steering the tribe towards shared horizons.

Sustainability challenges require foresight, strategic direction, and collaboration. The Navigator plots a course toward a sustainable future, ensuring that organizational goals are aligned with global sustainability targets, such as the UN's Sustainable Development Goals. By inspiring collective alignment, they mobilize resources, technologies, and people toward sustainable innovations, ensuring the journey is shared, collaborative, and driven by a unified vision.

4. **The Facilitator:** Shifting away from traditional top-down leadership, the facilitator prompts leaders to lead from within. They are the vigilant sentinels, attuned to existing dynamics and emerging trends, orchestrating efforts to harness the collective intelligence and energy of the tribe. The facilitator in action adeptly connects the dots between the "Strategizers" in the boardroom and the "Executors" on the ground, eliminating impediments that stifle performance and profitability.

   Sustainability leadership is not a solitary endeavor. It requires collective intelligence, expertise, and diverse skills. The facilitator in sustainability leadership ensures that all stakeholders, from policymakers to grassroots workers, are involved, heard, and empowered. They break down silos, encourage cross-disciplinary collaborations, and ensure that solutions are holistic and inclusive. By reducing barriers, they ensure that sustainable practices are integrated at all levels, from strategic planning to ground-level execution.

5. **The Healer:** Integral to fostering a resilient, sustainable culture, the healer dimension in a conscious leader brings a holistic touch. They aren't swayed by personal conflicts or overwhelmed by emotional dramas. Instead, they employ a balanced detachment – fusing empathy and compassion with

professionalism. Recognizing the intrinsic human spirit in every individual, they act, ensuring the organization's holistic interests are met by establishing a harmonious blend of personal regard and respectful organizational culture.

The healer's role is crucial in a world grappling with the scars of environmental degradation, societal inequalities, and historical wrongs. In sustainability leadership, the healer acknowledges past mistakes, seeks reconciliation, and works toward restoration. They promote mental and emotional well-being, recognizing that a sustainable future is not just about environmental and economic metrics but also about healing and harmony. By blending empathy with professionalism, they ensure that sustainability initiatives address ecological and economic needs and the deep-seated emotional and societal wounds.

Conscious Leadership and Sustainability

The intersection of conscious leadership and sustainability is gaining increasing traction in academic and professional literature, signaling a paradigm shift in leadership thought.

For instance, Kirilyuk's (2014) *Complex-Dynamic Origin of Consciousness and Sustainability Transition* explores the fundamental connections between consciousness and sustainable transitions, shedding light on the intricate dynamics that drive both entities. [5] Similarly, Chapman, Dethmer, and Klemp's (2015) *The 15 Commitments of Conscious Leadership* offers a new framework that underscores the importance of consciousness in achieving sustainable success. [6] Additionally, Shelley Reciniello's (2014) *The Conscious Leader* delves deep into the intricate psychological landscape of the modern workplace, offering core principles and practices to foster an alert and efficient environment. [7] Her work serves as a compass for leaders to navigate the complex emotional terrains of their teams, ensuring collective success by prioritizing psychological well-being and self-awareness. This trend continues with Tavanti and Sfeir-Younis's (2020) piece on *Conscious Sustainability Leadership*, suggesting a renewed leadership paradigm for emerging leaders navigating our increasingly complex world and offering values and principled-centered models for understanding leadership and sustainability with a renewed sense of planetary awareness. **8** Together, these works provide compelling evidence of the growing recognition of the conscious leadership paradigm as instrumental in fostering a sustainable future.

Drawing from diverse perspectives and disciplines, these studies collectively argue that when rooted in consciousness, leadership can create sustainable practices and decisions that honor both the present and future generations.

Traits of Conscious Leaders for Sustainability

As we delve deeper into this leadership model, a consensus emerges on certain foundational attributes that are important in shaping this paradigm. While the literature touches upon many traits, our subsequent section will spotlight five pivotal characteristics for coherence and clarity. These traits are the basis which conscious sustainability leadership is created. They are self-awareness, relationships, systems thinking, purpose, and integrity.

1. **Self-awareness**: Conscious leaders are deeply in tune with their strengths, vulnerabilities, and core values. More importantly, they comprehend the ramifications of their decisions and actions on others. Regarding sustainability, leaders with strong self-awareness understand the broader implications of their decisions on the environment, society, and future generations. Conscious leaders can make ethical and sustainable decisions by being attuned to their values and the effects of their actions. This introspective clarity enables them to recognize the need for sustainable solutions, ensuring decisions benefit the present and future.

2. **Relationships**: The foundation of conscious leadership is made up of strong, meaningful relationships. These leaders nurture bonds with their team's, clients, partners, and other stakeholders. By doing so, they cultivate a sense of unity and belonging. Building and nurturing strong relationships means considering the needs and perspectives of various

stakeholders about sustainability. A conscious leader engages with communities, understands their concerns, and collaborates with partners to drive eco-friendly initiatives. Strong relationships also foster trust, which is essential for moving any sustainability initiative forward. By valuing relationships, leaders can rally diverse groups towards shared sustainable goals.

3. **Systems thinking**: Rather than viewing challenges in isolation, conscious leaders comprehend the intricate interplay between different organizational components, and the need to move towards alignment on shared objectives. They understand sustainability is inherently a complex web of interconnected challenges and solutions both for their organization and society. Conscious leaders who use systems thinking sees the ripple effects of actions taken in one area on another. For example, they can anticipate how a decision impacting water resources might, in turn, affect local communities or ecosystems. They are better equipped to formulate sustainable strategies by understanding these interconnections and therefore avoiding unintended negative consequences.

4. **Purpose**: Profit is not the sole driver for conscious leaders. A deeper sense of mission motivates them. They want to make a lasting and positive mark on the world. Leaders driven by purpose, rather than solely by profit are more likely to prioritize sustainability. Recognizing that their mission goes beyond the bottom line, these leaders can institute practices that protect the environment, uplift communities, and promote long-term viability. A purpose-driven approach ensures organizations thrive economically and contribute positively to the world by addressing pressing challenges such as climate change, resource scarcity, and social inequality.

5. **Integrity**: Unwavering in their commitment to honesty and ethical behavior, conscious leaders are models of integrity. They take responsibility for their deeds and inspire the same accountability in others. Integrity is at the heart of

sustainability. Leaders committed to honest and ethical behavior are more likely to uphold sustainable practices, even when they are challenging or less profitable. Such leaders set the standard for their organizations, ensuring transparency, ethical sourcing, and accountability. When faced with sustainability challenges, their unwavering commitment to doing the right thing ensures they make choices that benefit the planet and its inhabitants.

Linking conscious leadership to sustainability leadership, the emphasis is on shaping an equitable future for all stakeholders. This means decisions are taken with three underlying considerations: environmental stewardship, societal well-being, and economic viability. By adopting conscious leadership principles, leaders can foster an organizational culture that celebrates sustainable innovation, encourages synergistic collaboration, and is anchored in long-term, holistic thinking.

Examples of Conscious Sustainability Leaders

In today's globalized world, we need a new set of conscious leaders who recognize the interconnectedness of business, society, and the environment. The following leaders model conscious sustainability leadership characteristics:

1. **Christiana Figueres:** She stands out as a prominent conscious sustainability leader. As the Executive Secretary of the United Nations Framework Convention on Climate Change (UNFCCC) from 2010 to 2016, she played a pivotal role in the 2015 Paris Agreement, the historic treaty that united nearly 200 countries in a global action plan to combat climate change.

   Figueres's leadership is marked by her unwavering optimism, tenacity, and collaborative spirit. Recognizing the challenges of bringing together disparate countries with varied economic backgrounds and climate vulnerabilities, she focused on collective ambition and the shared responsibility of addressing global climate threats. Her approach often transcended traditional diplomacy. By engaging a broad spectrum of stakeholders, including businesses, activists, and regional leaders, she ensured that the conversation about climate change was inclusive, holistic, and action oriented.

After her tenure at the UNFCCC, she co-founded "Global Optimism," an initiative that seeks to instill hope and inspire action, emphasizing the idea that challenges, no matter how daunting, can be overcome with persistent effort and collective will. Her journey exemplifies a conscious leadership model rooted in purpose, collaboration, and a deep understanding of the interconnectedness of our global community. Through her actions and initiatives, Christiana Figueres has illuminated the path forward in the fight against climate change, showcasing the true essence of stewardship leadership.

2. **Marc Benioff:** Marc Benioff, the CEO of Salesforce, is known for his focus on creating a culture of trust and transparency at Salesforce. He has also emphasized the importance of corporate social responsibility and embedded philanthropy. In his book *Trailblazer* he wrote, "It's about creating a culture where doing well is synonymous with doing good to thrive in a world where a company is only as strong as the principles it adopts." **9** He believes today's leaders must be trailblazers for sustainability and global responsibility. It's no longer just about profit; it's about benefiting the planet and society. Businesses have the resources and influence to drive significant change, and they must lead this charge for a better future.

3. **Mary Barra:** As the CEO of General Motors, she exemplifies conscious leadership by emphasizing transparency, accountability, and a deep commitment to diversity and inclusion. Under her guidance, GM has championed open communication and trust-building, understanding that diverse teams foster innovation and better represent the company's global clientele. **10**

Additionally, Barra has positioned GM at the forefront of sustainable mobility, showcasing a forward-thinking approach to reducing transportation's environmental impact. Her leadership reflects a modern corporate ethos where businesses, while profit-driven, are also connected with societal and environmental responsibilities, proving that sustainability and profitability can coexist harmoniously.

4. **Paul Polman:** Recognized as a visionary in corporate leadership, Paul Polman's tenure as the former CEO of Unilever symbolizes his profound commitment to sustainability and social responsibility. Taking the helm in challenging times, Polman steered Unilever with the conviction that businesses can, and should, be a force for good. [11]

The landmark initiative of his leadership was the Unilever Sustainable Living Plan. This ambitious strategy aimed not only at diminishing the negative ecological footprint of the company but also magnifying its positive contributions to society. Addressing critical areas such as health and hygiene, nutrition, and environmental protection, the plan set out clear goals to make Unilever's operations more sustainable. Polman's efforts reflect his belief that businesses are pivotal in tackling global challenges and that long-term success is linked with societal well-being.

5. **Indra Nooyi:** Heralded as one of the most influential business leaders of her time, Indra Nooyi's leadership at PepsiCo was characterized by her tireless push for innovation and fostering a culture of collaboration. Recognizing that the future of businesses hinges on their ability to evolve and be agile, Nooyi drove PepsiCo to diversify its portfolio, introducing healthier product options and rethinking traditional business strategies. [12]

Beyond the boardroom, she was vocal about the indispensability of sustainability and the moral imperative for businesses to shoulder social responsibilities. Nooyi envisioned a profitable and purpose-driven PepsiCo, seeking a balance between short-term results and long-term sustainability. Under her guidance, the company launched initiatives addressing environmental stewardship, nutritional challenges, and community upliftment, illustrating her belief that businesses should be agents of positive change.

6. **Satya Nadella:** As the CEO of Microsoft, one of the world's leading tech giants, Satya Nadella stands out for his technological acumen and deeply human-centered approach to leadership. Nadella champions the idea that empathy is an invaluable asset in the modern corporate world. He contends that understanding and relating to customers' and employees' needs, desires, and aspirations is key to driving innovation and fostering a sense of belonging. **13**

Under Nadella's guidance, Microsoft has experienced a cultural transformation. The emphasis has shifted from a purely profit-driven approach to one that values empowerment, inclusivity, and personal growth. By fostering a workspace where everyone feels valued and heard, Nadella has redefined Microsoft's mission and vision, aligning it more closely with the global community's needs and the aspiration to empower everyone.

7. **Eileen Fisher:** A pioneer in sustainable fashion, Eileen Fisher is not just the name behind the brand Eileen Fisher, Inc., but also embodies a conscious and mindful approach to fashion. She recognized the devastating effects of fast fashion on the environment and labor early, leading her to establish a brand that directly counters such practices. **14**

Fisher's commitment goes beyond mere words—every garment tells a story of organic materials, ethically sourced and woven with care. Her brand also spearheads initiatives to promote fair labor practices, ensuring everyone in the production chain is treated with dignity and respect. Furthermore, with recycling programs such as "Renew," Eileen Fisher encourages consumers to return gently worn garments, thus extending their lifecycle, and reducing waste.

Fisher's brand is a beacon of fleeting trends, illuminating path for a more sustainable and ethical fashion future.

8. **Yvon Chouinard**: An iconic figure in sustainabl entrepreneurship, Yvon Chouinard's creation, Patagonia, more than just a brand—it's a movement. Chouinard commitment to the planet is unwavering, and this ethc permeates every aspect of Patagonia. The company has bee a vocal advocate for preserving the environment, often takin stands on controversial issues, and advocating for protecte lands. **15**

Furthermore, Patagonia's dedication to using 100% renewabl and recycled materials showcases Chouinard's vision of business that doesn't profit but contributes positively to th planet. Beyond sustainable practices, he believes in fostering sense of responsibility, encouraging other entrepreneurs an businesses to follow suit, and proving that success an sustainability can go hand in hand.

Rose Marcario stepped into Yvon's visionary leadership an became the CEO of the company, expanding its values int corporate activism. Under her leadership, the company mad groundbreaking decisions, such as pledging a significar portion of its profits to grassroots environmental movement This wasn't mere philanthropy—it reflected Patagonia's cor beliefs that corporations aren't just bystanders but activ participants in global movements.

9. **Natura & Co Leadership**: Hailing from the vibrar landscapes of Brazil, Natura stands as a testament to th power of harmonizing business with nature. As the parer company of brands such as The Body Shop and Aesop Natura & Co has woven the threads of sustainabilit biodiversity, and ethical sourcing into its corporate identity Their products, inspired by the richness of nature, are ofte sourced from sustainable ingredients, emphasizing th company's commitment to protect and preserve biodiversit **16**

Moreover, in a world where indigenous communities are frequently sidelined, Natura & Co takes deliberate steps to recognize, respect, and support the rights of these communities, often collaborating with them and ensuring that their wisdom and rights are prioritized. Such endeavors have positioned Natura & Co as a trendsetter in cosmetics and spotlighted the company as a beacon for those aspiring to intertwine profitability with responsibility.

10. **Dr. Bronner's Leadership Team**: Rooted in a legacy of purity and ethical craftsmanship, Dr. Bronner's is not merely a brand—it's a philosophy. As a family-owned entity specializing in organic soap and personal care items, the brand has consistently advocated for practices that are kind to the planet and its people. A staunch believer in the principles of fair trade, the leadership team ensures that every product that bears Dr. Bronner's name is a testament to ethical sourcing and organic production. **17**

Their commitment to regenerative agricultural practices further underscores the brand's dedication to sustainability, ensuring the earth's resources are consumed and replenished. Beyond their exceptional products, the leadership at Dr. Bronner's has never shied away from amplifying their voice for justice. They actively engage in various social and environmental justice campaigns, reinforcing that businesses can and should be vehicles for positive societal change.

The list could continue as conscious leadership for sustainability is more than a trend— and it is becoming a necessary evolution in the business world. The leaders above, among many others, exemplify how businesses can thrive while also making meaningful contributions to society and the environment.

The spirit of conscious leadership for sustainability is wider than the corporate sector. Leaders in nonprofit and governmental realms have spearheaded many of the most profound impacts on sustainability. In the nonprofit sector, figures like **Wangari Maathai**, founder of the Green Belt Movement, have been instrumental in promoting reforestation and women's rights in Africa. **18** **Dr. Jane Goodall** has transformed our understanding of primates and has been a fervent advocate for conservation and environmental education through the Jane Goodall Institute. Another inspiring example comes from **Malala Yousafzai,** who has tirelessly championed girls' education rights, ensuring that young women worldwide have opportunities for empowerment and learning. **19** Another notable figure is **Kailash Satyarthi,** Nobel Peace Prize laureate, who has dedicated his life to the global pursuit of eradicating child labor and exploitative practices through the Kailash Satyarthi Children's Foundation. **20**

In government, leaders like **Jacinda Ardern,** former Prime Minister of New Zealand, has received international acclaim for her commitment to climate change initiatives and prioritizing well-being alongside economic growth. **21** Similarly, **Sadiq Khan,** Mayor of London, has been pushing for cleaner air policies and promoting green transportation alternatives. **22** **Carlos Alvarado Quesada,** the President of Costa Rica, also deserves to be mentioned. Under his leadership, Costa Rica has been striving to become one of the first carbon-neutral countries in the world, emphasizing renewable energy and biodiversity conservation. **23** **Erna Solberg,** Prime Minister of Norway, is another leader worth noting. **24** She has been at the forefront of promoting sustainable ocean management and has strongly advocated for global education, especially for girls, through initiatives like the Global Partnership for Education.

These leaders, among many others in the business, nonprofit, and governmental sectors, are powerful reminders that commitment to sustainability and conscious leadership can be championed across all arenas of influence. Their stories inspire and challenge us to reimagine the essence of conscious sustainability leadership in the 21st century. They have made an impact in their respective fields. By adopting conscious leadership practices, leaders can create a culture that promotes innovation, collaboration, and long-term thinking.

Leading with Mindfulness, Consciousness, and Sustainability

In the evolving leadership landscape, mindfulness is a foundational pillar that integrates consciousness and sustainability seamlessly. As leaders strive for more intentional, purposeful approaches, mindfulness fosters a deepened awareness of self and surroundings. This heightened consciousness then serves as a basis for sustainability, prompting leaders to make decisions that are beneficial for the immediate environment and resonate with long-term ecological and societal well-being. When leadership is immersed in mindfulness, the connection of consciousness and sustainability becomes evident, creating a holistic approach that champions personal growth and global progress.

Consciousness, mindfulness, and sustainability while individually meaningful, make impactful leadership when combined. Here is a closer look at their integrated significance on leadership:

1. **Mindfulness in Leadership:** Achieving mindfulness means anchoring one's awareness firmly in the present and observing feelings, thoughts, and sensations without judgment. Beyond meditation, a mindful leader can be fully present in decisions and actions. When leaders incorporate mindfulness, they become acutely aware of their consumption habits, introspect their organizational impact, and lean towards sustainable leadership strategies. Mindful leaders maintain a keen awareness of their actions, words, decisions, and the ripple effects they create, considering both immediate and distant stakeholders and future generations.

2. **Consciousness in Leadership:** Central to consciousness is the keen awareness of one's existence, perceptions, and thoughts. Leadership with heightened consciousness understands the broader implications of one's actions on the environment, society, and the legacy for future generations. Conscious leaders transcend mere mindfulness. Instead of being driven by image-centric motivations, they operate with an eco-centric focus grounded in fundamental principles and core values.

3. **Sustainability in Leadership:** Grounded in the commitment not to compromise the ability of future generations to flourish, sustainable leadership integrates environmental, social, economic, and social justice considerations. This approach aims for a balance that

guarantees a resilient future for the world and its inhabitants while actively addressing issues of equity and justice.

Both consciousness and mindfulness in leadership center on an elevated sense of awareness. Consciousness offers leaders a panoramic view of their impact on the larger ecosystem, while mindfulness sharpens their focus on immediate decisions and their repercussions. This dual awareness makes leaders acutely conscious of actions and subsequent outcomes. Leaders infused with consciousness discern the intricate mosaic of life and the essence of sustainable stewardship. Such leaders inherently grasp the ripple effects of their decisions, steering towards eco-friendly and socially commendable choices. Leaders practicing mindfulness, attuned to the nuances of the present, can discern the tangible consequences of their actions more distinctly. For example, a mindful leader might see the excesses in organizational waste and champion waste-reducing initiatives. With an anchored presence, their decisions naturally resonate with sustainable tenets.

In other words, these dimensions play value-centered influences on sustainable leadership practices. Consciousness offers leaders a panoramic lens to visualize their broader global role and influence. Mindfulness acts as a compass, directing leaders to remain grounded and aware of their immediate actions and implications. Together, they move forward mentally, emotionally, and ethically to champion sustainability in their leadership narrative.

From Sustainability Mindsets to Conscious Leadership

There are common links between Dr. Rimanoczy's sustainability mindset model and conscious leadership. Both concepts are a holistic, self-aware approach to leadership, emphasizing broader understanding and purposeful action. Here's a deeper exploration of their commonalities:

1. **Holistic Viewpoint**: Both conscious leadership and the sustainability mindset model urge individuals and organizations to view situations holistically. While the sustainability mindset model highlights the

interconnectedness of ecological, systemic, emotional, and spiritual dimensions, conscious leadership emphasizes understanding oneself, the team, and the broader organizational and societal ecosystem.

2. **Self-awareness & Reflection**: Emotional Intelligence, which forms one of the pillars of the sustainability mindset model, resonates strongly with conscious leadership. Both emphasize introspection, self-awareness, and understanding one's emotions, motivations, and beliefs. This self-awareness is crucial in guiding decisions and actions that benefit the broader community and environment.

3. **Ethical Decision-making**: The sustainability mindset model emphasizes ethical principles and societal and environmental well-being considerations. Similarly, conscious leadership involves making beneficial decisions for the organization, society, and the environment.

4. **Purpose-driven Actions**: Both frameworks underscore the significance of purpose. The sustainability mindset model speaks to the broader purpose of ensuring ecological balance and social justice. At the same time, conscious leadership emphasizes alignment with personal and organizational purpose, ensuring meaningful and impactful decisions and actions.

5. **Long-term Perspective**: Through its Systems Perspective, the sustainability mindset model encourages long-term thinking. Similarly, conscious leadership is about seeing beyond short-term gains and understanding the long-term implications of decisions on stakeholders, the environment, and society.

6. **Integrative Thinking**: The sustainability mindset model emphasizes "Both and Thinking," understanding paradoxes, and seeking inclusive solutions. Conscious leaders often display this quality, seeking integrative solutions that address various stakeholder needs.

7. **Transformational Change**: Both the sustainability mindse model and conscious leadership are transformative. They air to change individual behaviors, reshape organizationa cultures, influence societal norms, and drive broader systemi change.

In summary, Dr. Rimanoczy's sustainability mindset model an conscious leadership provide frameworks for leading with awareness purpose, and a commitment to the broader good. While they ma approach the topic differently, their essence is aligned, advocating fo considerate, holistic leadership and sustainable and ethical principles.

Conscious Sustainability Leadership: A Path Forward

We must consider some emerging core elements as we conclud these reflections on the mindsets and consciousness characteristics c leaders striving for sustainable values and outcomes. While leadershi practices can take many shapes and adaptations across diverse bu connected values, there are some core characteristics that leader would need to consider in their development. Our challenging time characterized by rapid environmental change, societal shifts, an complex global challenges, require new mindsets, mindful awareness and conscious identities. In this context, conscious sustainabilit leadership emerges as a beacon of hope. Such leadership is not just strategy or a skill but a mindset, a way of being that embodies profound understanding of our place within the global ecosystem. **25**

In summary, we identify seven core elements of consciousness fo sustainability that delineate the foundational principles that underpi this form of leadership:

1. **Interdependence Awareness**: We recognize that nothin exists in isolation. Every action taken reverberate influencing outcomes in distant corners of our interconnecte world. The application of this principle to organizationa leadership is evident. For example, a multinational compan that sources raw materials from various countries decides t invest in the communities from which they extract th resources. They recognize that the well-being of thes

communities affects the quality of their products, their brand image, and overall company success. By doing so, they acknowledge the interconnectedness of their supply chain and the broader ecosystem.

2. **Empathy & Compassion:** Beyond mere understanding, conscious sustainability leadership operates from a heartfelt connection, fostering genuine concern for the well-being of all life forms and the planet. Applying this principle for organizational leadership is exemplified by a clothing brand that doesn't just modify contracts upon learning about the working conditions of laborers in their overseas factories. They visit these places, engage with workers, understand their challenges, and develop humane policies that ensure fair wages, safe working conditions, and overall well-being.

3. **Holistic Thinking:** Rooted in systems thinking, this perspective appreciates the intricate dance of cause and effect, discerning patterns and relationships often overlooked in traditional leadership models. An example of applying this principle could emerge when a tech company, while developing a new product, considers the potential profit and the environmental impact of the product's lifecycle, societal implications, and potential misuse scenarios. They develop a comprehensive strategy that includes recycling initiatives, ethical usage guidelines, and community engagement to ensure balanced benefits.

4. **Long-term Vision:** Prioritizing future generations ensures that today's decisions do not inadvertently mortgage tomorrow. They demonstrate a commitment to enduring value and impact. A possible application could emerge when a beverage company, witnessing plastic waste's increasing detrimental environmental impact, shifts its packaging strategy. Instead of using cheaper single-use plastics, they invest in developing biodegradable packaging, understanding that the long-term sustainability of our planet is linked with their business's future.

5. **Global Responsibility**: This principle transcends borders, recognizing that our shared planet demands shared stewardship. It is a call to align actions with a global vision of sustainability. An example could be an automobile manufacturer, though based primarily in one region, understands the global implications of climate change. They transition to electric vehicles, support global environmental initiatives, and collaborate with other industry players worldwide to promote green transportation.

6. **Adaptive Learning**: The world is constantly changing, and what worked yesterday may not work tomorrow. A conscious sustainability leader is agile, open to feedback, and willing to pivot when circumstances demand. An example could be a pharmaceutical firm that stays open to post-market feedback after launching a new drug. When some adverse reactions are reported, rather than ignoring or downplaying the issues, they promptly reassess, make necessary formulaic modifications, and ensure transparent communication with the medical community and public.

7. **Cultural Sensitivity**: In our globalized era, solutions cannot be one-size-fits-all. They must be co-created with local stakeholders, honoring traditions, histories, and perspectives unique to each community. An example could be an international fast-food chain expanding into new countries, which doesn't just impose its existing menu. They research local food preferences, respect religious and cultural dietary restrictions, and even include regional delicacies. They ensure their outlets resonate with local sensibilities, thus ensuring better acceptance and success.

In the unfolding theory of "Sustainability Leadership," the consciousness paradigm emerges an imperative call to the heart of every leader. In a world where the ripples of our actions reverberate through intricate webs of interdependence, leadership requires a profound shift in perception. It calls for a transition from isolated decision-making to a holistic, systemic approach grounded in empathy, compassion, and a profound understanding of our shared human journey. For a leader, the call is clear: envisioning a future through the lens of long-term sustainability, seamlessly integrating pressing immediate concerns without losing sight of the horizon. To be truly effective in this transformative era, our identity must evolve; global responsibility, adaptive learning, and cultural sensitivity aren't mere add-ons but foundational elements of leadership.

In conclusion, conscious sustainability leadership represents a paradigm shift in leadership studies and practices. It redefines success, measures progress regarding holistic well-being, and challenges leaders to step forth with both head and heart. As individuals and institutions put these seven core elements into their ethos, a transformative ripple effect is set in motion. The culmination is a world where sustainability is not just an agenda but a lived reality, where leaders act as stewards for the present and countless future generations.

As we close this chapter, let it not be the end of a discussion but rather the beginning of a new leadership ethos, inviting all to a renewed consciousness where the interconnectedness of our world isn't a challenge but a guiding compass for a brighter, more sustainable future.

Key Takeaways: Consciousness Paradigm

1. **Holistic Approach to Sustainability**: Sustainability is not just environmentally focused but also represents an expansive consciousness about our actions' long-term impacts. It embodies a holistic understanding that links ecological, social, and economic considerations.

2. **Leadership Transformation**: Embracing sustainability demands a transformative leadership approach. Leaders need to adopt a forward-thinking mindset, recognizing that their decisions today can have lasting consequences on future generations.

3. **Exemplary Conscious Leaders**: Throughout history and in contemporary settings, some leaders have epitomized the principles of conscious sustainability. Their actions and

decisions serve as real-world examples and inspire others to emulate them.

4. **Mindfulness in Action**: Leading with mindfulness means making decisions with awareness, empathy, and foresight. It emphasizes the importance of being present and thoughtful in leadership roles, allowing for more compassionate and sustainable choices.

5. **The Evolutionary Path**: There's an ongoing evolution from mere sustainability mindsets to full-fledged conscious leadership. This transition signifies a global shift in understanding and acting upon sustainability principles, paving the way for a more harmonious coexistence with our planet.

CHAPTER 3

WELL-BEING DIMENSIONS

FOR HAPPINESS, THRIVING AND PROSPERITY

Overview

Well-being is more than just the absence of illness; it's about nourishing in all dimensions of life. This chapter discusses the multifaceted nature of well-being, emphasizing that genuine thriving encompasses physical, mental, emotional, and social health. It explores well-being concerning happiness and the Gross National Happiness (GNH) measurements. It reviews well-being concerning other correlated dimensions of thriving and flourishing, prosperity, and empowerment. It makes implications for sustainability leadership and its responsibility to nurture these aspects so that individuals and societies can achieve a state of holistic wellness.

Defining Well-being

Well-being is more than just an individual's mind; it's an intricate blend of personal emotions, societal conditions, and external environments. It encapsulates experiences like joy, happiness, and contentment, emphasizing personal growth, autonomy, a sense of purpose, and nurturing relationships. [1] The World Health Organization defines well-being as a positive state that individuals and communities experience influenced by social, economic, and environmental determinants. At its core, WHO's definition of well-

73

being encapsulates the quality of life, united with the ability c individuals and entire societies to impart meaningful contributions t the world. **2** They state:

> Well-being is a positive state experienced by individuals an societies. Like health, it is a daily life resource determine by social, economic, and environmental conditions. Wel being encompasses quality of life and the ability of peop and societies to contribute to the world with a sense c meaning and purpose. Focusing on well-being suppor tracking the equitable distribution of resources, overa thriving, and sustainability. A society's well-being can k determined by its resilient nature, builds capacity for actio and is prepared to transcend challenges. **3**

Furthermore, well-being offers a lens through which we can monitc the fair distribution of resources, the holistic thriving c communities, and sustainability principles. A community's well-beir is not just about how happy its members feel; it's measured by i resilience, proactive capacity-building, and preparedness to naviga and overcome challenges. Emphasizing well-being means ensurin that societies aren't just surviving and thriving with purpose an unity.

The benefits of well-being stretch across various aspects of lif Individuals with high well-being often display heightene productivity at work, engage in effective learning, showcase creativit and foster positive interpersonal connections. This state of mind an being isn't limited to the present; evidence suggests that a child's wel being can foretell their well-being trajectory into adulthood. Beyon the psychological realm, enhanced well-being correlates wit improved physical health, increased longevity, and broader societ outcomes such as superior national economic metrics. **4**. Well-beir isn't just about personal contentment; it's a powerful predictor c success across various life domains.

Well-Being and Happiness Dimensions

In the evolving discourse on sustainability leadership, well-being an happiness have emerged as pivotal constructs. Well-being is comprehensive metric that evaluates individual and collective health, development, and contentment. Rather than limited to physical health or material affluence, it delves into diverse aspects of human existence, including emotional well-being, social relationships, and a life driven by purpose. Happiness is linked with well-being. More than a fleeting feeling of joy, happiness in the context of well-being denotes a lasting state of life satisfaction and connection. **5**

While well-being encompasses a broader range of factors, including physical, mental, and social aspects, happiness can be seen as a component or an outcome of well-being. In other words, when various dimensions of well-being are fulfilled, happiness is often a result. Here are some core dimensions intersecting between the definition of well-being and happiness:

1. **Emotional Well-being:** This involves individuals experiencing more positive emotions (e.g., joy, contentment, love) than negative ones (e.g., sadness, anger, fear).

2. **Life Satisfaction:** A broader evaluation of one's life. People assess the overall quality of their lives and their satisfaction levels with their current life.

3. **Social Connectedness:** The quality and depth of social relationships and feelings of belonging contribute significantly to happiness.

4. **Purpose and Meaning:** Engaging in activities or having beliefs that give one's life purpose and significance.

5. **Personal Development:** Growth, learning, and the ability to utilize one's potential also play roles in the experience of happiness.

6. **Physical Health:** Good health and vitality often contribute to overall happiness.

In its broader sense, happiness provides valuable insights into the qualitative aspects of well-being. It serves as a barometer for the success of policies and initiatives to improve the quality of life. The pursuit of happiness, linked with the broader dimensions of well-being, requires a supportive environment where individuals can connect, grow, and find purpose. This realization has profound implications for sustainability leadership. **6**

For leaders in the realm of sustainability, the paradigm shift towards well-being and happiness demands a more integrative approach. No longer can decisions be made based solely on economic outcomes or short-term gains. Sustainability leadership now requires a nuanced understanding of the factors contributing to well-being and happiness. Leaders must foster environments where individuals can access basic needs and opportunities for personal growth, meaningful engagement, and emotional fulfillment.

Incorporating well-being and happiness into the core of sustainability leadership means prioritizing policies and strategies that create resilient, inclusive, and connected communities. It means recognizing that our planet's health is intrinsically linked to the well-being of its inhabitants. Above all, it emphasizes that true sustainability goes beyond conserving resources and mitigating negative impacts—it is about creating a world where every individual has the chance to lead a happy, fulfilling life.

Aristotle's Framework for Sustainable Well-Being

Aristotle's teachings on Eudaimonia (often interpreted as "flourishing," "thriving" or "happiness"), Phronesis ("practical wisdom"), and Arete ("virtue" or "excellence") offer guidance for understanding the dimensions of sustainable well-being. These principles, rooted in ancient philosophy, are remarkably relevant in today's quest for a balanced and prosperous life, individually, corporately, and communally. **7** Aristotle's framework for well-being and ethical leadership is elegantly constructed around these three core dimensions that build on each other. Arete forms the ethical foundation, representing the virtues and values essential for principled leadership and moral excellence. Phronesis, or practical wisdom, is pivotal in applying these virtues through discerning and ethical decision-making in complex situations. These two principles coalesce in the pursuit of Eudaimonia, transcending individual achievement to encompass the collective well-being and prosperity of the community and society at large. Together, these dimensions offer a holistic approach to leadership, where moral integrity, practical wisdom, and the shared flourishing of society are inextricably linked, guiding leaders toward a harmonious and impactful synergy of personal, collective, and globally responsible success. These principles offer a profound and interconnected framework for understanding the core values, discernment processes, and higher purposes of sustainability leadership through these specific characteristics and implications:

1. **Arete as Virtuous Excellence:** In Aristotle's philosophy, Arete signifies achieving one's highest potential and embodying the best qualities. In sustainability leadership, Arete is about committing to integrity, ethical behavior, and excellence in resource management. It calls for a balanced approach that values social justice, environmental care, and economic objectives. Arete emphasizes pursuing excellence through ethical practices, transparency, and accountability. Sustainability leaders who center around Arete lead by example in reducing carbon footprints, promoting diversity and equality, and ensuring fair trade. They also commit to continuous learning and improvement in sustainability practices. They inspire others through their commitment to ethical standards and drive for innovation in sustainable solutions. This principle also encourages collaboration across sectors and communities, recognizing that excellence in sustainability is a collective effort. **8**

2. **Phronesis as Practical Wisdom:** Phronesis involves making informed decisions about the delicate balance between individual well-being, societal needs, and environmental preservation. It encourages a lifestyle harmonizing personal health with communal welfare and ecological responsibility. This concept underscores the importance of ethical, socially responsible, and environmentally sound practices in achieving sustainable well-being. Phronesis involves the application of practical wisdom in sustainability, guiding leaders to make strategic decisions that balance immediate needs with long-term environmental and societal goals. It calls for understanding complex systems and foresight in anticipating the consequences of actions on future generations. The practical applications of Phronesis in

sustainability leadership decision-making may result in embracing renewable energy, sustainable resource management, and policies that mitigate climate change impacts. Phronesis also entails educating and empowering communities to make sustainable choices, fostering a culture where environmental consciousness is a norm. **9**

3. **Eudaimonia as True Happiness and Flourishing:** Eudaimonia represents the pinnacle of human aspirations – the quest for genuine happiness and well-being. It transcends the pursuit of momentary pleasures and material wealth, advocating for a holistic approach that combines environmental sustainability, social equity, and economic stability. Eudaimonia emphasizes sustainable development that nurtures individual and community growth, advocating for policies and practices that foster long-term happiness and prosperity. In the context of sustainability, Eudaimonia extends beyond personal happiness to encompass the well-being of the entire community and the environment. It promotes a vision where environmental health, social justice, and economic prosperity are inextricably linked. Leaders embracing Eudaimonia strive for policies and actions that achieve long-term ecological balance, social inclusivity, and economic growth, recognizing that true happiness arises from a healthy, vibrant community and planet. This principle advocates for practical leadership applications prioritizing long-term welfare over short-term gains in corporate or societal initiatives. **10**

This three-layered Aristotelian approach fosters a vision of comprehensive well-being that includes economic prosperity, social equity, environmental stewardship, and individual fulfillment. It nurtures a society where every facet of human flourishing is valued, leading to a sustainable and fulfilling future.

Arete, Phronesis, and Eudaimonia can be combined into a concentric circle model representing a renewed perspective of interconnected values and responsibilities for collective well-being. This model recalls the Egg of Sustainability, which emerged as a response to the three-pillar and triple-bottom-line models, which sometimes has been riticized for suggesting that the three dimensions of sustainability are eparate and equally balanced. By contrast, the Egg of Sustainability 1odel, like the Doughnut Economics model, emphasizes how the ocial and economic systems perspective limits and regulates the conomic activities that necessarily need orientation toward social nd environmental (common) good. Understanding the haracteristics and relations among these well-being dimensions are undamental to sustainability leadership development and practices.

Multi-dimensional Views of Well-Being

Bhutan's Gross National Happiness (GNH) is a pioneering ramework that shifts the focus from purely economic metrics of evelopment to a more holistic assessment of well-being and societal rogress. The GNH framework breaks down into nine domains, each apturing different dimensions of well-being and sustainability. **11** ach domain contributes to the understanding of well-being and reates implications for the priorities in sustainability leadership:

1. **Living Standards:** At the heart of the GNH framework is the recognition that while economic metrics are essential, they cannot stand alone as indicators of societal health. The "Living Standards" domain evaluates the material well-being of individuals, capturing elements such as income, housing, and employment security. For sustainability leadership, this domain underscores the necessity of ensuring that economic growth translates into tangible benefits for all members of society. It reminds leaders that a comfortable standard of living, with access to essential amenities and services, is crucial for a nation's well-being.

2. **Education:** GNH's "Education" domain emphasizes the transformative power of knowledge and learning. This domain goes beyond measuring literacy rates or school enrollments; it evaluates the quality, relevance, and accessibility of education at all levels. Recognizing that educated citizens are empowered to make informed decisions, innovate, and drive change, this domain asserts the importance of lifelong learning opportunities and the cultivation of intellectual and ethical values.

3. **Health:** Physical well-being is an integral part of the GNF The "Health" domain encapsulates traditional metrics such a life expectancy and morbidity rates, access to medical car and broader social determinants of health. Leaders leveragin this domain are reminded to promote preventive healt measures, ensure universal healthcare access, and understan that a nation's health directly influences productivity an vibrancy.

4. **Environment:** In the GNH framework, the "Environment domain, often called "Ecological Diversity and Resilience, draws attention to the intrinsic relationship between huma well-being and environmental health. It evaluates the state c ecosystems, promotes sustainable environmental practice: and underscores the importance of biodiversity. This domai serves as a reminder that sustainable leadership cannc sideline environmental considerations without jeopardizin the very foundation of societal well-being.

5. **Community Vitality:** Communities form the bedrock c societies, and the "Community Vitality" domain explores th strength, quality, and depth of social connections withi them. This includes evaluating trust, mutual support, and th sense of belonging among community members. Drawin insights from this domain, sustainable leaders are urged t foster cohesive and resilient communities, recognizing thei pivotal role in navigating societal challenges.

6. **Time-use:** The "Time-use" domain delves into hov individuals allocate their time between work, leisure, and res It brings to light the significance of work-life balance i influencing well-being. Leaders are reminded that relentles productivity and long working hours can harm societal healtf Ensuring individuals have time for recreation, rest, an personal pursuits is vital for their overall well-being.

7. **Psychological Well-being:** Moving beyond external metric: the "Psychological Well-being" domain evaluates intern; states of satisfaction, emotions, and spiritual health. I underscores the importance of mental and emotional healt in the broader picture of well-being. This domain guide

leaders to consider psychological support, mental health infrastructure, and initiatives that nurture the inner well-being of their populace.

8. **Good Governance**: Governance plays a pivotal role in shaping the trajectory of societies. The "Good Governance" domain assesses governance structure functionality, responsiveness, and ethical nature. Emphasizing transparent, inclusive, and participatory governance, this domain informs leaders about the value of fostering trust and stability through ethical leadership practices.

9. **Cultural Resilience and Promotion**: The "Cultural Resilience and Promotion" domain cherishes preserving and promoting cultural heritage and traditions. Recognizing that culture enriches the societal tapestry and provides a sense of identity, this domain highlights the importance of fostering cultural diversity, celebrating traditions, and ensuring they evolve and remain relevant in changing times.

The nine domains of GNH offer a multi-dimensional view of well-being, emphasizing that a truly sustainable and happy society requires a balanced and holistic approach. For sustainability leadership, GNH provides a roadmap to guide decisions, ensuring that an individual's well-being and an ecosystem's health are front and center in all developmental initiatives.

The GNH Leadership Implications

The significance and dimensions of the GNH framework have numerous implications for sustainability leadership. Sander Tideman (2016) argues that GNH provides a revolutionary approach to understanding sustainable development and leadership. Unlike traditional models, GNH accentuates a hierarchically nuanced interdependence between ecology, society, and economy. This perspective challenges the common Triple Bottom Line approach, suggesting that the environment (planet) is foundational to societal health and paramount for a sustainable economy. Rather than positing an adversarial relationship between humanity's desires and nature's limited resources, GNH envisions a harmonious coexistence where balanced needs across all societal and ecological stakeholders lead to sustainable value creation.

Furthermore, GNH introduces the critical dimension of governance, emphasizing its pivotal role in orchestrating the other three pillars. It recognizes the importance of transparent governance, citizen participation, and institutional trust as driving forces for sustainable development. At its core, GNH promotes the holistic pursuit of happiness, blending tangible material benefits and an individual's subjective well-being. It emphasizes the cultural importance of emotional well-being, mental health, and spiritual engagement, positing that genuine happiness requires both external provisions and internal mind-training. For sustainability leadership, GNH offers a comprehensive and forward-thinking guide to creating harmonious and thriving societies. **12**

The GNH framework, while innovative, faces critiques that could hold implications for sustainability leadership. These limits are inherent to these dimension's difficult-to-measure, subjective, and culturally framed interpretations. **13** Governments could also exploit significant concern about GNH's subjective nature to mask governance flaws, as observed in Bhutan's treatment of Nepalese minorities. While GDP offers an objective and globally recognized measure, the subjective elements of GNH challenge its application in international comparisons. It is commendable that numerous alternatives and more comprehensive measurements are advanced to measure sustainable and human development beyond economic indicators. **14** However, the friction between GNH and GDP remains evident. This tension, representative of the broader debate between tangible economic goals and holistic sustainable development, can lead to fragmented leadership approaches and policy oversights. For sustainability leaders, it emphasizes balancing and reconciling economic imperatives with broader well-being objectives, ensuring innovative frameworks like GNH remain relevant and actionable in policymaking. It indicates the need for revising leadership with more inclusive, humanistic, resilient, and sustainable (economic, social, environmental) dimensions. **15**

Thriving Dimensions

At its core, thriving signifies a state of optimal existence where individuals maintain balance and excel in various life dimensions. It is an elevated state, often seen as the pinnacle of personal and collective evolution, encompassing growth, vitality, and the ability to adapt and evolve amidst challenges.

Concerning well-being, thriving can be seen as an advanced continuum. While well-being often encapsulates the basic aspects of a good life — physical health, emotional stability, and social connection — thriving goes further. It involves harnessing these foundational elements and pushing boundaries to achieve more. In a thriving state, one's well-being isn't just maintained; it's continuously enhanced.

Compared to flourishing, the concepts might seem synonymous, but subtle nuances differentiate them. Flourishing primarily focuses on the optimal range of human functioning, which includes positive emotions, relationships, purpose, and accomplishment. Thriving, on the other hand, not only includes these elements but also denotes resilience, adaptability, and the pursuit of excellence. While flourishing can be seen as the blossoming of one's potential, thriving can be understood as the continued growth and adaptation beyond that blossoming stage.

In terms of realization, thriving aligns closely. Realization is the conscious act of recognizing and achieving one's potential. In a state of thriving, this realization is continual. There's an ongoing process of setting higher benchmarks, achieving them, and setting new ones. The realization is not a destination in the context of thriving; it's an ongoing journey.

In essence, thriving can be visualized as a dynamic and ever-ascending spiral, capturing the sense of well-being, the peak experiences of flourishing, and the continuous journey of realization. It represents the holistic integration of these elements, propelling individuals, and communities to seek higher grounds of existence perpetually.

Embracing the dimensions of thriving about well-being offers sustainability leaders a holistic roadmap. It emphasizes a comprehensive approach beyond economic or environmental factors, prioritizing socio-emotional and psychological aspects. This thriving-centric perspective advocates for long-term vision and resilience, ensuring adaptability to challenges. It underscores the importance of empowering individuals and communities, highlighting the interconnectedness of various well-being facets and the need for a systems-thinking approach. Continuous learning becomes crucial, with success metrics extending beyond traditional indicators to encompass factors like community cohesion and ecosystem resilience. Ultimately, by weaving education and awareness into their strategies, leaders can ensure active community participation and a more holistic commitment to sustainability.

Prosperity Dimensions

Prosperity is another dimension of well-being, carrying numerous important implications for sustainability leadership. In the context of sustainable development, the United Nations underscores "prosperity" as a more holistic and encompassing term than "profit." While profit often connotes a singular focus on immediate financial gains and short-term economic outcomes, prosperity paints a broader picture. It encapsulates material wealth and extends to health, education, well-being, environmental sustainability, cultural richness, and social cohesion. Such a comprehensive perspective ensures that growth remains inclusive, addressing the root causes of societal challenges and championing human-centric solutions. As such, prosperity serves as a core concept for sustainability leadership. **16** Embracing it emphasizes a commitment to long-term, shared growth that respects human and environmental well-being instead of transient economic success. This alignment with holistic development makes prosperity a pivotal focus for leaders envisioning a sustainable future.

Prosperity traditionally focuses on material wealth. Yet, when viewed in relation to well-being, it encompasses far more. It's not merely about amassing wealth but ensuring that such affluence genuinely enhances life quality, providing comfort and security. Another integral component of prosperity is health and longevity. A prosperous society emphasizes the importance of a healthy populace,

nking economic growth with robust health infrastructures and broad
ccess to healthcare services.

Moreover, the dimension of educational and personal growth
becomes pivotal. True prosperity fosters an environment that
promotes education and skill development, enabling individuals to
realize their potential fully. Hand in hand with this is the
acknowledgment of environmental harmony. A genuinely prosperous
society values its natural ecosystems, not just exploiting resources for
immediate gains but ensuring their sustainability for future
generations.

Adding depth to this view of prosperity is the importance of social
and cultural richness. The essence of a prosperous society lies in its
ability to maintain, celebrate, and even enrich its cultural identities,
weaving them into the fabric of a cohesive society. Lastly, beyond
tangible assets and accomplishments, prosperity delves deep into
emotional and psychological realms, emphasizing the need for
societies where individuals find contentment, fulfillment, and
emotional balance.

Empowerment Dimensions

Empowerment relates to the pursuit of prosperity. Empowerment is
about granting individuals and communities the confidence,
resources, and tools to influence their path in life. When empowered,
people can actively shape their environments, make choices, and
recognize their potential. Take, for instance, the women's self-help
groups in rural India. These groups have empowered countless
women by providing access to microfinance, enabling them to start
small businesses, make financial decisions, and uplift their families
and communities. This autonomy isn't just an assertion of agency; it's
a tangible step towards prosperity, viewed as realizing one's potential
and a life of fulfillment. **17**

An empowered society is an active participant in its destiny. Such
active involvement transcends mere economic growth. In Brazil, for
example, community-led initiatives in favelas have empowered
residents to take charge of their localities, leading to community
gardens, local businesses, and enhanced safety. This increased

participation nurtures innovation, fortifies democratic processes, and fosters conditions ripe for shared growth and prosperity.

Empowerment also bolsters resilience and adaptability. When communities are empowered, they're better poised to confront challenges head-on. The Indigenous communities worldwide, from the Maori in New Zealand to the Native Americans in the U.S., offer illuminating examples. Drawing from their profound knowledge of local ecosystems, they have stewarded and preserved their environments, ensuring sustainable resource use and resilience against environmental challenges.

For those at the helm of sustainability leadership, empowerment isn't just an end goal; it's a fundamental approach. Such leaders understand that the complexities of sustainability require collaborative action. By empowering others, they are fostering collective wisdom and effort. They invest in building capacities and providing education, training, and resources to equip individuals and communities to tackle challenges head-on. A noteworthy example is the Green Belt Movement in Kenya, initiated by Wangari Maathai. By empowering local women to plant trees, the movement not only combatted deforestation but also provided these women with a source of income, reinforcing the relationship between empowerment and sustainable prosperity. **18**

In creating opportunities, empowerment-driven leadership aims to level the playing field. It is about removing barriers and ensuring equitable resource access. Sustainability leaders recognize that genuine prosperity emerges when everyone is given an equal shot at success and contribution. In other words, empowerment isn't just a buzzword in the lexicon of sustainable development. It's the bedrock on which prosperous, resilient, and inclusive societies are built. Leaders championing this cause are not just aiming for transient economic milestones but envisioning a world where everyone has the platform and potential to thrive.

Key Takeaways: Well-Being Dimensions

1. **Holistic Perspective on Well-being**: Well-being transcends the absence of disease, focusing instead on flourishing across

diverse life facets. Genuine thriving is a composite of physical, mental, emotional, and social health.

2. **Happiness and Well-being**: The chapter delves deep into the relationship between happiness and well-being, drawing references from the Gross National Happiness (GNH) metrics prioritizing societal well-being over mere economic measures.

3. **Correlations with Thriving and Flourishing**: An exploration of well-being is complete when we understand the interplay between thriving, flourishing, prosperity, and empowerment. While distinct, these elements intersect to paint a fuller picture of an individual's or society's well-being.

4. **The Role of Sustainability Leadership**: Leaders in sustainability play a pivotal role in fostering and nurturing well-being. Their responsibility extends beyond short-term solutions, focusing instead on ensuring holistic wellness for communities and individuals.

5. **The Vision of Holistic Wellness**: As described in this chapter, the goal is to achieve holistic wellness. This state, championed by sustainability leadership, integrates the various dimensions of well-being, creating an environment where individuals and societies can survive and thrive.

CHAPTER 4

RESILIENT ADAPTATIONS

FOR ADAPTIVE CONTEXTUALIZATIONS

Overview

In exploring the Resilient Adaptations paradigm, we delve deep into the confluence of resilience and leadership in the face of mounting global challenges. The chapter underscores a leader's need to cultivate a holistic understanding of resilience, transcending mere recovery to embody evolution and growth. Emphasizing the critical role of contextualized leadership, the narrative showcases how adapting strategies to specific circumstances fosters trust and aids in managing multifaceted challenges. Moreover, exploring the "Crossing Boundaries" paradigm reveals the transformative power of transcending traditional barriers, be they cultural, disciplinary, or resistive to change. This interweaving of diverse perspectives and knowledge realms is portrayed as instrumental in driving innovative solutions, drawing parallels between historical polymaths and contemporary leaders. In navigating our volatile, uncertain, complex, and ambiguous (VUCA) world, the chapter champions adaptive leadership, advocating for agility and proactivity.

Introduction to the Resilient Adaptations Paradigm

As the stressful environmental conditions will likely continue impacting the VUCA (Volatile, Uncertain, Complex, Ambiguous) and dynamic landscape of our rapidly changing world, resilience has emerged as a cornerstone of sustainable thinking and action. **1** As unprecedented challenges threaten the ecological balance, economic stability, and social cohesion, the ability of systems, communities, and organizations to adapt, recover, and thrive becomes paramount. In this context, resilience is not just about enduring; it's about evolving in the face of adversity, turning challenges into catalysts for growth and innovation.

For sustainability leadership, this emphasis on resilience introduces a paradigm shift. Leaders can now focus more than on maintaining the status quo or achieving static goals. Instead, they must cultivate an environment of flexibility, innovation, and adaptive thinking. This mindset ensures that organizations and communities withstand shocks, learn, innovate, and emerge stronger.

The implications of the resilient adaptation paradigm are profound. It challenges traditional leadership models, pushing for greater agility, foresight, and a commitment to continuous learning. It emphasizes the importance of understanding and navigating complex, interdependent systems, ensuring decisions are both locally relevant and globally informed. As we delve deeper into this chapter, we'll explore the intricate relationship between resilience and sustainability, the leadership models it creates, and the transformative potential it holds for a future where change is the only constant.

Resilience and Sustainability

Resilience, at its core, is the inherent ability of a system—be it ecological, social, or organizational—to anticipate potential threats, absorb and counteract their impacts, and, most crucially, adapt and evolve in the aftermath of persistent stress or sudden disturbances. While this concept has become an essential principle in various fields, its conflation with sustainability is not uncommon. Both terminologies share overarching similarities, often becoming ntertwined in discussions and strategies without clearly distinguishing their implications and objectives.

However, it's crucial to discern that while they intersect, sustainability and resilience are distinct entities, each offering a unique perspective on how systems interact with their environments. Overlooking their differences can lead to oversimplified approaches that might not achieve the intended outcomes.

A critical distinction arises in the realm of spatial and temporal scales. Numerous studies have highlighted how sustainability, in essence, peers into the future, setting sights on enduring, long-term benefits. In contrast, resilience often deals with more immediate, localized challenges, aiming to fortify systems against existing and imminent threats. **2**

Furthermore, a nuanced understanding reveals that efforts to bolster resilience at a particular spatial or temporal scale might inadvertently undermine it at another. For instance, rapid localized solutions to address immediate vulnerabilities might not be sustainable in the long run, or addressing a problem in one area might shift the challenge to another region. **3**

Thus, while resilience and sustainability are critical for a harmonious existence within our ever-changing environment, recognizing their distinct characteristics and applications is paramount. Only then can we craft strategies that harness the strengths of both paradigms, ensuring that our systems are enduring but also adaptive and robust in the face of unforeseen challenges.

Resilience and Leadership

Resilience presents some real connotations for leadership in crisis management and change management. Navigating the complexities and uncertainties of the modern era necessitates a paradigm shift in leadership—a move towards resilience as an indispensable quality. Beyond sheer skill and strategy, effective leadership now calls for an intrinsic ability to rebound from adversities, adapt, and continue forward with an unwavering spirit.

In 2022, bestselling author and influential economic thinker Jerem Rifkin published a book entitled *The Age of Resilience* highlighting th necessity of resilient systems, the transition to renewable energy, an the interconnectedness of global systems. Rifkin advocates for balance between economic growth and environmental sustainability emphasizing the importance of collaborative approaches to addres complex challenges like climate change. His focus on innovativ technology use and future-oriented thinking provides a framewor for sustainability leaders to drive change. Additionally, his insight into policy and social change are crucial for leaders aiming to foste long-term environmental and social impacts, making his work foundational guide for those in sustainability leadership. **4**

Three other seminal works, namely Duggan and Theurer's *Resilien Leadership 2.0*, Drath's *Resilient Leadership*, and Everly and Athey' *Leading Beyond Crisis*, offer insights into the evolving intersection c resilience and leadership.

In *Resilient Leadership 2.0: Leading with Calm, Clarity, and Conviction i Anxious Times*, Duggan and Theurer construct a compellin framework around emotional intelligence. They champion tha influential leaders confront challenges with determination, clarity, an conviction. This triumvirate, according to them, forms the core c resilient leadership. By championing calm, leaders are better poised t navigate crises, warding off the paralyzing anxieties that typicall accompany them. Clarity ensures decisions remain informec strategic, and purpose driven. Conviction becomes the driving forc that ensures perseverance through even the most daunting c challenges. **5**

In *Resilient Leadership: Beyond Myths and Misunderstandings*, Drath offer a unique perspective, suggesting resilience extends beyond person; attributes. He argues that many existing leadership models ar steeped in misconceptions, which, in turn, hinder genuine resilienc A holistic leadership approach, as per Drath, involves a willingness t break free from these myths, embracing adaptability, flexibility, an longevity in leadership endeavors. **6**

The narrative further deepens with Everly and Athey's *Leading Beyor Crisis: The Five Pillars of Transformative Resilient Leadership*. The introduce a structured approach to resilience, outlining five essenti;

pillars that leaders must embrace to transcend crises. Their model underscores that resilient leadership is not just reactive but transformative, focusing on creating positive changes that endure beyond immediate challenges. Everly and Athey's contributions emphasize the symbiotic relationship between crisis management and transformative leadership, suggesting that resilience can be both a protective mechanism and a catalyst for growth. **7**

Drawing from these works, it's evident that resilient leadership is multifaceted. It encompasses attributes such as calm, clarity, and conviction but also champions adaptability, continuous growth, and transformative thinking. In today's volatile landscape, leaders poised to make a difference will combine skill with resilience, viewing challenges not as impediments but as opportunities for innovation and growth.

The Adaptive Leadership Paradigm

These notions of resilient leadership parallel the values and characteristics explored in the "adaptive leadership theory studies." **8** It is obvious that in today's VUCA world, the challenges leaders face is multifaceted and ever evolving. The traditional, linear approaches to leadership, which often focus on rigid strategies and predefined outcomes, find themselves ill-equipped to tackle the unpredictability inherent in our contemporary context. This is where the Adaptive Leadership Paradigm emerges as a game changer. **9**

Adaptive leadership, at its core, is about navigating complexity and molding and thriving within it. It recognizes that the solutions of the past might only sometimes address the present or future challenges. This paradigm encourages leaders to be forward-thinking, constantly attuning themselves to environmental shifts and recalibrating their strategies accordingly.

A hallmark of adaptive leadership is its emphasis on resilience. But it's not resilience in the face of adversity alone; it is resilience combined with agility. This means leaders aren't just withstanding pressures; they're pivoting, learning, and growing amidst them. They are flexible in their approaches and willing to abandon outdated strategies in favor of innovative solutions.

Moreover, adaptive leadership demands an intimate dance with ambiguity. Instead of perceiving ambiguity as a threat, adaptive leaders see it as an opportunity—a canvas on which new ideas can be painted, a space where innovation flourishes. Such leaders are reactive and proactive, often anticipating changes and crafting responses even before challenges manifest.

This paradigm also fosters a culture of continuous learning. Leaders who adapt are voracious learners, always seeking insights, whether from successes or failures. They cultivate environments where feedback is cherished, risks are taken, and failures are not shunned but seen as steppingstones to greater achievements.

The Adaptive Leadership Paradigm is a clarion call for leaders to evolve. In a world marked by VUCA, it is not the strongest who survive but the most adaptable. And this adaptability, punctuated by agility, resilience, and a love for innovation, will shape tomorrow's success stories.

The Crossing Boundaries Paradigm

As our global environment's complexities deepen and we find new interconnected, interdisciplinary, and international solutions, leadership cannot remain confined within traditional boundaries. Instead, it must venture beyond, crossing previously thought distinct and separate realms. This shift is encapsulated in the "crossing boundaries paradigm," a notion that extends the principles of resilience and adaptive leadership into uncharted territories. **10**

At the core of this paradigm lies the recognition that innovative solutions often emerge at the intersections. Fresh perspectives are birthed at the crossroads of disciplines, cultures, and worldviews, pushing the horizons of what's possible. This is particularly vital in sustainability leadership, where the challenges are inherently multifaceted and require holistic, integrative solutions.

One of the most profound boundaries leaders face is that of cultural biases. Our cultural lenses shape our perceptions, influencing our reactions to change and our understanding of what's "normal" or "acceptable." However, resilient leadership recognizes that these lenses can sometimes be limiting, acting as blinders that restrict our vision. Crossing this boundary (cross-culturally) means actively challenging one's cultural biases and seeking to understand and appreciate perspectives that might seem foreign or even contrary. In a world that's becoming increasingly globalized, such cross-cultural agility is not just beneficial—it is imperative. **11**

Beyond cultural boundaries, leaders also face the challenge of resistance to change. Humans, by nature, often gravitate towards the familiar, and changes, especially transformative ones, can induce fear or apprehension. Yet, adaptive leadership understands that evolution is an inevitable part of growth. The crossing boundaries paradigm thus encourages leaders to bridge the gap between the known and the unknown, making the unfamiliar more accessible and the intimidating more approachable.

Furthermore, the importance of interdisciplinary boundaries cannot be overstated, especially in the context of sustainability leadership. Solutions to complex environmental, social, and economic challenges rarely lie within the purview of a single discipline. Instead, they demand a fusion of insights from multiple domains, be it science, humanities, technology, or arts. Leaders who embrace multidisciplinary and transdisciplinary approaches are better equipped to devise innovative strategies that address the root causes of issues rather than just their symptoms.

The crossing boundaries paradigm has frequently birthed resilient solutions and groundbreaking innovations throughout history. Historical polymaths like Leonardo da Vinci seamlessly blended art and science, with his anatomical sketches revolutionizing both fields. Similarly, Benjamin Franklin's multifaceted genius led to inventions like the lightning rod, demonstrating the power of interdisciplinary thought.

In contemporary times, this spirit of boundary-crossing is evident in our response to pressing crises. The swift development of COVID-19 vaccines was a collaborative triumph, blending expertise from bioinformatics, molecular biology, and logistics. Meanwhile, the fight against climate change sees engineers, biologists, and urban planners unite to devise green urban solutions. Modern innovators, akin to past polymaths, exemplify this ethos. Elon Musk's ventures, spanning diverse fields, and Tim Berners-Lee's invention of the World Wide

Web underscore the transformative potential of crossing traditional boundaries. [12]

In other words, the crossing boundaries paradigm is a testament to the evolution of leadership in our contemporary era. It beckons leaders to be boundary-spanners, to embrace the richness that lies beyond their immediate contexts, and to weave a tapestry of solutions that are as diverse as the challenges they aim to address. In doing so, it strengthens the principles of resilience and adaptability and elevates the vision of sustainable leadership, grounding it in an interconnected and interdependent reality.

The Contextualization Paradigm

The essence of the contextualization paradigm is deeply rooted in the appreciation that leadership cannot adopt a universal, one-size-fits-all approach. Instead, it must be a mix of strategic foresight, cultural sensitivity, and adaptability tailored to the intricacies of each unique situation. In this lens, leadership is as much about reading and interpreting as it is about guiding and directing.

Building upon the principles of the contextualization paradigm, we find a seamless connection with the Zeitgeist Theory of Leadership. [13] This theory posits that the spirit of the times, or the 'Zeitgeist,' essentially molds and determines emerging leaders. The collective consciousness of a particular era or culture shapes its leaders rather than individuals shaping the times. In this framework, leaders are both a product and a reflection of their socio-cultural, economic, and political contexts. These contextualization paradigms later generated the situational and contingency theories we examined in Chapter 1. The Zeitgeist and context-oriented leadership theories share a core belief: leadership is intrinsically tied to its environment. Leaders aren't isolated entities; they are deeply interwoven into the fabric of their times, continually influenced by, and influencing the contexts in which they operate. As such, a truly effective leader is one who not only understands and adapts to their context but also recognizes that they are, in many ways, a manifestation of that very context. This symbiotic relationship between leaders and their environments underscores the profound significance of contextual awareness in leadership dynamics.

Resilient leadership, which calls for the ability to handle diverse challenges, is a testament to contextualization's importance. The strategies that prove effective during a financial crisis might be incongruent with those needed in the face of a natural calamity. Furthermore, cultural nuances significantly influence the fabric of resilience. Consider the starkly different approaches during the COVID-19 pandemic: nations with communal cultures, like New Zealand and Taiwan, underscored collective responsibility and care, significantly aiding their successful containment strategies. Conversely, societies with a more individualistic bent had to pivot, emphasizing personal responsibility linked to individual freedoms.[14]

Turning our focus to sustainability leadership, the value of contextual understanding becomes even more palpable. The challenges and solutions of sustainability are deeply regional, if not local. Addressing desertification in Africa's Sahel Region demands a different leadership approach than combatting Amazon Rainforest deforestation. Moreover, true sustainability leadership requires an acute understanding of local stakeholders. It is about ensuring initiatives resonate with local values and get the crucial buy-in from communities. Scandinavian nations, for instance, leverage their high societal trust and communal ethos to pioneer sustainable initiatives. Yet, in regions where institutional trust might be lower, the goal of sustainability is often started by grassroots movements. Parts of India stand out in this context, where community-led endeavors have driven impactful reforestation projects.

In summary, the importance of the contextualization paradigm in leadership dynamics must be considered. It is a potent reminder for leaders: true success isn't merely about vision or strategy. It is about understanding, adapting, and resonating with the ever-evolving landscapes of challenges, cultures, and opportunities. In the vast arenas of resilience and sustainability, such contextual leadership is a hallmark of effectiveness and an imperative.

Conclusion: The Imperative of Contextualized Resilience

In exploring resilience as contextualization, we've emphasized the importance of aligning leadership strategies with the unique facets of ever-evolving contexts. The distinct challenges and opportunities that emanate from diverse situations require leaders to exercise agility, adaptability, and acute contextual awareness. Tailoring responses based on the specificities of organizations and communities doesn't merely help weather the storm; it builds robust resilience that stands the test of time.

Resilience is destined to become a more integral element in our VUCA future. Leadership would need to adapt and integrate these new paradigms and promote initiatives that produce systemic results across diverse but interconnected contexts. An example is the World Economic Forum, which introduced the Resilience Consortium during the 2022 annual gathering in Davos, Switzerland. This initiative aims to unite visionary leaders from both public and private sectors to bolster resilience on a global scale—spanning various regions, economies, and industries.

McKinsey & Company rightly positions contextualization as a cornerstone for resilience aimed at sustainable and inclusive growth. Leaders cultivate an environment that fosters continuous learning and iterative refinement by moving beyond reactive approaches and stepping into proactive anticipation of disruptions. The COVID-19 pandemic stands as a vivid testament to this. Those at the helm who managed to create their strategies into the unique approach of their contexts navigated the crisis more effectively and fortified trust and adaptability within their ecosystems. **15**

However, the essence of contextualized leadership transcends adaptability alone. As research by Fischhoff and Roxane Cohen Silver suggests, the tenet of honesty during turbulent times adds another layer of trust-building. **16** Context-aware leaders, in their truthfulness and clarity, fortify the bridges of trust with stakeholders. This trust is not just a bond; it's the bedrock upon which resilient structures can be built and sustained.

In wrapping up this chapter, it's worth reiterating that our era underscores the urgent need for contextualized leadership. Whether steering the ship through global crises or charting paths for sustainable futures, leaders who embrace and embody contextualization are poised to make lasting impacts.

Key Takeaways: Resilient Adaptations

1. **Holistic Understanding**: Resilience isn't just about recovery; it's about comprehensively understanding and adapting to ever-changing contexts. This means bouncing back from setbacks and evolving in response, often becoming stronger.

2. **Context is King**: Contextualized leadership proves to be imperative in times of crisis. Leaders who tailor their strategies and actions according to the unique circumstances of their organizations and communities are more adept at fostering trust and navigating complex challenges.

3. **Crossing Boundaries for Innovation**: Breaking down barriers—cultural biases, resistance to change, or interdisciplinary divides—is pivotal to fostering resilience. Drawing inspiration from polymath innovators like Leonardo da Vinci, modern leaders can harness diverse knowledge areas and perspectives to drive forward-thinking solutions.

4. **Adaptive Leadership in a VUCA World**: In an environment characterized by volatility, uncertainty, complexity, and ambiguity (VUCA), adaptive leadership becomes non-negotiable. It promotes agility, embraces change, and ensures a proactive response to unforeseen challenges.

5. **Collaboration for Global Resilience**: Global initiatives, like the Resilience Consortium launched by the World Economic Forum, underscore the importance of collaborative efforts across sectors and regions. Such global consortiums highlight the need for shared wisdom and collective action to build resilience that transcends borders.

CHAPTER 5

STEWARDSHIP AS CARE

FOR GOVERNING THE COMMONS

Overview

Stewardship is a deep-rooted sense of responsibility and care towards whatever one oversees, whether a project, team, or the planet. By nurturing a stewardship mindset, one becomes intrinsically motivated to protect, preserve, and enhance, ensuring the well-being of current and future generations. This chapter focuses on the profound essence of stewardship, transcending mere management to encompass a genuine dedication to whatever one is charged with. Central to this idea is the belief that everything, from teams to projects to the Earth itself, deserves respect, protection, and conscious cultivation. By embracing stewardship, individuals are moved by immediate objectives and a deeply ingrained desire to foster long-term well-being and prosperity. This chapter offers insights into the transformative power of such a mindset, emphasizing its significance in ensuring a balanced and thriving environment for both present and upcoming generations. The narrative underscores the importance of acting with passion and responsibility, revealing the impact of a stewardship-centered approach on sustainability and holistic development.

Leadership as Stewardship

We need new paradigms for leadership that meet the sustainability challenges of our times. Leadership and management are essential for sustainability implementations but demand fresh perspectives. Traditional paradigms often saw leadership through dual lenses: the pragmatic control that ensured the cogs of an organization turned efficiently (leadership as management) and the heroic visionaries whose foresight guided these cogs towards a grand future (leadership as visionaries). However, the challenges of the 21st century, underscored by the urgent need for sustainable solutions, call for a different kind of leadership. This is where our perception needs a shift from mere pragmatic controllers and visionaries to embrace the profound ethos of stewardship. With its foundational values of nurturing, empowering, and caring, Stewardship aligns seamlessly with the core tenets of sustainability leadership. Unlike the siloed, top-down approaches of old, stewardship fosters an inclusive, holistic approach. It recognizes the intricate interconnectedness of our world and emphasizes collective well-being and long-term health. As we delve deeper into management, leadership, and stewardship, it becomes evident that the stewardship paradigm offers the most aligned and effective approach to leadership for a future that prioritizes sustainability.

Let's review these paradigms in their distinctive elements and how they indicate a correlated evolution of values and practices:

1. **Management Controls and Optimizes Efficiency**: Management is the gear mechanism of an organization. It focuses on the specifics, laying out the steps and procedures that ensure the machinery runs smoothly. Management adopts a controlling stance when operating with a close lens on the day-to-day operations. This is essential to address immediate tasks, uphold standards, and achieve short-term goals. The essence of management is not just about ticking boxes but optimizing processes to ensure the utmost efficiency. When managed properly, every cog in the machinery, every employee, and every task contributes to the organizational structure's streamlining and productivity. It's

SUSTAINABILITY LEADERSHIP

about making the best use of resources and ensuring that the organization's path aligns with its tactical objectives.

2. **Leadership Guides, Envisions, and Harnesses Effectiveness**: Beyond the immediate and tactical, leadership sets its eyes on the horizon. Leaders provide the larger vision and guide their teams towards it. While management deals with the "how," leadership is concerned with the "why" and "what." It's about painting a picture of the future, instilling a shared mission, and steering the organization toward that envisioned future. Leadership delves into the dynamics of human interactions, influencing them, providing incentives, and embedding shared values. While leaders cannot guarantee fixed outcomes, they shape the journey, ensuring that every step taken is meaningful, purposeful, and effective. Leadership is the compass that points out the direction and ensures the organization remains true to its strategic vision.

3. **Stewardship Nurtures, Empowers, and Exudes Care**: At the heart of every thriving organization lies the essence of stewardship. Beyond the tactical efficiencies and strategic visions, stewardship focuses on the overall health and well-being of the organizational ecosystem. The gentle hand nurtures growth, the protective shield that empowers every member, and the underlying force that cares for the collective good. Stewards operate from a place of deep understanding and empathy. They create conditions ripe for innovation, ensuring every member feels valued, heard, and motivated. By fostering a culture of encouragement, invitation, and continuous learning, stewardship ensures that the organization doesn't just function but thrives and flourishes. It's a role that cherishes the intrinsic potential of the system and every individual within, ensuring holistic growth and sustainability.

Leaders play a pivotal role in crafting legacies that extend beyond their immediate realm of influence to touch the lives of future generations. By embodying stewardship behaviors, they foster a positive and continuous loop of intergenerational reciprocity. Such leaders prioritize the present needs of their organizations or communities and anticipate and address the potential challenges and requirements of those who will come after them. This forward thinking approach ensures that decisions made today are beneficial in the short term and resonate with lasting positive impacts. In essence through genuine stewardship, leaders commit to the well-being o future generations, ensuring that they inherit a world that's been cared for and thoughtfully sustained.

Defining Stewardship

The essence of stewardship, as displayed in literature, is a clear shif from the self to others. It is not just about personal gains, ambitions or agendas; rather, it underscores a profound commitment to broader vision that benefits all. Traditionally, stewardship i characterized by its dedication to safeguarding the well-being of every stakeholder within an organization or community. This approach recognizes that every entity, regardless of its stature or role, hold intrinsic value. Thus, true stewards seek to ensure their actions and decisions prioritize collective welfare over isolated benefits. Thi selfless orientation, deeply embedded in the fabric of stewardship differentiates it from other leadership paradigms and makes i particularly relevant in contexts where holistic well-being and sustainable growth are paramount.

In his 1993 pioneering book *Stewardship: Choosing Service Over Self Interest* Peter Block argues that "the alternative to leadership i stewardship." **1** Moving beyond traditional paradigms of leadership and management, Block introduces a fresh perspective that center on the role of stewardship in guiding organizational behaviors and outcomes. His argument isn't merely about integrating stewardship a a peripheral value but about placing it at the core of an organization' ethos. It is about altering the very DNA of organizational culture. He defines this new paradigm with sustainability values identifiable as the responsibility to serve and empower the next generations.

> Stewardship is the umbrella idea that promises the means of achieving fundamental change in how we govern our institutions. Stewardship is to hold something in trust for another. Historically, stewardship was a means to protect a kingdom while the rightfully in charge were away or, more

often, to govern for the sake of an underage king. The underage king for us is the next generation. We choose service over self-interest more powerfully when we build the capacity of the next generation to govern themselves. **2**

Block, already known for his book, *The Empowered Manager*, **3** takes his understanding of empowerment to the next level, where organizational hierarchies are flattened, and the traditional power dynamics are replaced with the stewardship model. Under this paradigm, private, public, and nonprofit organizations don't just chase short-term gains but look at the larger picture, ensuring their actions resonate with a purpose and benefit all stakeholders involved. Doing so can make their operations more transparent, inclusive, and, most importantly, service oriented. Block makes a compelling case for stewardship to become a central paradigm for the next levels of leadership and management, where they rethink their role in the spirit of service, partnership, and shared responsibility.

Unfortunately, the concept of "stewardship" has been hindered by misinterpreting criticisms. For one, "stewardship" has been criticized for its narrow Christian Biblical (Genesis) interpretations of God's given human dominance over nature. Even within the differences between Benedictine stewardship and Franciscan conservation, it has consequently been understood as an inadequate paradigm for effective environmental stewardship. **4** Some critics have pointed out potential drawbacks in the stewardship concept, associating it historically with tendencies that may be seen as sexist, speciesist, or anthropocentric. **5** There's also an argument that without a foundational belief in a creator, the concept of "environmental stewardship" lacks substance and meaning. **6** However, other studies that have analyzed the concept's recent developments and nuances advance a more in-depth conceptual exploration, providing an adequate comprehensive framework. **7**

Stewardship Leadership for the Commons

Stewardship leadership is emerging as an imperative for businesses and organizations in the 21st century. As articulated by Rajeev Peshawaria in a recent *Forbes* article, steward leadership is about a genuine commitment towards shaping a collective, brighter future for stakeholders, the environment, society, and future generations. **8**. Leaders must transition from traditional norms and values to truly live up to this role, understanding that external mechanisms like financial incentives or regulatory compliance aren't sufficient. The heart of this transition lies in understanding and practicing four pivotal stewardship values:

1. **Interdependence:** Recognizing that the world is a complex, interconnected web where one's success is intertwined with the success of others. For businesses, this means collaborative strategies, partnerships, and co-creating value.

2. **Long-term View:** Commitment to ensuring that actions and strategies create sustained value for the present stakeholders and future generations. This is akin to safeguarding the commons for the next generation, as emphasized by Elinor Ostrom.

3. **Ownership Mentality:** Embracing an active role in steward leadership, stepping up, taking responsibility, and driving change, rather than waiting for it to happen or be mandated.

4. **Creative Resilience:** Displaying the resolve to overcome unforeseen and disruptive challenges by innovating and finding new pathways and solutions.

Drawing parallels to Elinor Ostrom's influential work on governing the commons, we can deduce some enriching insights for stewardship leadership. Her groundbreaking research debunked the prevailing belief that common resources were doomed to overuse and destruction (Garret Harden's *Tragedy of the Commons*) unless they were regulated by the government or privatized. Instead, she found that communities could, and did, self-organize to manage common resources sustainably under certain conditions. **9** These insights can be summarized and adapted to stewardship leadership as follows:

1. **Trust and Reciprocity:** Central to effective commons management, mutual trust, and reciprocity can also be foundational for steward leaders. This can be fostered through transparent communication, clear decision-making, and consistent actions.

2. **Collective Decision Making:** Ostrom emphasized decisions made by those most affected by them. In the context of steward leadership, this underscores the importance of stakeholder engagement and participatory leadership.

3. **Boundaries and Membership:** Clear demarcations and roles are vital in commons management and stewardship leadership. Ensuring that resources aren't over-utilized requires clear accountability structures.

4. **Monitoring and Sanctioning:** Steward leaders should have robust monitoring systems akin to effective commons management. Any deviation from organizational or environmental responsibilities should be met with corrective measures.

5. **Nested Enterprises:** Larger commons are often governed effectively when broken into nested, smaller units. From this, steward leaders should promote decentralized decision-making, aligning local units with overarching organizational objectives.

6. **Long-term Thinking:** Ostrom's principles lean heavily towards sustainable resource management. Guiding by their long-term view value, Steward leaders must similarly make decisions that might sometimes require preceding short-term gains for the broader, long-term good.

Integrating the four stewardship values with the six principles from commons governance offers a refined view of stewardship leadership. This model emphasizes collaboration, sustainability, and visionary thinking. Such leadership champions responsibility and sustainability and encourages collaborative efforts and long-term planning, safeguarding the immediate commons and the wider community's future.

Stewardship as Leadership that Cares

Pope Francis's Encyclical *Laudato Sí: On Care for Our Common Home* (2015) reframes the notion of "stewardship" as a proper relationship of "care" for the Earth and its inhabitants. **10** These relationships "should be understood more properly in the sense of responsible stewardship" (sec. 116). He makes the case that stewardship is embedded in a "culture of care" (sec. 231). The "care of creation" (sec. 14), "care for safeguarding species" (sec. 42), "care for nature" (sec. 64), and "care for the environment" (sec. 64) are integrated with other forms of social care such as "care for the vulnerable" (sec. 10), care for our neighbors (sec. 70), "care for our brothers and sisters" (sec. 208), care for the interior of homes of the poor (sec. 148), and care for indigenous communities and traditions (sec. 146). In other words, the value message of *Laudato Sí* is to inspire us all to embrace stewardship as a "care for all that exists" (sec. 11), "care for our own lives" (sec. 70), care for a fragile world (sec. 78), "care for the world" (sec. 144), care for the land (sec. 146), care for the care for our body (sec. 155), "care for the ecosystem of the entire earth" (sec. 167), care for the natural environment (sec. 208), "care for creation" (sec. 211), "care for other living beings" (sec. 211), "care for all creatures" (sec. 213), "care for ecology" (sec. 225). Stewardship is interpreted as a necessary relation of reciprocity and universal care where the care for our common home (sec. 3) is balanced with the care for our common good (sec. 23), and our common destiny "which cannot exclude those who come after us (sec. 159). **11**

From these perspectives, stewardship emerges from an "Ethics of Care" called "Seva Ethics" in the Sanskrit lexicon. **12** This notion is distinct from anthropocentric views, which place human interests at the pinnacle, and biocentric standpoints, which revere the inherent worth of all living entities; stewardship revolves around the notion of "care" of our interconnected ecosystems. It emphasizes the mutual dependence and shared destinies of every being and ecosystem on Earth. Stewardship posits that humanity isn't an external force but an integral thread in this vast tapestry of life, bestowing us with the role of caretakers.

At the heart of stewardship ethics lies the notion of "caretaker ship," displacing the conventional idea of ownership. It challenges the erroneous belief that Earth, and its infinite resources are human properties to exploit. Instead, it advocates for a role of guardianship, where our primary duty is to protect and nurture – to care for. It underscores the value of reverence towards our planet, its diverse lora and fauna, and the essence of treating every life form with unwavering compassion and care. Leaders embracing stewardship move beyond mere directives, fostering a culture of collective care, responsibility, and sustainable guardianship for the world we all share.

Leadership in this perspective of stewardship-as-care comprises the personal, collective, and universal levels of responsibilities across the common good, common home, and common destiny. This comprehensive and universal level of care requires an inclusive awareness of our interdependence and co-responsibility. In ethics, these levels correspond to *cura personalis* (care for the whole person) and what Aristotle refers to as *Arete* (virtuous leadership development), *cura apostolica* (care for the service of others), and what Aristotle refers to as *phronesis* (practical wisdom) and *eudemonic* purposes (virtuous habits). Finally, it includes a third level of care that is expressed as *cura universalis* (care for the whole world), which Aristotle expresses as *eudaimonia* (true happiness, well-being, prosperity, and 'blessedness') and modern literature identifies as global responsibility through a sense of global citizenship. **13**

Rediscovery of the Leadership of Care Paradigm

Numerous studies and reflections emerged on the "leadership of Care" as a paradigm to make sense of the COVID-19 pandemic. **14** Some even observe that this event has brought forth the rediscovery of a broad range of caring leadership behaviors. Due to these events, they envision that "deep caring values, compassion for humankind, empathy for the human condition, honesty, and humility will be at the heart of future transformational leadership and inspire others to act ethically, positively, and responsibly." **15**

Although not without its leadership issues, COVID-19 was an unprecedented global event that shook the very foundation of our societies, economies, and healthcare systems. More than just a health crisis, it was a sociocultural awakening, illuminating the deep interconnections between communities and nations and emphasizing the inherent responsibility of every individual to preserve the collective well-being. The pandemic highlighted the crucial need for a paradigm shift in leadership, away from traditional, profit-driven, and individualistic approaches towards one that emphasizes care, compassion, and community-centric values. Not just for the healthcare sector, this "leadership of care" paradigm is influencing other fields and making a mark in our understanding of sustainability leadership.

In the shadow of the global pandemic, Leadership of Care emerged as a poignant paradigm, revealing the intricate weave of interdependencies that defines our global community. Though not an entirely new concept, the pandemic's trials and tribulations brought its essence to the forefront, spotlighting its foundations in empathy, altruism, and community-centric values. This approach to leadership is deeply rooted in the understanding that every decision reverberates, influencing the well-being of individuals, communities, and entire nations. Such a perspective aligns closely with the stewardship paradigm for sustainability leadership, emphasizing the guardianship of resources and the profound responsibility leaders have toward the holistic well-being of the interconnected web of life. The emphasis is on a harmonious coexistence, where decisions are made with an acute awareness of their far-reaching consequences, underscoring the importance of nurturing, and caring as fundamental leadership attributes.

The leadership of Care Characteristics

Here are some core "caring" characteristics of the stewardship paradigm and their correlations to sustainability leadership. This list expands on the 10 Caritas Processes (*in italics*) elaborated by Dr. Jean Watson in her study of caring science and nursing practices **16**

1. **Humanistic-Altruistic Values** *(Sustaining humanistic–altruistic values–the practice of loving kindness-compassion and equanimity for self/other):* Stewardship places a premium on serving others and promoting well-being, aligning with the principle of fostering love, kindness, and equanimity for oneself and others. Care leadership emphasizes a duty to serve, not command.

2. **Authentic Presence** *(Being authentically present, enabling faith/hope/belief system; honoring subjective inner, lifeworld of self/others):* Sustainability leadership underscores the

importance of being present, attentive, and responsive to the ecosystem's needs. By honoring the inner world of others and oneself, leaders can truly understand the depth of challenges faced and respond with hope and faith.

3. **Self-Sensitivity and Transpersonal Presence** *(Being sensitive to self and others by cultivating spiritual practices; beyond ego-self to transpersonal presence):* Effective sustainability leaders transcend ego, embracing a broader perspective that encompasses self-awareness and a profound understanding of the larger global community.

4. **Relationship Development** *(Developing and sustaining loving, trusting-caring relationships):* Sustainable practices thrive on collaboration. A caring leader fosters loving, trusting relationships, ensuring teamwork is underpinned by mutual respect and understanding.

5. **Expression of Feelings** *(Allowing for expressing positive and negative feelings — authentically listening to another person's story):* Transparency and open communication are pivotal for care leadership and stewardship. Leaders can authentically listen and value feedback to address concerns and build trust.

6. **Creative Problem-Solving** *(Creatively problem-solving "solution-seeking" through the caring process; complete use of self and artistry of caring-healing practices using all ways of knowing/being/doing/becoming):* Sustainability challenges demand innovative solutions. Leaders who engage in "solution-seeking" through a caring lens will leverage creativity to address complex issues holistically.

7. **Transpersonal Teaching-Learning** *(Engaging in transpersonal teaching and learning within the context of caring relationships; staying within other's frame of reference; shift toward coaching model for expanded health/wellness):* Sustainability leadership involves mentoring and empowering others. A shift towards a coaching model facilitates mutual growth, enhancing collective capacity to address challenges.

8. **Healing Environment Creation** *(Creating a healing environment at all levels; subtle environment for energetic, authentic caring presence):* A caring leader recognizes the significance of creating

environments that promote well-being at all levels, reinforcing the sustainability aim of holistic health.

9. **Reverential Assistance with Basic Needs** *(Reverentially assisting with basic needs as sacred acts, touching the mind of others, sustaining human dignity):* Sustainability is rooted in meeting basic needs without compromising future generations. Leaders uphold the sanctity of life and the environment through sacred acts that honor human dignity.

10. **Openness to the Existential and Spiritual** *(Opening to spiritual, mystery, unknowns — allowing for miracles)*: Embracing life's mysteries and unknowns means recognizing the interconnectedness of all things, a core principle of sustainability.

As the world continues to grapple with the aftershocks of the COVID-19 pandemic and learn to become more resilient for future pandemics, leaders must recognize and live these values, steering communities towards a sustainable and compassionate future. We also need to better integrate these relational, compassionate, emphatic, and human-centered values with perspectives of stewardship and sustainability leadership values. The notion of quantum leadership and conscious leadership we examined earlier provides those value integrations that better explain these dimensions of sustainability leadership.

Leadership of Care & Quantum (Conscious) Leadership

Quantum Leadership is rooted in the principles and theories of quantum physics. In this model, leadership doesn't merely draw parallels from the quantum world; it seeks to embody the foundational truths of our universe. One key quantum idea is interconnectedness: particles can be entangled, meaning one particle's state immediately affects another's, regardless of the distance between them. This phenomenon moves beyond the material world, suggesting a universal consciousness or an interwoven fabric of existence. **17**

The "Leadership of Care" paradigm, emphasizing compassion, interconnected well-being, and collective responsibility, resonates deeply with the principles of Quantum Leadership and offers insights for understanding how sustainability leadership incorporates these tenets. Here's how these realities merge into these interconnected values:

1. **Holism Over Reductionism:** Traditional leadership often tries to break down problems into smaller, independent parts (reductionism). However, both care leadership and quantum leadership recognize that everything is interconnected. A problem isn't just an isolated event; it's a symptom of the entire system.

2. **Non-locality and Being Present:** Quantum physics introduces the concept of non-locality, where particles influence each other regardless of spatial separation. In care leadership, the idea is reflected in the emphasis on being authentically present and understanding that actions have wide-reaching consequences, regardless of the immediate context.

3. **Potentiality and Creative Problem-Solving:** In the quantum world, particles exist in a state of potentiality, materializing based on observation. Care leadership encourages tapping into untapped potentials, seeking creative solutions, and believing in what's possible rather than just what's observable.

4. **Observer Effect and Authentic Listening:** Quantum theory posits that the mere act of observing affects the observed. Similarly, in care leadership, truly listening (observing) can bring about change, healing, and transformation in the observed (those being led).

5. **Entanglement and Relationship Development:** Quantum entanglement signifies an inseparable relationship between particles beyond space and time. Similarly, care leadership emphasizes the development of deep, meaningful relationships, recognizing that we're all entangled in a web of mutual influence and responsibility.

6. **Universal Consciousness and Transpersonal Presence:** Quantum Leadership posits a universal consciousness beyond

mere matter, echoed in care leadership's emphasis on self-sensitivity and a transpersonal presence that transcends ego and material desires.

Incorporating the interconnected values of Quantum Leadership into the leadership of care paradigm adds a profound layer of depth, emphasizing that leadership isn't just about navigating the material world. Instead, it's about recognizing and operating within the interconnected web of universal consciousness. Such a leadership style is more attuned to the complexities of the modern world and speaks to deeper truths about the nature of existence. By aligning with these principles, leaders can drive organizations and communities towards more holistic, compassionate, and sustainable futures.

The "I CARE" Paradigm for Sustainability Leaders

In 2023, Italian President Sergio Mattarella celebrated the 100th anniversary of Don Lorenzo Milani's (1923-1967) birth with a reverential speech at his village school. After World War II, Benito Mussolini's fascist ideologies still lingered in the air of 1950's Italy. Don Milani, a young Catholic priest and a strong critic of fascism, was reassigned by his superiors to work in the remote village of Barbiana in the Mugello Region outside Florence in order to silence him. In spite of this ostracism, Don Milani and his staff became a guiding light for the community of Barbiana, evoking civil participation and justice in a time of indifference.

Today, visitors to the Barbiana School can see their "I CARE" sign in the classroom. They wrote this sign as a deliberate objection to Mussolini's popular fascist slogan, "Me ne frego," literally meaning "I don't care." Don Milani wanted to encourage his students and community to resist such apathy and used his "I CARE" slogan to signify hope. This simple yet powerful phrase symbolized Don Milani's empathy, unity, and educational paradigm. **18**

He and his staff focused their attention on the entire village. Barbiana, cut off from the rest of the world and the eyes of the press, resembled all types of marginalized communities.

Disenfranchisement and circumstance-induced apathy are all too common, but they are neither irrevocable nor endemic.

Don Milani's teamwork-based pedagogy reflects that of Brazilian educator Paulo Freire (1921-1997). In this effort, everyone, irrespective of age, gender, or status, was a participant. Everyone was a learner, and everyone was a teacher. Don Milani's educational approach was a collective, collaborative endeavor, breaking down the traditional barriers between teacher and student and making every voice pivotal in the educational process. It is this process that brought fame and curiosity to the school. An example of this collaborative approach was their book *Lettera a una Professoressa (Letter to a Teacher)*, co-written by Don Milani and his students. They began the process in 1966 and published the book in 1967, one year before the 1968 student movement protests. It was quickly translated into several languages, touching a nerve worldwide. In addition, the students' collective letters to newspapers also gave them notoriety for their innovative thinking and writing. In this holistic model, education was about individual advancement, community upliftment, social justice, and a brighter collective future.

In emphasizing this interconnectedness, Don Milani was ahead of his time. He recognized that for education to be truly transformative, it had to be rooted in real-world contexts, in the lived experiences of its recipients, and address not just academic but socio-economic and cultural disparities. In doing so, he didn't just transform the Barbiana community but demonstrated a blueprint for social justice education that remains relevant today.

Drawing from Don Lorenzo Milani's Barbiana School model, sustainability leadership can be enriched by several poignant lessons. First, true stewardship requires a radical shift from individualistic endeavors to collective ones; it underscores the necessity of encompassing entire communities in our sphere of influence and concern. Second, leaders should actively strive to cultivate environments where every voice is valued, and every person plays a part, recognizing that the potency of leadership often lies in its ability to galvanize and uplift rather than merely dictate. Moreover, the Barbiana School model underscores the power of context in shaping sustainable decisions. For sustainability leaders, it is imperative to ground their actions and strategies in the nuanced realities of thei communities. Finally, Don Milani's legacy compels us to prioritiz long-term growth and systemic change over transient successes. Tru sustainability lies not in short-lived initiatives but in creating resilien ecosystems where communities can learn, adapt, and thrive fo generations.

As we conclude our exploration of the "stewardship as care" paradigm for sustainability leadership, Don Lorenzo Milani stands a: a towering example of what it truly means to care. His life and worl challenge us to expand our circles of concern, to see beyonc immediate contexts, and to recognize the profound impact o! nurturing holistic, community-centered ecosystems of learning anc growth.

Key Takeaways: Stewardship as Care

1. **Foundational Paradigm for Sustainability Leadership:** The stewardship paradigm is intrinsic to sustainability leadership. True leaders in this realm do not merely manage resources or guide communities but act as guardians. They understand the profound responsibility of ensuring the well-being of the present and future generations, aligning their actions with long-term preservation and communal growth.

2. **Laudato Sí's Call to Action:** Pope Francis's encyclical, "Laudato Sí," amplifies the stewardship message, emphasizing that it is a moral and spiritual responsibility to care for our "common home." Sustainable leadership isn't just a professional endeavor deeply intertwined with ethical and spiritual dimensions. Recognizing our interconnectedness with nature and all living beings, leaders are called to engage in stewardship that harmonizes human advancement with ecological balance.

3. **Characteristics of Leadership Rooted in Care:** Leadership rooted in care extends beyond strategy and vision; it embodies compassion, empathy, and genuine concern for all stakeholders. Such leaders prioritize the well-being of their communities, understanding that true progress is holistic and

inclusive. They see their roles not as dominators but as facilitators of collective growth.

4. **Integration of Quantum (Conscious) Values**: Care leadership embraces Quantum values, recognizing our universe's non-linear, interconnected nature. This means valuing the intangible as much as the tangible and appreciating the unseen connections that bind communities, ecosystems, and the broader cosmos. Such leaders tap into collective consciousness, valuing collaboration and shared wisdom and leading with intuition and holistic insight.

5. **Don Milani's "I-CARE" Motto as a Leadership Guide**: Don Lorenzo Milani's transformative "I CARE" motto challenges leaders to move beyond indifference and take active responsibility. It serves as a reminder that genuine care, underpinned by active participation and responsibility, is the cornerstone of sustainable leadership. In the face of adversity or societal apathy, embracing an "I CARE" ethos means committing to active, compassionate, and forward-thinking leadership that opposes inertia or neglect.

PART II

PRACTICES
AND
APPLICATIONS

CHAPTER 6

PURPOSE: CARING FOR PRINCIPLES

HIGHER PURPOSE MATTERS FOR PRACTICES

Overview

This chapter delves into the foundational role of a higher purpose in shaping sustainable and ethical business practices. It shows the need f going beyond mere corporate social responsibility, emphasizing he necessity of intertwining purpose and sustainability at an organization's core. Beginning with the intrinsic value of a higher urpose, we explore its transformative potential in organizational onduct and culture. By examining the principles vital to sustainable perations, we underscore their role in guiding leaders toward thically sound decisions. Through real-world examples, we showcase ow organizations can move from merely adhering to sustainability rinciples to pioneering systemic societal changes, forging ethical ultures that ripple beyond corporate boundaries.

The chapter culminates in exploring sustainability reporting, ositioning it not as a perfunctory exercise but as a reflective and ransparent demonstration of a company's commitment to its ustainability principles. Together, the sections of this chapter onstruct a holistic view of how purpose, embedded deeply within an rganization, can reshape its relationship with the world, aligning profit with principles, action with accountability, and business wit benevolence.

Higher Purpose Matters

In sustainability leadership practices, "purpose" and "highe purpose" are foundational pillars. On the one hand, "Purpose" ca be understood as the central reason an organization operates, whic transcends mere profit-seeking. It's the core driving force, a missio that clarifies actions and decisions. On the other hand, "highe purpose" elevates this concept further, connecting an organization mission not just to its stakeholders but to broader societal an environmental imperatives. Such a purpose doesn't just guide th company's operations but seeks to impact the world at large addressing overarching challenges like climate change, socia inequality, or community development. In this context, let's delv deeper into how sustainability leadership practices rooted in a "highe purpose" stand apart and influence positive, large-scal transformations. **1**

Higher purpose sustainability leadership extends beyond traditiona corporate social responsibility (CSR). At its core, this leadership styl is about connecting an organization's operational strategies an identities with broader missions that aim to deliver profound socia and environmental impacts. **2**

Take, for example, **Interface**, a company that champions th ambitious goal of reversing global warming and shaping a climate f for life. Rather than just reducing its carbon footprint, Interfac pushes boundaries by focusing on producing carbon-neutra products, turning waste into valuable raw materials, and restorin natural carbon sinks. This commitment demonstrates tha sustainability and profit coexist harmoniously, setting a precedent fo other industries and fostering significant brand loyalty.

Similarly, **Etsy** has a driving mission to champion creativ entrepreneurs and prioritize individual craftsmanship ove impersonal mass production. This commitment is not just in word Etsy offsets 100% of carbon emissions resulting from shipping ensuring every purchase supports sustainable choices. Such practice have sculpted a unique marketplace that values uniqueness and sustainability, drawing sellers and buyers with shared values.

The Body Shop presents another compelling case. With its mission to "enrich, not exploit," the company is a good example of ethical practices in the beauty industry. They take pride in ethical sourcing, cruelty-free beauty standards, and regenerative practices. In doing so, The Body Shop attracts customers and partners who prioritize sustainability, building a community geared towards positive change.

Another standout example is the **Seventh Generation**, which envisions nurturing the health of the next seven generations. Instead of merely marketing green, they produce household products rooted in sustainability, utilizing plant-based ingredients and recyclable packaging. They don't just sell products; they sell a commitment to a circular economy. This approach has rightly positioned them as frontrunners in sustainable consumer products, garnering trust among a rapidly growing eco-conscious consumer base.

Notably, **TOMS Shoes** has pioneered a unique approach to business with its One for One program. The company's mission isn't just about selling shoes but is grounded in believing that businesses can be transformative for good. Each purchase goes beyond the transaction, extending help to someone in need through shoes, sight, water, or safe birth services. This model has driven sales and made customers feel they are a part of a larger, meaningful cause.

Embedding "higher purpose" in the Organizational DNA

Furthermore, the rise of Benefit Corporations and Social Enterprises underscores this shift towards purpose-driven business. These entities, by design, blend profit with purpose. An illustrative example is **Kickstarter**, which transitioned to a Public Benefit Corporation in 2015. Their mandate ensures that while shareholders are important, societal, and environmental impacts aren't side notes but central to their decision-making. This legal transformation sends a clear message to users and stakeholders about Kickstarter's unwavering commitment to prioritizing mission over mere margins.

When a "higher purpose" is embedded in the organizational structure through alternative legal forms, it can result in a tangible sustainability impact. While the size and visibility of large corporations engaged in CSR may be featured in newspapers, the impact and value of dedicated organizations cannot go unnoticed. This is the case for many benefit corporations and social enterprises worldwide, reshaping traditional business paradigms by integrating profit with a higher purpose, particularly in sustainability. **3**

A notable example is **Ecolife Recycling**. They are not only dedicated to the production of eco-friendly products but also champion recycling by providing comprehensive guides on material recycling. Their dual approach of offering sustainable products and educating the public has substantially increased recycling awareness and adoption.

Another transformative brand in this space is **Warby Parker**. With a vision to tackle global vision impairment, they introduced the "Buy a Pair, Give a Pair" initiative. Every sale ensures a pair of glasses is donated to someone in need, translating to millions of pairs distributed and effectively bringing clear sight to countless individuals worldwide.

Meanwhile, **Method Products** is revolutionizing the cleaning industry. They've set themselves apart with biodegradable products sourced from recycled materials and sustainably designed packaging. Their endeavors have reduced the environmental impact of cleaning products and inspired other companies in their industry to adopt sustainable practices.

Ice cream giants **Ben & Jerry's** seamlessly blends delectable treats with a drive for positive societal change. Their commitment goes beyond ethically sourced ingredients; they're vocal advocates for climate justice and various social causes. Their global influence has not only shifted consumer expectations around corporate responsibility but has also played a significant role in advancing global conversations on pressing issues.

In the realm of renewable energy, **d.light** stands out. Dedicated to improving lives in off-grid communities, they have provided solar-powered products to millions, simultaneously improving living conditions and championing the use of renewable energy.

On a more tactile front, **BOMBAS** has addressed the homeless community's often-overlooked needs. They identified socks as one of the most requested items in homeless shelters. Donating every item, they sell ensures warmth and comfort for many facing harsh conditions.

Lastly, **Lemonade Insurance** is redefining transparency in the often-opaque insurance sector. They've adopted a unique model that uses a flat fee, promises rapid claim responses, and, most intriguingly, gives back unclaimed money to charitable causes chosen by their policyholders. This innovative approach streamlines consumer insurance and sends significant funds into various philanthropic endeavors.

These are just a few examples of how the many benefits corporations and social enterprises connect their profit motives with a deeper, more profound societal and environmental purpose, especially in sustainability. Their modus operandi starkly contrasts with other corporate entities that engage in CSR as a mere supplement to their existing practices.

Besides their distinctive organizational (legal) identity, benefit corporations and social enterprises are often subject to standardized reporting beyond financial performance. This reporting examines their tangible impact on their chosen societal or environmental betterment domains. In many jurisdictions, benefit corporations are legally required to produce annual benefit reports, which assess their performance against third-party standards. These rigorous evaluations provide a transparent account of their activities, outcomes, and impacts.

In contrast, while many corporations engaged in CSR produce ESG and other sustainability reports, they don't always adhere to a standardized criterion. This can sometimes lead to discrepancies in reporting and leave room for potential greenwashing. **4**

Another distinguishing factor is the certifications often associated with benefit corporations and social enterprises. Certifications like the B Corp Certification ensure that these businesses meet the highest standards of verified social and environmental performance, public transparency, and legal accountability. Such certifications are not just badges of honor; they are rigorous validations of a company's commitment to genuine impact. **5**

It is this combination of an inherently purpose-driven organizational structure, stringent reporting requirements, and rigorous certifications that set benefit corporations and social enterprises apart. While traditional corporations may engage in CSR activities, often driven by market demands or public relations strategies, benefit corporations and social enterprises are built from the ground up to create positive change. Their operations, strategies, and legal structures are all aligned to ensure they walk the talk, making them less susceptible to the pitfalls of greenwashing and more authentic in their pursuit of a better world. They are inspiring examples of businesses that integrate "higher purpose" into their organizational DNA. These companies stand as testaments to the power of purpose, showcasing how it can differentiate businesses in the marketplace and establish deeper, more meaningful connections with their stakeholders. **6**

Sustainability Principles Matter

In organizational leadership, "principles" influence action and direction. These principles become even more impactful when linked with sustainability, steering companies toward holistic growth and responsible stewardship. Here are a few examples of organizational leadership practices aligned with core sustainability principles:

1. **Resource Efficiency Principle:** This principle propels businesses to use resources optimally and responsibly. **Interface**, has been a pioneer in this area. Their mission to achieve a closed-loop production system sees them using discarded fishing nets to produce carpet tiles. Similarly, **Apple** embodies this principle through its commitment to a closed-loop supply chain, aiming to produce products from recycled or renewable materials. Such an approach, though challenging, embodies the resource efficiency principle and demonstrates a long-term commitment to sustainable operations.

2. **Stakeholder Inclusivity Principle:** This principle ensures that all voices—employees, shareholders, local communities, or even future generations—are given due consideration. The outdoor gear company **REI** exemplifies this principle with its cooperative model. Instead of a typical corporation, REI operates as a co-op, involving members in decision-making processes and returning a portion of profits to the members, thereby weaving community inclusivity into its business fabric. Similarly, **Patagonia** exemplifies this principle in the decision to donate 100% of its Black Friday sales to grassroots environmental groups. This is reflected in their commitment to the broader community and environmental well-being, seamlessly integrating stakeholder interests into their business strategy.

3. **Ecological Resilience Principle:** This principle emphasizes the creation of systems capable of withstanding environmental challenges, which is vital in today's rapidly changing climate. **Seventh Generation**, a green cleaning products company, has long focused on creating products that don't harm the environment and have minimal carbon footprints, displaying a commitment to ecological balance and resilience. Similarly, with its Sustainable Living Plan, Unilever showcases a holistic approach incorporating ecological resilience, influencing market trends, and cultivating a workforce deeply aligned with sustainability.

4. **Long-Term Thinking Principle:** This other tenant of sustainability leadership transcends the impact measurement beyond immediate gains or quarterly results. The global furniture retailer **IKEA** embodies this principle with its ambitious sustainability strategy. Aiming to make sustainable living accessible to millions, they've ventured into offering eco-friendly products, sustainable sourcing, and even renewable energy solutions for households, portraying a vision far beyond the immediate horizon. Another example is **Tesla,** which, with its overarching goal of transitioning the world to sustainable energy, has continuously innovated in transportation and energy, looking decades into the future rather than just the next financial quarter.

As we venture deeper into sustainable business and leadership practices, we need to recognize that the framework of sustainability principles extends far beyond these initial concepts. The subsequent chapters will explore the more nuanced principles driving global initiatives.

The chapter on "prosperity practices" will explore the tenets of the **United Nations Global Compact** and the **Principles for Responsible Investing**. These frameworks underscore the necessity of aligning business operations and investment strategies with universally accepted human rights, labor, environment, and anti corruption principles. They argue for a world where businesses pursue profits and consider their broader societal impacts, aiming for a prosperous future where both businesses and society thrive symbiotically.

Following this, our exploration into the "peace practices" chapter will shed light on the **Guiding Principles of Business and Human Rights**. These principles outline the role of businesses in respecting human rights and provide a framework for addressing adverse human rights impacts associated with business activities. The emphasis here is on ensuring that businesses don't inadvertently become complicit in human rights abuses in the pursuit of economic objectives.

For leaders championing sustainability, these principles are more than mere guidelines; they're the ethos of their leadership style. Every strategy, decision, and partnership are crafted with these principles at the forefront. By genuinely embracing and embedding these principles into their operations, organizations do more than just business—they carve out a legacy of positive impact and responsible growth in the global landscape.

Ethical Decision Making

While values, (higher) purposes, and principles are integral to shaping the foundation of sustainability leadership practices, they only represent the theoretical framework. The true test of sustainability leadership lies in its application—how these principles and purpose translate into real-world decisions. It is through ethical decision making that these abstract concepts come to life and genuinely impact organizations and the broader communities they serve.

Ethical decision-making is the bridge between understanding sustainability principles and implementing them effectively. Without this capacity, leaders risk falling into a pattern of "all talk and no action," where grand statements of purpose remain just that—statements. Realizing this potential requires a structured approach to decision-making that consistently reflects the established principles and purposes.

There are critical steps that sustainability leaders and their organizations can do to ensure their decisions align with their sustainability purpose and principles. Here are the steps with examples:

Step 1: Awareness: Recognize and acknowledge the ethical dilemma. This step is fundamental; effort toward an ethical decision can only be made by recognizing a situation's ethical dimensions. An example is the company, Shell, when, in 2015, it recognized the ethical implications of its operations in the Arctic. Amid concerns about environmental impacts and Indigenous rights, the company chose to halt its drilling operations, prioritizing ecological and social concerns. [7]

Step 2: Gather Information: Understand the context, stakeholders involved, and the potential impacts of the decision. An example emerged in the late 2000s when Nike faced criticism for its labor practices. In response, the company undertook extensive research into its supply chain to fully understand the root causes and implications of the issues raised. [8]

Step 3: Evaluate Alternatives: Consider various courses of action, weighing the pros and cons of each in terms of sustainability principles. An example of this step is when Starbucks was confronted with the environmental impacts of its single-use cups; it evaluated multiple alternatives, from cup recycling to promoting personal tumblers, before rolling out strategies to reduce waste. [9]

Step 4: Make the Decision: Choose the action that best aligns with the organization's sustainability principles, ensuring it is ethically and practically sound.

Step 5: Implement the Decision: This step requires courage and conviction, as leaders may face resistance, especially if the decision involves short-term sacrifices for long-term sustainability. An example emerges from Adidas when, in its commitment to sustainability, it decided to produce shoes made from recycled ocean plastic. Implementing this decision meant investing in new materials and technologies, a testament to the company's dedication to its principles. **10**

Step 6: Review and Reflect: Post-decision, it's crucial to assess the outcomes, gather feedback, and learn from successes and failures to inform future decisions. An example is when, after the Deepwater Horizon oil spill, BP had to reflect on its operational practices and safety standards, leading to significant changes in its approach to offshore drilling. **11**

For sustainability leaders, ethical decision-making transcends a mere procedural approach. It epitomizes a profound dedication to ensuring actions consistently mirror deeply entrenched values, even in intricate and demanding situations. This commitment means that leaders don't merely pay lip service to sustainability; they make it an intrinsic part of their operational fabric. By weaving ethical considerations into the DNA of decision-making, they champion a brand of leadership where words meet actions. Consequently, these leaders shape an organizational culture that champions sustainability and paints a broader vision for the business world. It's a vision where profitability and growth don't match ecological and social responsibility. Instead, they complement each other, heralding an era where business success and sustainable practices are two sides of the same coin, mutually reinforcing and driving each other forward. **12**

Building Sustainability Ethical Cultures

Ethical compliance, though essential, represents merely the baseline for sustainability leaders. It's the strict adherence to rules, laws, and standards. However, in an age where businesses wield considerable influence over societal trends, expectations, and behaviors, merely "doing no harm" or "playing by the rules" is no longer sufficient. Ethical sustainability leaders recognize this, and instead of solely focusing on meeting compliance requirements, they strive to do good and instill positive change.

This endeavor is about building an ethical culture of sustainability that permeates every layer of the organization and spills over into the broader community, influencing suppliers, customers, stakeholders, and even competitors. Such leaders don't see their organizations as isolated entities; they view them as interconnected components of a larger ecosystem. Their vision is comprehensive, aiming to transform not just their internal processes and cultures but also the systems in which they operate.

Here's why this expanded focus is crucial:

1. **Resilience and Longevity**: Organizations deeply rooted in ethical sustainability practices are better equipped to weather economic, environmental, and social storms. Their adaptive capacities are enhanced and aligned with future societal needs and demands.

2. **Stakeholder Trust**: Going beyond compliance fosters greater trust among stakeholders. When a company consistently demonstrates a commitment to broader societal good, it solidifies its reputation as a responsible and forward-thinking entity.

3. **Innovation**: A culture of sustainability often breeds innovation. When organizations aim to solve larger systemic issues, they uncover new market opportunities, novel product ideas, and transformative business models.

4. **Systemic Impact**: Ethical sustainability leaders who extend their influence beyond organizational boundaries can drive industry-wide changes. They can reshape entire sectors by

setting new standards, advocating for robust policies, or pioneering innovative practices.

For instance, consider **Patagonia**, the outdoor apparel company. Its mission statement, "We're in business to save our home planet," transcends mere compliance. They actively advocate for environmental causes, donate a percentage of their profits to grassroots activists, and encourage other businesses to adopt sustainable practices. Their influence isn't limited to their immediate operations; they aim to inspire an industry and society.

Similarly, **Dr. Daniel Goleman**, renowned for his pioneering work on emotional intelligence, ventured into environmental consciousness with his book *Ecological Intelligence*. He doesn't just raise awareness about environmental costs but propels the narrative towards radical business transparency. By doing so, Goleman nudges consumers and industries to understand and adjust the environmental implications of their actions, fostering a shift in consumer behavior and industry benchmarks.

Meanwhile, **Jeffrey Hollender's** leadership at Seventh Generation showcased a broader vision than merely creating eco-friendly products. Hollender heralded an era of full ingredient disclosure, sparking a broader discourse about the depth of corporate responsibility. This wasn't just a brand-specific initiative; it set the stage for transforming how products are designed with sustainability at their core.

In the realm of food, **Kimbal Musk** emerges as a leader. While he champions ventures like Square Roots and The Kitchen Restaurant Group, Musk's objective transcends selling food. He aims to overhaul the food system's roots by emphasizing urban farming and fostering connections with local producers, underlining the significance of a sustainable food supply chain.

Chetna Sinha's Mann Deshi Foundation is revolutionizing more than banking for rural women in India. Sinha demonstrates that financial empowerment and sustainability are not mutually exclusive by embedding sustainable business practices among women entrepreneurs. Her initiatives symbolize a blueprint for how financial services can dovetail with sustainability.

Through her organization Navdanya, **Vandana Shiva** takes the sustainable agriculture conversation a notch higher. She doesn't merely advocate for practices like seed freedom and organic farming; she mounts a formidable challenge against the industrial agriculture behemoth. Her mission is both a protest and a proposal, urging industries and societies to rethink their agricultural paradigms.

Joel **Makower** of GreenBiz Group Inc. is rounding off this list of sustainability leaders. His insights and reports aren't mere documentation; they're instruments of change. Through highlighting green business innovations and curating influential sustainability conversations, Makower aspires for businesses to reimagine and realign their core with a sustainable ethos.

These are just a few examples of ethical sustainability leaders who do more than being executives of their enterprises and initiatives; they're visionary change-makers for their entire industries and society at large. They have the foresight to understand that real success isn't about thriving in isolation but ensuring that the entire ecosystem— the industry, community, and planet—thrives. By fostering sustainable, ethical cultures, they embed sustainability principles within organizational walls and into the very fabric of society.

The Purpose of Sustainability Reporting

Sustainability reporting is an organization's public disclosure of environmental, social, and governance (ESG) performance. Historically, business reporting focused predominantly on financial results. However, the need for a comprehensive reporting form grew as the interplay between business activities and broader societal and environmental impacts became more evident. Sustainability reporting emerged as a response to this need, providing stakeholders, including investors, customers, employees, and the broader public, with a holistic view of an organization's performance in terms of financial results and its commitment to creating a sustainable future.

For instance, the global furniture giant IKEA has consistently utilized its sustainability reports to share its progress toward becoming a more circular business. Their commitment to using sustainable materials and reducing waste isn't just rhetoric; it's a quantified purpose. In their reports, tangible metrics, such as the percentage c products made from sustainable or recycled materials, clarify thei commitments, anchoring their purpose in real-world impacts. **13**

Novo Nordisk, a global healthcare company, provides anothe illustrative example. Their Triple Bottom Line principle, integrate into their business operations, dictates that they must conside financial, social, and environmental factors in their decision-makin This principle is reflected in their annual sustainability report, whe they present data and narrate stories that provide context, illustratin how they are making a difference in real-world scenarios, fro patient access to their products to their efforts in reducing the carbon footprint. **14**

Best practices in sustainability reporting often revolve aroun transparency, stakeholder engagement, and alignment wit recognized standards. **Danone**, for example, follows the GR framework for its reporting, but to ensure its purpose is at th forefront, it integrates feedback from diverse stakeholders. Thi practice of active engagement means their sustainability journey informed by and accountable to those it impacts. **15**

Furthermore, some trailblazing companies take reporting to the ne level by seeking third-party verification of their sustainability report **L'Oréal**, for instance, has its reports externally verified, ensuring tha its disclosures aren't just based on in-house assessments but meet th rigorous criteria of independent experts. **16**

These leading organizations recognize that sustainability reporting not merely a tick-box exercise or a public relations tool. When don genuinely and purposefully, it further influences an organization culture, embedding accountability deep within its DNA. Reportin based on standards like ESG, Global Reporting Initiative (GRI), o the United Nations Global Compact (UNGC) requires a organization to track and disclose specific metrics and reflect on it broader societal role. This reflection drives companies to reevaluat their purpose, ensuring that it aligns with broader societal an environmental objectives.

The act of reporting amplifies an organization's commitment to it stated purpose. When a company proclaims its dedication t sustainability, reporting requires it to measure and disclose its progress against that commitment. This measurement and its transparency ensure that purpose is not just a statement on paper but a tangible, measured, and accountable goal. **17**

Moreover, adherence to standards like ESG, GRI, or UNGC elevates the rigor and comprehensiveness of sustainability reporting. These frameworks demand a level of detail and accountability that pushes organizations to think deeply about their impacts and to strive for improvement continually. In this way, sustainability reporting becomes a powerful tool for making an organization's purpose manifest in its day-to-day operations and long-term strategy. The promise of a better world, enshrined in an organization's purpose, is thus not just a vision but a measured and reported reality.

Key Takeaways: Purpose and Principles

1. **Purpose Transcends Profit:** An organization's higher purpose is more than just a mission statement; it serves as a compass that directs every business decision and action. When genuinely integrated, this purpose drives sustainable practices and outcomes, ensuring that profitability coexists harmoniously with ecological and social responsibility.

2. **Principles as Guardrails:** Sustainable organizations define and embrace guiding principles as essential to their operations. These principles, whether based on environmental stewardship, social equity, or ethical governance, offer a clear path for leaders, ensuring that sustainability isn't merely a goal but an intrinsic part of an organization's identity.

3. **Ethical Decision Making is Crucial:** An organization's dedication to sustainability principles and higher purpose necessitates a consistent commitment to ethical decision-making. This involves recognizing and navigating complex dilemmas, ensuring that choices align with deeply held values and result in tangible, positive impacts on society and the environment.

4. **Culture of Ethical Sustainability:** Beyond individual decisions, sustainability leaders have the potential and responsibility to foster a culture that prioritizes ethical practices within their organization and the larger business ecosystem. By championing systemic changes and influencing industry norms, these leaders expand the scope and depth of sustainability, ushering in transformative shifts in how business intersects with society.

5. **Reporting Reflects Accountability:** Sustainability reporting is more than a disclosure tool; it's a testament to an organization's commitment to its purpose and principles. By aligning with recognized standards like ESG, GRI, or UNGC, companies ensure transparency, measure their real-world impact, and hold themselves accountable. This continuous action, reflection, and disclosure cycle underscores an organization's dedication to a sustainable future.

CHAPTER 7

PEOPLE: CARING FOR THE COMMUNITY

SOCIAL SUSTAINABILITY PRACTICES

Overview

This chapter delves into the vital role of community welfare in achieving social sustainability. We trace the journey of societal care from its origins, emphasizing its prominence in global sustainability agendas. We highlight corporate responsibility and discuss transitioning from philanthropic actions to transformative systemic changes. By spotlighting solutions to societal challenges, we underscore the essential role of businesses and leaders. The chapter culminates by emphasizing the connected relationship between businesses and their communities, asserting that genuine community care stems from valuing, respecting, and providing equal opportunities for all members.

The Evolution of Social Sustainability

In short, social sustainability is a multifaceted concept that stems from recognizing the interdependency between human societies, economies, and the environment. It is a theory that sums up the many ways human societies, economies, and the environment intersect. It emerges from the understanding that our individual and collective well-being (community) is intrinsically tied to the well-being of our planet and the equitable distribution of resources and opportunities.

Within this framework, social responsibility becomes a key pillar. It refers to the ethical obligations of individuals, communities, and institutions, especially businesses, to act for the collective good. This sense of responsibility is grounded in realizing that societal and community well-being directly affects long-term success and stability, whether economic or environmental. It is not just about charity or philanthropy; it is about understanding and addressing the root causes of societal challenges, from education to healthcare to housing.

Meanwhile, social justice is the moral compass that guides the quest for social sustainability. It emphasizes the fair distribution of resources, opportunities, and privileges within a society, regardless of background, gender, ethnicity, or socioeconomic status. Social justice seeks to challenge and rectify systemic inequalities and create an environment where all individuals can thrive, free from discrimination and prejudice. **1**

Together, these elements underline the essence of social sustainability: building societies that are equitable, resilient, and harmonious, where every individual has the chance to thrive, and where communities work in tandem with their environment for a better future.

Historically, communities have always sought ways to ensure their longevity and welfare, but it's only in the more recent past that these ideas have been formalized and globally recognized. **2**

1. **Pre-Industrial Era:** Before the Industrial Revolution, businesses were typically smaller, local entities. Leadership was often autocratic, with decisions made by the owner or a small group. CSR was more personal in these times. For instance, philanthropic acts were often driven by religious or community values. Business owners might support local charities or help build community infrastructures like churches or schools. **3**

2. **Industrial Revolution (Late 18th to Early 20th Century):** As the Industrial Revolution progressed,

leadership transformed with the ascent of vast industrial conglomerates. Hierarchical management took root, centralizing decision-making. This period also saw heightened societal and environmental challenges from industrial activities, including worker mistreatment and environmental degradation. However, early Corporate Social Responsibility (CSR) gestures emerged. Robert Owen, a mill owner, took steps to enhance the living conditions for his workers, while George Cadbury envisioned a community with improved housing and facilities for his employees. Similarly, organized charities like the Hull House by Jane Addams emerged in Chicago, rapidly morphing into the manufacturing nexus of the U.S. by the late 1800s. The Hull House exemplified a progressive approach to mitigating poverty, focusing on offering social services and educational opportunities to working-class immigrants and laborers in the city. **4**

3. Post-World War II (Mid-20th Century): Post-World War II (Mid-20th Century): The aftermath of WWII marked the rise of multinational corporations and a shift in leadership approaches towards more inclusive and democratic models. "Corporate Social Responsibility" (CSR) emerged during this era. Companies started recognizing duties that extended beyond mere profit-making. Kaiser Industries, for instance, played a pivotal role in establishing health services and actively incorporating women into the labor market. Similarly, Johnson & Johnson's credo, drafted in 1943, highlighted the company's obligations to customers, employees, communities, and shareholders. **5**

4. 1970s to 1990s: Leadership saw the introduction of transformational and servant leadership theories. Leaders like Herb Kelleher of Southwest Airlines exemplified putting employees first, believing that satisfied employees would lead to satisfied customers. CSR became more structured during this period. The idea that businesses owed something back to society became more widely accepted. The environmental movement of the 1970s put pressure on companies to adopt green practices. Companies like Ben & Jerry's emerged with

CSR as a core part of their mission, focusing on social missions and fair trade.

5. 2000s to Present: Leadership in today's age is marked by resilience, inclusivity, and an emphasis on sustainable practices. The surge of the digital age and global interconnectivity underscore the significance of ethical stewardship and transparency in corporate functions. Leaders like Tim Cook of Apple prioritize values and privacy, while Satya Nadella of Microsoft emphasizes empathy and continuous learning. The landscape of CSR has expanded, often becoming intrinsic to an organization's fundamental vision. The advent of frameworks like the Triple Bottom Line (TBL), highlighting People, Planet, and Profit, showcases this evolution. Corporations like Patagonia, Unilever, Tesla, and Ben & Jerry's exemplify this by setting rigorous sustainability targets across their operations, supply chains, and product lifespans. **6**

Social Sustainability in Development Priorities

With the UN's Sustainable Development Goals (SDGs) unveiled in 2015, the global community recognized the importance of placing social sustainability at the heart of development strategies. These goals transcended traditional economic indicators, embedding within them the essence of international development—inclusive, equitable, and environmentally conscious prosperity. The SDGs underline that the path to meaningful progress is inextricably linked to social well-being, from eradicating poverty and hunger to fostering peace and ensuring justice.

Furthermore, this global framework outlines how social development—advancements in the quality of human life—is not just a by-product but an integral driver of community development. When fostered with equitable opportunities, education, and health services, these communities become the foundation of robust nations. In this context, the SDGs offer both a vision and a roadmap. They guide state leaders in policy direction, inspire businesses to integrate sustainability into their core strategies and remind every stakeholder of their shared responsibility toward creating a resilient and inclusive global society.

No Poverty (Goal 1): Priority - Prioritizing basic needs and financial stability. Companies can concretely contribute to this goal and its targets by offering fair wages, creating jobs in impoverished areas, and supporting microfinancing initiatives. Leaders can rally for wage reforms and engage in public-private partnerships to tackle poverty.

Zero Hunger (Goal 2): Priority - Ensuring food access and improving agricultural methods. Companies can invest in sustainable agricultural technologies, support local farmers, and reduce food waste. Business leaders can advocate for improved food distribution systems and sponsor food security initiatives.

Good Health and Well-being (Goal 3): Priority - Enhancing healthcare accessibility and promoting preventative care. Businesses can provide health benefits to employees, sponsor medical research, and partner with NGOs to improve healthcare access. Leaders can push for better health regulations and awareness campaigns.

Quality Education (Goal 4): Priority - Ensuring equitable education and lifelong learning access. Companies can offer scholarship programs, support educational NGOs, and establish worker training programs. Leaders can promote educational reforms and support the digitization of education for wider access.

Gender Equality (Goal 5): Priority - Eliminating gender-based discrimination and violence. Businesses can establish gender-equal hiring practices, create safe workplaces, and support women in leadership roles. Leaders can champion gender equality in all sectors and support initiatives addressing gender violence.

Clean Water and Sanitation (Goal 6): Priority - Safe water access and sanitation facilities. Companies can reduce water waste, support clean water initiatives, and introduce eco-friendly sanitation solutions. Leaders can drive policies ensuring water management and infrastructure development.

Decent Work and Economic Growth (Goal 8): Priority - Promoting job opportunities and economic prosperity. Businesses can adopt sustainable practices, support SMEs, and create inclusive workplaces. Leaders can focus on labor laws and push for economic policies that foster sustainable growth.

Reduced Inequalities (Goal 10): Priority - Addressing income disparities and promoting social inclusion. Companies can support underrepresented groups in the workforce and advocate for equal opportunity. Leaders can rally against discriminatory policies and promote inclusive economic strategies.

Sustainable Cities and Communities (Goal 11): Priority - Creating resilient urban areas with adequate infrastructure. Companies can invest in sustainable architecture, promote green transportation, and collaborate with urban planners. Leaders can advocate for urban policies that prioritize sustainability and community involvement.

Peace and Justice Strong Institutions (Goal 16): Priority - Ensuring societal peace and institutional transparency. Businesses can adopt transparent practices, support peace initiatives, and establish mechanisms for conflict resolution. Leaders can work towards building trust in institutions and champion policies that promote justice.

Incorporating these social sustainability goals into a company's operations and strategies showcases a commitment beyond profits. By actively working towards these SDGs, business leaders play a crucial role in shaping a more inclusive and equitable future. The establishment of these SDGs not only reflects our historical understandings but sets a roadmap for our collective journey toward a socially sustainable future. By acknowledging the intricacies of social well-being and community development through the SDGs, humanity has embarked on a concerted effort to ensure that everyone, regardless of their background, has an equitable chance at a prosperous and fulfilling life.

Interrelated Approaches for CSR Practices

The concept and practices of CSR have expanded and diversified in our current era to result in various approaches adopted by businesses. Two notable approaches include the "philanthropic" and "systemic" models. Let's distinguish between these two to understand their practical leadership implications for sustainability solutions:

1. Philanthropic CSR Approach

In this model, businesses prioritize direct charitable contributions to social causes or the community. These actions are often additional to their main line of business and might need to be integrated into their core strategy.

Many American corporations have initiated charitable foundations to streamline their philanthropic activities. The Walmart Foundation is a prime example, offering grants to community organizations focusing on education, workforce development, and environmental sustainability. Across the Atlantic in Spain, the Inditex Group, the conglomerate behind brands like Zara, has established the Amancio Ortega Foundation. This foundation channels its resources primarily towards education and health, sponsoring a variety of educational schemes and healthcare projects.

Adding to these examples, Salesforce, under the leadership of Marc Benioff, has taken a unique and systematic approach to philanthropy with its 1-1-1 model. This model dedicates 1% of Salesforce's equity, 1% of its products, and 1% of employees' time to charitable causes. This commitment ensures that as Salesforce grows, its impact on various communities scales proportionally. The 1-1-1 model has fortified Salesforce's CSR footprint and inspired other companies to adopt similar integrated philanthropic strategies, amplifying corporate contributions to global challenges. **7**

2. Systemic CSR Approach

Here, businesses aim to address social issues at a structural level, integrating solutions into their core strategy and operations. This approach recognizes that businesses are part of a larger system and can influence positive changes through policy advocacy, partnerships, and long-term initiatives. Using policy advocacy for community well-being and taxation as a mechanism for redistribution are examples of systemic CSR.

Microsoft has engaged in policy advocacy around privacy, cybersecurity, and digital skills training. Their efforts aim to shape policies that protect consumers, promote equitable access to digital resources, and foster a more inclusive digital economy. Unilever, a British-Dutch multinational, has advocated for policies that combat climate change and promote sustainable agriculture. Their leadership has actively engaged with governments and international bodies to drive environmental sustainability.

While taxation in the U.S. is a complex issue, some leaders like Warren Buffet have advocated for higher tax rates on the wealthy, arguing that they have a responsibility to pay more to support societal infrastructure and welfare. His perspective suggests a systemic approach to CSR, emphasizing the broader redistribution mechanisms available to society. In Europe, although criticized in the past for complex tax structures, IKEA has in recent years made efforts to advocate for fair taxation and ensure that they pay taxes transparently in all the countries they operate. European countries generally have a tradition of higher taxation, especially in the Nordic regions, which is often seen as a mechanism for redistribution to support social welfare systems. **8**

While the philanthropic approach often provides immediate relief and showcases corporate goodwill, the systemic approach seeks to address the root causes of societal challenges. Both approaches have their merits, but the systemic perspective, by its nature, tends to offer more sustainable and long-term solutions.

Leadership Solutions to Pressing Social Challenges

Effective leadership, spanning private, public, and social sectors, bears the weighty responsibility of cultivating the well-being and sustainability of communities on both local and global scales. Navigating the complexities of social challenges and proposing innovative solutions is more than just a policy directive or corporate initiative; it's the hallmark of visionary leadership. By addressing these challenges, leaders pave the way for a brighter, more inclusive future for everyone involved.

1. **Poverty, Wage Inequality, and Debt Crises:** Over 700 million individuals, representing 10% of the world's populace, endure extreme poverty, subsisting on less than $1.90 daily. The ramifications of the COVID-19 pandemic, coupled with the persistent challenges of conflicts and climate change, are anticipated to exacerbate these numbers further. **9** Innovative companies, such as Danone, are stepping up with initiatives like the "Ecosystem Fund," which is dedicated to establishing sustainable ecosystems based on inclusive business models. Another inspiring leadership example is the microfinance organization Grameen Bank, founded by Nobel Peace Prize laureate Muhammad Yunus. It offers small loans to impoverished individuals without collateral, enabling them to kick-start or grow small businesses. Unilever's "Shakti" initiative in India is another inspiring solution to poverty. It allows women in rural areas to act as direct-to-consumer retailers, offering employment and improved accessibility to essential products. Another notable initiative is the Mastercard Center for Inclusive Growth, which focuses on advancing equitable economic growth and financial inclusion around the globe, empowering people through access to the digital economy and capital.

2. **Food Insecurity:** An estimated 9% of the global population is undernourished. In 2021, the reach of global hunger extended to approximately 828 million individuals, reflecting an increase of around 46 million from 2020 and 150 million since the COVID-19 pandemic's onset. **10** A concerning trend emerges from a recent United Nations report, suggesting that global efforts are straying from the ambition of eradicating hunger, food insecurity, and all manifestations of malnutrition by 2030. In the United States, a report from the USDA revealed that about 33.8 million Americans were deprived of adequate access to food. **11** One significant contributor to this challenge has been the existence of food deserts, regions where affordable and nutritious food remains elusive. Companies like Everytable have responded, aiming to

145

make nutritious food affordable and accessible, especially in underserved communities. On the global front, organizations such as the World Food Programme (WFP) are championing the cause by supporting smallholder farmers in market access and adopting sustainable practices. PepsiCo, through its "Sustainable Farming Program," joins the effort by collaborating with farmers worldwide to bolster agricultural sustainability and productivity. Meanwhile, Bayer's "Food Chain Partnership" initiative focuses on delivering integrated crop solutions, stressing sustainable food production. These initiatives underscore the vital role of corporate and sustainability leadership in tackling global hunger, resonating with the UN's SDG 2 of Zero Hunger.

3. **Migrant and Refugee Rights:** "By the end of 2022, 108.4 million people were forcibly displaced worldwide due to persecution, conflict, violence, or human rights violations. This includes 35.3 million refugees. 62.5 million internally displaced people." **12** Initiatives like Techfugees harness technology to equip refugees with skills and employment opportunities in host nations. Similarly, the Tent Partnership for Refugees mobilizes businesses to include refugees in their core business operations, from hiring and investing to sourcing and service provision. Additionally, the International Rescue Committee (IRC) collaborates with companies like Starbucks to create employment pathways for refugees, thus aiding in their smoother integration into new communities.

4. **Health and Public Health Concerns:** The COVID-19 pandemic highlighted significant health inequalities worldwide. It exacerbated difficulties for populations already struggling to access healthcare systems, leading to disproportionate effects on their well-being. "And 381 million people were pushed or further pushed into extreme poverty in 2019 due to out-of-pocket payments for health." **13** Nevertheless, the collaborative spirit was evident in public-private partnerships, which expedited vaccine development and distribution. For instance, Gavi, the Vaccine Alliance, partnered with multiple stakeholders to ensure vaccines reached even the most vulnerable

populations in lower-income countries. Johnson & Johnson collaborated with global health entities to amplify testing capabilities and accelerate vaccine trials. Similarly, AstraZeneca partnered with various nations and international health organizations to produce and supply its vaccine at scale, ensuring broad and equitable access. These endeavors underscore the power of leadership when tackling monumental health challenges.

5. **Disability Rights, Racism, and Diversity Inclusion**: Discrimination remains deeply rooted, particularly against disabled individuals; nearly one in five grapple with considerable life challenges. "Around 15 percent of the world's population, or an estimated 1 billion people, live with disabilities." [14] In response, Microsoft stands out with its dedication to inclusivity, developing tools and workspaces specifically designed to cater to those with disabilities. Similarly, Accenture's "Getting to Equal" initiative champions a comprehensive approach to ensure that people with disabilities have equal employment opportunities. Meanwhile, Airbnb has launched the "Open Doors" policy, pledging to accommodate guests who feel discriminated against, emphasizing their commitment to combatting racism and fostering an inclusive community. Such corporate initiatives spotlight the essential role of leadership in creating a more inclusive world.

6. **Children's Rights**: A distressing fact remains that over 150 million children worldwide are trapped in labor practices. "In the world's poorest countries, slightly more than 1 in 5 children are engaged in child labor." [15] UNICEF and its business partners are working to eradicate child labor and create environments where children can thrive. Similarly, the LEGO Foundation focuses on learning through play, investing in global projects to support children's cognitive, emotional, and social development. H&M's "Fair Living Wage" strategy addresses the root causes of child labor in the textile industry, focusing on sustainable supply chains and ensuring ethical practices. Additionally, The Cocoa Initiative, a collaboration between the world's leading chocolate and

cocoa companies, aims to make sustainable cocoa the norm, directly targeting and working to eliminate child labor in the industry. These concerted efforts underscore the role of leadership in championing children's rights and welfare.

7. **Homelessness and Housing Rights**: Homelessness starkly exemplifies the severe impacts of poverty, prejudice, and disparity, touching individuals across all ages, genders, and backgrounds. Around the world, 1.6 billion individuals grapple with substandard housing, and as highlighted by UN-Habitat, nearly 15 million face forced evictions annually. Alarmingly, the past decade has seen a significant surge in homelessness. **16** Addressing this, the Tiny House Movement has become prominent in offering affordable, sustainable living spaces. In addition, social enterprises such as New Story are revolutionizing housing by 3D printing homes efficiently for marginalized communities. Moreover, Habitat for Humanity, a non-profit organization, partners with families, volunteers, and donors worldwide to construct and rehabilitate homes, emphasizing the significance of shelter as a human right. These innovative solutions spotlight the potential for leadership to address and alleviate housing challenges globally.

8. **Governance, Democracy, and Voting Rights**: Corruption's staggering annual cost sees an alarming $3.6 trillion lost to underhanded dealings and bribes. **17** Against this backdrop, digital platforms like DemocracyOS have emerged, providing tools to bolster transparent governance and invigorate citizen participation. Similarly, the Sunlight Foundation uses technology to make government data more accessible, championing transparency and accountability. The International Budget Partnership, on the other hand, collaborates globally to ensure public finances are open, accountable, and responsive to citizens. These initiatives exemplify the innovative ways leadership can promote democratic values and reinforce good governance.

9. **Women's Rights, Gender Equality, and Reproductive Justice**: Globally, the gender pay gap is stark, with women

earning approximately 77 cents for every dollar a man makes for equivalent work. **18** To address these disparities, the HeForShe movement, supported by UN Women, has risen to prominence, actively mobilizing men as allies for gender equality. Additionally, companies like Salesforce have taken a stand, auditing their pay structures and rectifying wage gaps between male and female employees. Meanwhile, Procter & Gamble's "#WeSeeEqual" campaign seeks to challenge and break down gender bias barriers through awareness. Lastly, the Gates Foundation's investments in family planning highlight the significance of empowering women through reproductive health education and resources. These combined efforts signify a global commitment to championing women's rights and achieving gender equality.

10. **Education and Accessibility**: Globally, more than 617 million children are not acquiring foundational skills in reading, writing, and math. **19** However, there are determined endeavors to counter this issue. The Malala Fund focuses on breaking barriers to girls' education in the most threatened regions. Platforms like Khan Academy are revolutionizing learning, offering free, world-class educational content to anyone, anywhere. EdTech start-ups like Coursera and Udacity are also redefining education by providing affordable upskilling and reskilling courses, crucial for adapting to the rapidly changing job market and automation. Through these combined efforts, the vision of universal quality education and lifelong learning, even in the face of automation and shifting labor demands, is becoming more attainable.

While the ten challenges outlined in this section underscore pressing social issues, they are just the tip of the iceberg. Other significant challenges, such as rapid urbanization and its accompanying strains on infrastructure, are being addressed by leveraging technological solutions, like smart city innovations that promote sustainable and livable urban centers. Additionally, in an era of globalization, the world grapples with concerns about diluting cultural identities and values. However, the current global movement towards preserving Indigenous cultures, languages, and traditions is a beacon of hope. Initiatives are underway to invest in cultural preservation projects, tourism drives, and digital archives to ensure the rich mosaic of global cultures continues to thrive for future generations. The breadth and depth of these challenges might seem daunting, but the host of leadership-driven solutions and innovative strategies highlighted here demonstrate humanity's resilience and determination. We carve a path toward a more socially sustainable future by embracing these diverse solutions. **20**

Rediscovery of Our Community Identities

Sustainability leadership highlights the inherent bond between businesses and the wider communities in which they operate. Recognizing that businesses are not isolated entities, but integral components of society is crucial. Every business depends upon its community for resources, workforce, consumer bases, and regulatory guidelines. However, some businesses have taken more than they give, failing to adopt a stewardship role.

This interconnectedness underscores a business's role in fostering societal welfare. Beyond mere profit, businesses must minimize harm and actively promote societal and environmental harmony. In the modern world, this responsibility goes beyond local communities due to the globalized nature of business operations. While CSR remains a priority, it is necessary to embrace a Global Social Responsibility (GSR) perspective and ensure companies remain accountable on an international scale. **21**

For sustainability leaders, this means creating strategies with a global perspective. This could involve partnering with international entities, adopting universal sustainability standards, or cross-border collaborations. A feedback loop is essential to gauge the impacts of such initiatives, and businesses should cultivate a culture celebrating global community engagement.

At the heart of sustainable practices is a call for leaders to connect with their communities, showcasing the balance between individual aspirations and collective welfare. This connection of local and global perspectives forms the bedrock of the next phase of sustainability leadership. Embracing our shared destiny and interconnectedness

nsures businesses and communities thrive in harmony, irrespective
f geographical boundaries.

ey Takeaways: Social Sustainability

1. **Integral Role of Community**: Community welfare is foundational to social sustainability, emphasizing the need for societies where everyone feels valued, respected, and has equal access to opportunities.

2. **Global Sustainability Agenda**: Social care has evolved over the years, becoming central to global sustainability goals, emphasizing addressing pressing societal challenges through local and global initiatives.

3. **Beyond Philanthropy**: Modern corporate social responsibility (CSR) transcends traditional philanthropic efforts, advocating for transformative systemic changes that promote holistic societal benefits.

4. **Leadership's Pivotal Role**: Effective solutions to societal challenges require proactive leadership that recognizes the symbiotic relationship between businesses and their communities, both locally and globally.

5. **Business-Community Interconnectedness**: Businesses draw their sustenance from society and thus have an inherent duty to act as stewards rather than exploiters, reinforcing the importance of both local CSR and Global Social Responsibility (GSR) in a connected world.

CHAPTER 8

PLANET: CARING FOR OUR ENVIRONMENT

ECO-LEADERSHIP FOR GOOD

Overview

Taking care of the environment is not just a moral duty but a necessity for the survival and prosperity of all living beings. The chapter introduces a holistic perspective, starting with the global climate's pressing concerns, discussing the interrelated risks and opportunities businesses face, and demonstrating the multi-dimensional aspects of environmental sustainability. Special attention is given to specific environmental goals, the transformative potential of regenerative leadership, and the paradigm shift from "Ego" to "Eco" leadership practices. We review comprehensive strategies and insights into proactive measures essential for our planet's health.

A Global Climate Imperative

The recent alarming call from the United Nations Global Compact (UNGC) has underscored our current environmental predicament. Their assessment is nothing less than a "Code Red for Humanity." Climate change is no longer a looming peril in the distant future but a pressing reality. The evidence is overwhelming, with the planet warming by a concerning 1.1°C and forecasts pointing towards a rise of roughly 2.7°C by the end of this century. Indeed, the UN has confirmed that 2023 was the hottest year in history. **1** These temperatures are manifesting, especially in the Global South, ever increasing inequalities and jeopardizing food and water security, health, and biodiversity. **2**

Facing these formidable challenges marks a pivotal role for businesses to spearhead change. The business community are not just mere bystanders but active players in the transitioning to a sustainable future. They are key to achieving a net-zero future by 2050, which demands a multifaceted approach: conservation, restoration, and a commitment to regenerative strategies. Several companies associated with the UNGC, whose collective market capitalization exceeds the U.S. GDP, align with this vision. Their involvement in initiatives like the Just Transition Think Lab, Ocean Stewardship Coalition, and Water Resilience Coalition showcases the potency of innovative and forward-thinking leadership. By 2021's close, over 1,000 companies had set science-based targets, reflecting a rising tide of corporate environmental commitment, especially within influential G20 nations.

The business landscape has opportunities to counteract and reverse climate change's impacts. Several organizations have adopted tangible measures: investing in electric vehicle infrastructure, transitioning to all-electric fleets, and restructuring supply chains, distribution channels, and facilities to foster sustainable behaviors among employees and broader industry networks.

Microsoft's exemplary stance shows that prioritizing carbon neutrality is an impactful business strategy. Their goal isn't merely carbon neutrality; they aim to be carbon-negative by 2030. Microsoft's ambition extends to removing all its historical carbon emissions by 2050. If more enterprises globally set similar or even more audacious goals, the pace of combating climate change can dramatically accelerate.

Today, businesses have access to a suite of resources and frameworks, ranging from the Science-Based Targets initiative to the Climate Ambition Accelerator. These aren't just tactical assets; they are essential for incorporating sustainability into the very DNA of corporate culture. To maximize their impact, businesses need to be agile, pioneering, and relentless in their pursuit of sustainability, leveraging these tools to set and achieve ambitious targets.

Climate Risks and Business Opportunities

The multifaceted implications of climate change stretch beyond immediate environmental repercussions, deeply influencing the social, economic, and peace factors. These climatic shifts, evident in many industries' daily activities and strategic planning, present a dual-faced scenario: challenges rooted in the pressing reality of a changing climate and potential growth avenues that arise from a world rapidly transitioning to sustainability.

Climate change amplifies environmental threats, leading to more frequent and severe weather events like flooding, which now puts about 23% of the global population, or 1.8 billion people, at risk during extreme scenarios. At the same time, intensified drought conditions resulting from rising global temperatures could displace roughly 700 million individuals by 2030. These immediate, tangible threats underscore the physical risks businesses face. 3

There are costs for transitioning the net-zero economy. Consulting giant McKinsey suggests that to achieve net-zero emissions by 2050, global expenditure across governments, corporations, and individuals on energy and land-use systems must increase by $3.5 trillion annually. 4 However, the financial consequences of not taking action are staggering. Deloitte's Global Turning Point Report estimates that if climate change remains unchecked, it could lead to a devastating economic loss of US$178 trillion over the coming five decades. This underscores the critical need for worldwide leaders to drive a comprehensive shift towards net zero collaboratively. 5

Furthermore, business leaders must remain vigilant about liability risks. These entail the legal ramifications they might face for not aligning with, disclosing, or adapting to evolving climate-related regulations and expectations. The growing trend of climate-related litigation, fueled by scientific advancements, changing legal paradigms, and public sentiment, adds another layer to these concerns.

In response, business leadership must take a big picture view of climate challenges. Instead of narrowly weighing immediate economic costs, leaders should consider the long-term risk implications at the physical, transitional, and liability levels.

Proactively addressing these risks safeguards businesses and pushes them to seize the immense growth opportunities presented by a world pivoting toward environmental sustainability. **6**

Multi-dimensions of Environmental Sustainability

Environmental sustainability is a multi-dimensional concept that refers to the responsible use and protection of the natural environment through conservation and sustainable practices. It involves making decisions and taking actions that are in the interest of protecting the natural world, with particular emphasis on preserving the capability of the environment to support human life. Leaders face both challenges and opportunities pursuing this challenge. They need to take a broad perspective. Each dimension needs careful consideration and has specific tools and certifications available to aid leaders in their commitment to a more sustainable future. Here are some dimensions of environmental sustainability and strategies to address sustainability in business operations:

1. **Resource Use:** When considering resource use, leaders should prioritize renewable resources or carefully use non-renewable resources to make them available for future generations. Tools such as Life Cycle Assessments (LCAs) can play a pivotal role, offering insight into the environmental impact throughout a product's life. In addition, acquiring certifications from organizations such as the Forest Stewardship Council (FSC) or the Marine Stewardship Council (MSC) can help a company follow through on its commitment to sustainable sourcing.

2. **Biodiversity Impact:** Biodiversity is another crucial dimension. Vibrant ecosystems, diverse species, and a rich genetic pool are foundations for a stable environment. Leaders should prioritize understanding and mitigating the impact of their operations on local ecosystems. The Biodiversity Impact Assessment is a valuable tool in this endeavor. Certifications like the Rainforest Alliance or the Bird Friendly Standard serve as badges of honor for companies adhering to biodiversity-friendly practices. Another tool is the Roundtable on Sustainable Palm Oil

(RSPO), the most well-known certification for sustainable palm oil. RSPO-certified producers must adhere to strict guidelines, which include biodiversity conservation and reduced environmental impact.

3. **Pollution Reduction:** The menace of pollution looms large, with businesses often being key contributors. Responsible leaders emphasize the Waste Hierarchy principle, prioritizing reducing, reusing, and recycling. Adopting standards like ISO 14001 can provide a structured approach to minimize environmental harm. Many organizations worldwide have reported tangible pollution reduction results after implementing ISO 14001. Examples include reduced greenhouse gas emissions, decreased water pollutants due to better wastewater management, reduced hazardous waste production, and improved air quality within and around operational sites.

4. **Carbon Footprint:** Carbon footprint reduction is a defining challenge in our contemporary age. Leaders are now recognizing the imperative of monitoring and curbing their organizational emissions. Carbon Footprint Calculators are and affiliations like the Carbon Trust Certification or the Science Based Targets initiative (SBTi) can bolster a company's green credentials.

5. **Circular Economy:** Connecting environmental concerns with economic factors in sustainability underscores the intricate relationship between ecological health and economic dynamics. The concept of a "circular economy" prioritizes longevity and regeneration over fleeting gains, focusing on how environmental decisions reverberate through economic wellness. Connected to it is the "green economy," which goes beyond short-term profits, emphasizing the long-term impacts of environmental decisions on economic health. Instruments such as Natural Capital Accounting equip leaders to merge environmental expenditures into economic planning seamlessly. Concurrently, the Global Reporting Initiative (GRI) standards present a comprehensive method for openly sharing accomplishments in economic sustainability.

6. **Environmental Equity:** Within the social sustainabilit framework, "environmental equity" links ecological issue with social fairness and justice principles. It emphasizes tha sustainability isn't just about being green—it's about bein equitable. This ensures a balanced distribution of th advantages and challenges stemming from environmenta endeavors, mirroring the ideals of environmental justice Instruments such as the Social Return on Investment (SROI empower leaders to measure the societal consequences o their green initiatives. In addition, Fair Trade certification and association with B Corporations are testaments to ; company's commitment to addressing ecological stewardshit with social accountability.

7. **Land Use & Planning:** The crucial aspect of land use anc strategy lies at the intersection of development and ecologica respect. Be it city blocks or agricultural fields, leaders with ; sustainability mindset place environmental vitality at the forefront. Instruments like Geographic Information Systems (GIS) provide invaluable support for judicious land allocation. The gold standard for land management practices is set by markers of excellence, such as LEED for urban realms and the Roundtable on Sustainable Palm Oil (RSPO) for responsible agriculture.

For contemporary leaders, environmental sustainability is not a passing trend—it is a pledge to our planet and its inhabitants. By using specific tools and earning pertinent certifications, leaders can champion the cause for a healthier planet and make lasting improvements for all stakeholders.

The Environmental (Planet) Specific Goals

The "Planet" priority in the 5P model emphasizes environmental protection and sustainability. While many SDGs have environmental aspects, some are more directly related to the environmental component of sustainability. Within this framework, the following six goals have been prioritized in terms of their direct implications for environmental sustainability:

1. **Goal 6: Clean Water and Sanitation:** Ensure availability and sustainable management of water and sanitation for all. Water quality and availability are essential for life, agriculture, and industries. Currently, about 2.2 billion people need access to safely managed drinking water. Nestlé's water stewardship practices ensure sustainable water use. Xylem's solutions for water scarcity and quality challenges. Levi Strauss & Co.'s Water<Less® techniques to reduce water use in denim production. [7]

2. **Goal 7: Affordable and Clean Energy:** Ensure access to affordable, reliable, sustainable, and modern energy for all. Transitioning to sustainable energy reduces environmental degradation and ensures long-term energy security. Around 789 million people lack access to electricity, while energy production represents 60% of global greenhouse gas emissions. Siemens Gamesa's innovations in wind energy solutions. Total's transition from an oil company to a broad energy company emphasizing renewables. Sunrun's residential solar panels and battery storage solutions. [8]

3. **Goal 12: Responsible Consumption and Production:** Ensure sustainable consumption and production patterns. This includes reducing waste and promoting sustainable practices at all stages of production and consumption. Sustainable consumption and production reduce waste, depletion of resources, and environmental harm. The global population is expected to reach 9.6 billion by 2050. If current consumption patterns continue, we'll need three planets to sustain our way of life—Patagonia's pledge to responsible production and encouraging consumers to buy used products. Coca-Cola's World Without Waste initiative is to collect and recycle a bottle or can for each sold by 2030. H&M's garment recycling program and push towards sustainable fashion. [9]

4. **Goal 13: Climate Action:** Take urgent action to combat climate change and its impacts by regulating emissions and promoting developments in renewable energy. One of the environmental leadership implications is that addressing climate change is a priority because of its widespread impacts

on all life and ecosystems. Leaders must drive efforts to reduce carbon emissions, adopt renewable energy, and build resilience against climate-related disasters. According to the Intergovernmental Panel on Climate Change (IPCC), global temperatures could rise by 1.5°C above pre-industrial levels by as early as 2030. This poses existential threats like rising sea levels, extreme weather events, and food and water source disruptions. Tesla's push for electric vehicles reduces carbon emissions from the transportation sector. Google's commitment to operate carbon-free by 2030. Ikea's pledge to become "climate positive" by reducing more greenhouse gas emissions than the IKEA value chain emits by 2030. **10**

5. **Goal 14: Life Below Water:** Conserve and sustainably use the oceans, seas, and marine resources for sustainable development. This includes issues like overfishing, pollution, and ocean acidification. Safeguarding marine ecosystems ensures biodiversity conservation, climate regulation, and sustenance for billions. Over 30% of marine habitats have been destroyed, and 90% of the world's fisheries are fully exploited or overfished. Adidas's commitment to using recycled ocean plastic in its products. MSC (Marine Stewardship Council) certification for sustainable fishing practices. Oceana's partnership with businesses to advocate for policy changes that protect marine life. **11**

6. **Goal 15: Life on Land:** Protect, restore, and promote sustainable use of terrestrial ecosystems, manage forests sustainably, combat desertification, and halt and reverse land degradation and biodiversity loss. This goal emphasizes the importance of biodiversity and the value of ecosystems for human well-being. Terrestrial ecosystems are vital for biodiversity, climate regulation, and human sustenance. 80% of the world's terrestrial biodiversity can be found in forests, but 13 million hectares of forests are lost annually. Unilever's commitment to zero deforestation in its supply chain by 2023. Conservation International's partnerships with companies like Starbucks for sustainable coffee production. Apple's commitment to protect and restore forests is used in its product packaging. **12**

This priority list underscores the interconnectedness of environmental goals. Each has its unique implications, but combined, they illustrate the global necessity of action to protect the planet. Effective leadership, both in the public and private sectors, can drive the transformative changes needed to achieve these goals.

While these SDGs are more directly oriented toward environmental sustainability, it's essential to recognize that the goals are connected. Achieving one goal can have spillover effects on others, and many environmental challenges are also intertwined with social and economic considerations. For instance, addressing climate change (Goal 13) can have direct impacts on No Poverty (Goal 1) and Zero Hunger (Goal 2), and vice versa.

Regenerative Leadership by Design

This refers to processes and systems that restore, renew, or revitalize their sources of energy and materials. Regenerative design goes beyond reducing the negative impact to actively creating a positive impact. In nature, ecosystems are regenerative.

We need to go beyond sustainability and invest in restoration. For decades, the narrative of environmental sustainability has been centered around halting and reducing harm. However, given the depth and breadth of ecological damage already incurred, the paradigm is rapidly shifting. It's becoming abundantly clear that more than simply slowing down our degradation rate is needed. As we face dwindling forests, diminishing freshwater sources, and surging carbon levels, the onus on leadership is not just about preservation but restoration.

At the heart of this renewed approach is the principle of "**regenerative design.**" Regenerative design is about sustaining and actively rejuvenating and revitalizing our environment. It's an approach that works with nature, rather than against it, to create systems that restore, renew, and revitalize their sources of energy and materials. In nature, ecosystems are regenerative. They don't just sustain themselves; they thrive and evolve. Regenerative practices in agriculture, for instance, would not only aim to maintain the health of the soil but to improve it year after year. In essence, it's a departure from linear processes and a reconnection with natural cyclical processes, emphasizing resilience, adaptability, and the capacity for self-renewal.

The principles of "regenerative design" provide a transformative framework that can be woven into numerous sectors. While traditionally associated with natural ecosystems, these principles hold tremendous potential when applied to various industries, ensuring they not only limit harm but actively contribute to healing and renewing the environment.

1. **Regenerative Forestry: Revitalizing the Green Gold** Forests, rightfully termed our planet's lungs, is a key component in global ecosystems. Within the timber and paper industries, leaders must re-envision their roles. Beyond mere conservation, there lies an immense opportunity for active forest regeneration. This encompasses the sustainable sourcing of wood, ensuring logged areas are replanted, nurturing the return of indigenous species, and investing in soil health innovations. For instance, the paper and packaging sector can adopt recycled materials and lead initiatives in afforestation, moving beyond the narrative of "less harm" to one of holistic renewal. **13**

2. **Water Regeneration: Beyond Conservation in Industries** The pressing concern of potable water scarcity demands immediate attention, especially in water-intensive industries like textiles, beverages, and agriculture. While conserving water remains essential, the emphasis should shift to water regeneration. For instance, breweries and beverage producers can invest in advanced purification technologies, ensuring wastewater is treated and returned to the environment cleaner than before. The textile industry, notorious for its water consumption, can pioneer watershed management projects, restoring aquatic ecosystems and ensuring their processes rejuvenate, rather than deplete, local water resources.

3. **Industrial Carbon Capture: Breathing Cleaner** The fight against mounting carbon levels in our atmosphere requires a dual approach, particularly within energy-intensive industries. Alongside emission reductions, energy, transportation, and

manufacturing sectors must prioritize active carbon removal strategies. Energy producers can restore natural carbon sinks like peatlands and mangroves while investing in cutting-edge direct air capture technologies. The automotive and aviation industries can research and fund projects that offset their carbon footprints, moving from mere carbon neutrality to active carbon negativity. **14**

As industries forge ahead, their trajectories must be realigned with regenerative principles, transforming them from mere economic participants to proactive healers of the environment. As stewards of the Earth, leaders now must transcend traditional boundaries and embrace regenerative strategies. It's not just about slowing the tide but actively reversing the waves of ecological damage, ensuring a harmonious coexistence of human progress and nature's well-being.

From Ego to Eco Leadership

The business world is witnessing a paradigm shift, moving away from self-centric leadership styles towards those emphasizing environmental stewardship. The contrast between 'Ego' and 'Eco' leadership lies at the heart of this transformation. Recognizing the distinctions and implications of these approaches is essential for companies committed to sustainability.

Ego Leadership: Traditionally, leadership in many organizations emphasized short-term gains, often sidelining environmental concerns. As the name suggests, ego leadership focuses on personal or organizational gain, prioritizing immediate profitability and often overlooking long-term environmental consequences. This can be seen in businesses that engage in excessive resource extraction without considering replenishment or ignore carbon-neutral alternatives due to cost concerns.

Eco Leadership: In contrast, Eco Leadership embraces a comprehensive perspective, emphasizing the interconnectedness of businesses, society, and the natural environment. At its core, Eco-leadership is rooted in networks, interdependence, and connectivity. It moves away

163

from traditional top-down models and embraces distribute leadership, recognizing that power and influence are ofte dispersed across an organization. "Ecosystems withi ecosystems" paints a vivid picture of this leadership style. **1** It underscores the idea that while an organization migl function as a self-contained ecosystem with its uniqu dynamics and relationships, it simultaneously exists withi and is influenced by a myriad of external ecosystems. Suc leaders prioritize the planet's long-term health, understandin that a sustainable approach is not just ethically sound bu crucial for continued business viability. An Eco leader migl opt for renewable energy sources, advocate for circula economy practices, or invest in green technologies, even these initiatives require a higher upfront investment. **16**

The two paradigms have different implications and consequence when applied to environmental actions for corporate leadership. Hei are how companies have adopted this eco-leadership approach an made important decisions and investments generating environment; sustainability outcomes.

1. **Sustainable Growth:** Eco leaders prioritize long-terr environmental sustainability over transient spikes in profit This means opting for business practices that reduce carbo footprints, limit waste, and conserve resources. Well-know examples emerge from eco leaders like Patagonia, whic prioritizes long-term environmental sustainability over brie profit surges, or IKEA's investment in wind and solar powe or conserving water in manufacturing processes, like Levi water-less jeans production, ultimately reducing carbo footprints, curtailing waste, and preserving resources. A les well-known but inspiring example is Echogen Powe Systems, which focuses on converting waste heat into clea electricity, making industries more energy-efficient and ecc friendly.

2. **Responsible Supply Chain Management:** While Egc centric firms might source materials from the cheapes providers, Eco leaders consider the environmental practice of their suppliers, ensuring sustainably sourced and ethicall

produced goods. Unlike Ego-centric firms that may source palm oil from deforested areas due to its low cost, Eco leaders, reminiscent of The Body Shop, ensure their suppliers uphold sustainable and ethical practices, resulting in sustainably sourced and ethically produced products. Another inspiring example is Thread International, which creates fabrics using recycled plastic bottles, providing jobs and cleaner neighborhoods in Haiti and Honduras by turning waste into valuable supplies.

3. **Waste Reduction and Recycling:** Eco leadership often entails a commitment to minimizing waste. This might involve adopting zero-waste practices, investing in biodegradable packaging, or implementing company-wide recycling programs. Companies influenced by Eco leadership, such as Zero Waste Market in Vancouver, reflect a genuine commitment to waste minimization. These companies might adopt a zero-waste framework, invest in alternatives like mushroom-based packaging to replace styrofoam, or champion company-wide recycling programs like those implemented by Starbucks. Another eco-leadership company is Terracycle, which specializes in recycling hard-to-recycle materials. Consumers can buy zero-waste boxes for specific waste streams, fill them, and return them to the company for proper recycling.

4. **Ecosystem Conservation:** Companies driven by Eco leaders are more likely to invest in preserving the ecosystems they operate within, whether by protecting local biodiversity, restoring natural habitats, or engaging in reforestation efforts. Firms led by visionary Eco leaders, like Brazil's Natura Cosmetics, often prioritize the conservation of the ecosystems they impact. These organizations might fund bee conservation initiatives, restore coral reefs, or initiate reforestation campaigns akin to the efforts of the One Tree Planted organization. Another example is Guayaki Yerba Mate, which, beyond selling beverages, is committed to reforestation in the South American Atlantic rainforest and aims to create a fair wage for the farmers they work with.

5. **Green Innovation:** Focusing on environmental sustainability often drives Eco leaders towards innovative solutions, from developing eco-friendly products to retrofitting offices and factories for energy efficiency. There are many examples of leadership for green innovation. Blueland, for example, offers cleaning products without single-use plastic packaging. Customers buy the bottle once and then purchase refill tablets, reducing plastic waste. Another example is Pela Case, a company that produces 100% compostable phone cases, helping to cut down on the vast amounts of plastic waste generated by the tech accessory industry.

Elon Musk's leadership style embodies a blend of 'ego' and 'eco' tendencies. On the one hand, biographical accounts, like that by Walter Isaacson, suggest personal experiences, including challenging familial relationships and bullying, influence Musk's leadership. These experiences, coupled with his admiration for dominant historical figures like Napoleon, often manifest as an autocratic, ego-driven approach to decision-making and interactions. Musk's confrontations with employees and his pronounced presence on social media further underscore this perspective. [17]

Conversely, Musk's commitment to sustainability, particularly through ventures like Tesla and SolarCity, paints a picture of an eco-leader. These endeavors, aimed at creating a sustainable future, emphasize collective well-being and long-term environmental viability. Therefore, while Musk's ambitions sometimes lead to ego-centric decisions, his overarching vision for a sustainable future position him within the eco-leadership paradigm. Like many visionary leaders, Musk is a complex individual, driven by a blend of personal experiences, situational approaches, contradictions and ambitions, and a genuine desire to foster positive change. It's essential to recognize that leaders can exhibit various behaviors and motivations, often merging intuition with data-driven decisions and 'ego' tendencies with 'eco' aspirations. [18]

While the practical examples of personal or organizational leadership may exhibit confluent and conflicting characteristics of this duality, it is important to understand their distinctive features clearly. The essence of leadership, particularly when analyzing eco-centered transformational leadership, hinges on the values and principles leaders uphold. Eco-leaders starkly contrast their ego-driven counterparts, emphasizing collective well-being, sustainable practices, and a long-term vision over immediate personal gratification. Their leadership lens is holistic, anchored in shared values and community welfare. Their decision-making processes don't merely revolve around hierarchical directives but involve active listening to stakeholders and deep empathy for those affected by their choices.

The emergence of Eco leadership isn't simply a trend but a paradigm shift, transcending environmental stewardship. It's about connecting stakeholder engagement, societal awareness, and pursuing a net-positive environmental footprint. Businesses championing this leadership style are forging a path of responsible action and strategic foresight. Their commitment ensures that they are doing what's right for the environment and aligning their operations for sustained success in a world where sustainability is increasingly becoming a baseline expectation, not just an admirable distinction. Using Musk as a nuanced example, it's evident that even visionary leaders can oscillate between ego and eco tendencies, underscoring leadership's complexity and multifaceted nature in today's world.

While sustainability leadership practices may exhibit different styles and paradigms as those that we have examined in Chapter 1 (shared values), the essence of sustainability leadership is anchored in the commitment to long-term holistic well-being, environmental stewardship, and a balanced consideration of social, economic, and environmental dimensions. Unlike traditional leadership models, which often prioritize short-term gains and hierarchical decision-making, sustainability leadership emphasizes collaboration, future-thinking, and the integration of values that ensure our planet's preservation and everyone's prosperity. At its core, sustainability leadership seeks not just to manage and direct but to inspire, empower, and bring about systemic change that aligns organizational objectives with the broader goals of global sustainability.

Key Takeaways: Environmental Sustainability

1. **A holistic Approach is Crucial:** Environmental sustainability extends beyond simple conservation practices, necessitating a holistic view that encompasses economic, social, and ecological dimensions, emphasizing the interdependence of these elements.

2. **Business Opportunities in Environmental Challenges:** While climate change poses significant risks, it simultaneously presents businesses with vast opportunities. Companies that adopt eco-leadership and prioritize sustainability can mitigate these risks and harness the potential for growth and innovation.

3. **Regenerative Leadership:** More is needed to sustain; there's a pressing need to regenerate and restore. Regenerative leadership emphasizes the proactive restoration of ecosystems, ensuring businesses give back to the environment, not just take from it.

4. **Shift from "Ego" to "Eco":** The chapter underscores the transformation from self-centered, short-term business decisions ("Ego") to a leadership style that prioritizes environmental well-being and long-term sustainability ("Eco"). This paradigm shift is essential for businesses to remain relevant in an evolving global landscape.

5. **Stakeholder and Community Involvement:** True environmental sustainability can only be achieved when businesses actively listen to and involve stakeholders and communities in their decision-making processes. This ensures that sustainability initiatives have a net positive impact and that long-term outcomes benefit all parties involved.

CHAPTER 9

PEACE: CARING FOR HUMAN RIGHTS

TOWARDS RIGHTS-BASED GLOBAL CITIZENSHIP

Overview

This chapter delves deep into the idea of fundamental human rights, emphasizing businesses' critical role in leading by example and setting standards that promote these rights. By embracing a holistic understanding of peace rooted in sustainable human security, freedoms from fear, want, shame, and vulnerability emerge as paramount. The United Nations Global Compact provides a clear framework, underpinning the importance of a principle-based and human rights-based approach in all sectors of society. Through this lens, we explore the collective responsibility of business and sustainability leaders in communities, governments, and institutions. These entities collaborate, using their unique strengths to build a society characterized by justice, respect, dignity, and sustainable peace.

The Global Citizenship Paradigm

As our world becomes more interconnected, the concept of citizenship has evolved. No longer is it sufficient to view oneself purely as a citizen of a particular nation; instead, there's a growing recognition of the responsibilities and rights that come with being a citizen of the world. This holistic perspective is embodied in the concept of 'Global Citizenship.' Linking this idea to peace, human rights, and sustainability leadership practices implies that being global citizen means actively fostering peace, championing human rights, and leading sustainable actions for the collective good. So what does it truly entail to assume this mantle of global citizenship i such a multidimensional context?

Global citizenship refers to belonging to a broader community an common humanity. It emphasizes individuals' interconnectednes regardless of nationality, culture, or religion. As a paradigm, encompasses the values, attitudes, and practices necessary fc individuals to understand, act upon, and engage constructively i world affairs.

The United Nations defines 'Global Citizenship' as the sustainabilit agenda and the responsibilities we carry for all societies, locally an globally.

> Global citizenship is the umbrella term for social, politica environmental, and economic actions of globally minde individuals and communities on a worldwide scale. The terr can refer to the belief that individuals are members c multiple, diverse, local, and non-local networks rather tha single actors affecting isolated societies. Promoting glob: citizenship in sustainable development will allow individua to embrace their social responsibility to act for the benefit c all societies, not just their own. **1**

Oxfam International has a similar definition for global citizenshi and recognizes its implications for our social-environment: responsibilities, common humanity, and human rights.

> Global citizenship is a term used to describe the socia environmental, and economic actions taken by individua and communities who recognize that every person is a citize of the world. It is about how decisions in one part of th planet can affect people living in a different part and abou how we all share a common humanity and are of equal wortl It means being open to engaging positively with othe identities and cultures and being able to recognize an challenge stereotypes. It is also about how we use and shar

the earth's resources fairly and uphold the human rights of all. **2**

The Sustainable Development Goals (SDGs) underscore the need for a global perspective in addressing worldwide challenges, with SDG 4 particularly emphasizing inclusive and quality education that promotes global citizenship. By 2030, the goal is for learners to embrace a worldview that aligns with sustainable development. The SDG Target 4.7 defines this responsibility to educate for 'global citizenship' and 'sustainable development' priorities.

> Target 4.7: by 2030 ensure all learners acquire knowledge and skills needed to promote sustainable development, including among others through education for sustainable development and sustainable lifestyles, human rights, gender equality, promotion of a culture of peace and non-violence, global citizenship, and appreciation of cultural diversity and of culture's contribution to sustainable development. **3**

Universities play a pivotal role in this vision, not just as educational institutions but as shapers of thought and cultivators of global thinkers. Through integrating global issues into their curriculum, fostering research on universal challenges, promoting collaborative international learning, and engaging in community-based projects, universities have the responsibility and power to guide students toward recognizing their potential as contributors to a larger global community.

Global Citizenship Dimensions

In a world that becomes increasingly interdependent and with common sustainability-related challenges, the concept of global citizenship takes on paramount importance. But what exactly does it mean to be a global citizen, and what are the practical implications for leadership, peace, and human rights? At its core, a global citizen is someone profoundly connected to the broader aspects of humanity, transcends borders, and perceives the world as an integrated whole. The world is viewed here in its interdependence and commonality rather than its barriers and differentiations. It is about understanding the world and recognizing one's role and responsibility. It is about actively making the world a better place in all aspects, including those that affect human security, human development, and human dignity. **4**

In other words, being a global citizen means being not merely an observer. Instead, you actively participate, leading the way in shaping the narrative of a world that aspires to peace, sustainability, and equity. This engagement isn't restricted to the global stage; it begins at home, in our local communities, extending outwards in concentric circles of influence. Global citizenship represents the complex "beyond-borders" responsibilities every individual possesses in this globalized era, a duty that is not confined to the borders of one's birth nation but spans across continents and cultures. Global citizenship also involves leadership expressed for the emergence and evolution of frameworks and institutions that allow individuals to exercise this responsibility effectively. Together, these concepts shape the contemporary understanding of global citizenship, urging individuals to recognize their role and influence in a world without walls. **5**

Let's discuss more what global citizenship involves to explain the concept further. It's about recognizing the intricate interplay between local actions and global repercussions. It requires introspection into our views, values, and assumptions, often challenging us to rethink our perspectives. Another essential dimension is exploring social justice within our immediate surroundings and globally. True global citizenship doesn't shy away from the complexities of international issues; it seeks to understand multiple viewpoints, fostering a more comprehensive and empathetic worldview. This informed perspective then finds application in real-world contexts, driving change where it matters most. Ultimately, global citizenship offers individuals the tools and platforms to act reflectively, ensuring their voices resonate in the call for a better, more united world.

We identify five dimensions that Global Citizenship represents and have practical implications for sustainability leadership practices.

1. **Awareness**: A global citizen is aware of the wider world and has a sense of their role as a world citizen. They recognize the interconnectedness of local and global contexts. For sustainability leadership, having a keen awareness means

recognizing that actions taken in one corner of the world can have ripple effects elsewhere. Leaders must understand the global context of their decisions, ensuring their actions are sustainable not just locally but on a global scale. For example, a company might decide to source its materials from a more sustainable and ethical supplier overseas, understanding that deforestation or labor exploitation in another country will have global environmental and societal impacts.

2. **Responsibility**: This entails understanding our role and responsibility for a better world and acting accordingly. Recognizing that one's local actions can have global consequences. Leaders in sustainability recognize the weight of their decisions, understanding that with the power to influence comes the responsibility to act in ways that benefit the greater good. For example, a fashion brand, acknowledging the environmental footprint of fast fashion, might commit to using recycled materials and reducing waste, knowing its actions will influence industry standards and consumer behavior globally.

3. **Participation**: Engaging with the global community in direct and meaningful ways. This can include voting, advocacy, community service, and other forms of active engagement. Sustainable leadership means actively engaging with global initiatives, communities, and frameworks. It's not just about the passive agreement but about tangible action. For example, a corporation might adhere to the Paris Agreement and actively participate in global climate change forums, contributing resources and knowledge to further the cause.

4. **Rights and Respect**: Recognizing and protecting the rights and dignity of all people, understanding that everyone has rights regardless of where they are from. For sustainability leaders, it's imperative to ensure that all actions uphold the rights and dignity of individuals everywhere. This includes considering the human aspect of sustainability ensuring that no community is adversely affected in the quest for environmental or economic gains. For example, instead of exploiting a resource-rich area in a developing nation, a

mining company collaborates with local communities to ensure their rights are protected, their culture is respected, and they benefit economically from the venture.

5. **Empathy and Solidarity**: Building emotional connections with people from different backgrounds, cultures, and beliefs, recognizing common human emotions and experiences, and supporting others in times of need. Leading sustainably means understanding and valuing the experiences of diverse groups. Leaders can make logical and compassionate decisions by fostering emotional connections ensuring holistic, sustainable outcomes. For example, after a natural disaster in a region, a multinational company might launch a global fundraiser among its employees, matching contributions and sending aid, showcasing solidarity and empathy with those affected.

In essence, global citizenship presents core dimensions that the shared values and multidimensions practices of sustainability leadership. It connects global perspective, responsibility, active participation, respect for rights, and empathetic solidarity into decision-making for a better world.

Global Citizenship for Human Rights

The nexus between global citizenship and human rights is profound, and its implications for sustainability leadership are vast. Embracing the ethos of global citizenship means leaders must broaden their horizons beyond the immediate or parochial, integrating human rights into the fabric of their sustainability missions. In the context of human rights, the Global Citizenship Paradigm plays a crucial role. As global citizens, individuals are more likely to:

1. **Advocate for the Rights Beyond Borders**: This means advocating for those beyond their immediate community or national borders. The practical implication for sustainability leaders is that they should transcend the confines of regional or national interests, actively championing the rights and welfare of individuals irrespective of geographical boundaries. An example of this practice is when a tech giant headquartered in North America could lobby against digital

censorship or surveillance in countries where online freedom is stifled, even if they don't have immediate business interests in those regions.

2. **Recognize and Challenge Global Injustices**: For sustainability leadership, this means addressing environmental issues and societal injustices. Leaders must actively oppose systems, practices, or policies that perpetuate inequalities on a global scale. An example is when a multinational coffee chain, realizing the injustices in global coffee trade dynamics, might pledge to source only from fair-trade farmers, ensuring equitable pay and fostering sustainable farming practices.

3. **Support International Human Rights Frameworks**: Instead of viewing international human rights conventions and frameworks as formalities, sustainability leaders should actively endorse, support, and adopt them, ensuring these principles guide their organizational strategy. A practical example is when a global fashion brand, aligning with the UN's Universal Declaration of Human Rights, undergoes regular third-party audits to ensure no child labor or forced labor is used in any part of its supply chain, from raw materials to retail outlets.

4. **Share Resources and Knowledge to Address Global Challenges**: This addresses global and sustainability challenges like poverty, inequality, and discrimination. To address overarching global issues, sustainability leaders should be committed to pooling resources, be it capital, technology, or knowledge, and fostering collaborative approaches. A practical example is when pharmaceutical companies, in response to a global health crisis, might collaborate to share research data, streamline clinical trials, and ensure that vaccines or treatments are distributed equitably, addressing challenges like health inequality, and ensuring the right to health.

n essence, the ethos of global citizenship mandates sustainability leaders to position human rights at the epicenter of their strategies. s guardians of the planet and its inhabitants, sustainable leadership,

guided by the principles of global citizenship, has the potential t
reshape our world, ensuring dignity, rights, and justice for all. **6**

Global Citizenship Education

In an increasingly interconnected world where human right
violations, inequality, and poverty pose significant threats t
sustainability and peace, UNESCO's Global Citizenship Educatio
(GCED) emerges as a beacon of hope. GCED is a transformativ
initiative that addresses these pressing global challenges b
emphasizing that they aren't merely local but universal concern
Drawing inspiration from key foundational documents lik
UNESCO's Constitution, the Universal Declaration of Huma
Rights, and the Education 2030 Agenda, GCED primarily focuses o
fostering values of peace, human rights, and sustainable developmen
Central to the sustainability agenda, GCED is designed to cultivate
deep sense of responsibility, creativity, and innovation, empowerin
learners to be champions of peaceful, tolerance, and inclusiv
societies. UNESCO's commitment to this mission is furthe
exemplified in its specialized themes under GCED, such as educatio
against violent extremism, promoting the understanding of th
Holocaust and genocide, and emphasizing the rule of law—all i
service of a peaceful and sustainable future. **7**

Embracing the Global Citizenship Paradigm is more than jus
understanding our interconnectedness; it's about taking active step
toward creating a world that respects and upholds the rights of all it
inhabitants. In this rights-based approach to global citizenship, peac
is not just the absence of conflict but the presence of justice, respec
and dignity for all. As we progress through this chapter, we wi
discuss how communities, governments, and institutions ca
promote and safeguard human rights within this paradigm.

The Human Rights-Based Approach

A human rights-based approach (HRBA) to sustainability leadershi
emphasizes the intrinsic human rights of all individuals as th
foundation of any sustainable development initiative. The approac
implies two interconnected practices. First, it means that individua

and communities should know their rights (rights holders claim their rights – empowerment process). Second, they should be fully supported to participate in developing policies and practices affecting their lives and claim rights where necessary (the duty bearer meets its obligations – accountability process). **8** Rooted in international human rights standards, HRBA integrates the international human rights system's norms, standards, and principles into the planning, implementing, and evaluating of sustainable initiatives and development projects. Rather than seeing individuals as passive recipients of charity or aid, a rights-based approach positions them as active holders of rights and central participants in the development process.

HRBA requires human rights principles (universality, indivisibility, equality and non-discrimination, participation, accountability) to guide United Nations development cooperation and focus on developing the capacities of both "duty-bearers" to meet their obligations and "rights-holders" to claim their rights.

Dimensions and Principles of the HRBA

The HRBA encompasses a set of principles that guide sustainable development and peace initiatives.

1. **Universality**: At its core, the HRBA hinges on the understanding that every individual inherently possesses human rights, regardless of distinguishing attributes like race or socio-economic background. This concept, known as universality, emphasizes that everyone is universally entitled to these rights. Leaders must recognize that any form of discrimination can trigger conflicts. For instance, when embarking on a project to provide clean water access, the universality principle would ensure that everyone receives equal benefits regardless of their background.

2. **Indivisibility**: Further building on this foundation is the principle of indivisibility, which asserts that human rights cannot be segmented or ranked. They exist as a holistic network, each one deeply interwoven with the others. Thus, while a reforestation initiative might seem environmentally driven at first glance, it must also factor in the economic and

cultural rights of Indigenous groups who depend on those forests.

3. **Participation**: Then there's the emphasis on participation. It's not enough for rights to merely exist; they need to be exercised and lived. Ensuring all stakeholders, especially the most vulnerable, are involved in decision-making. In scenarios like urban planning, active community involvement not only fosters a sense of belonging but also guarantees that plans align with the actual needs of the residents.

4. **Accountability**: The pillar of accountability ensures that organizations or entities spearheading development initiatives remain transparent and answerable. Such a stance builds trust. For instance, mining companies can't just focus on extraction; they must prioritize environmental care and the rights of local communities.

5. **Non-Discrimination and Equal Access**: Equal access to resources and opportunities lies at the heart of the nondiscrimination and equal access principle. Equity and inclusivity are essential for peace, as they prevent grievances that might escalate into unrest. This is evident when distributing resources, like renewable energy solutions, where urban centers and remote villages should experience equal benefits.

6. **Empowerment**: Empowerment takes the HRBA a step further. It's not just about providing rights or resources but enabling individuals to claim and utilize them. Empowered communities are more resilient and active in peacekeeping and conflict resolution. Take, for instance, sustainable farming programs that arm farmers with new techniques, ensuring not just better crops but also community-wide food security.

7. **Linkage to Rights**: Lastly, the linkage to rights principle reminds us that all these efforts are tied to a global framework of recognized human rights. Adhering to these standards offers a solid foundation and common ground,

making endeavors like international trade agreements more harmonious by safeguarding workers' rights across the board.

By understanding and integrating these HRBA dimensions, sustainable peace leaders can promote initiatives that advance development and reinforce the foundations of lasting peace.

Leadership for Sustainable Human Security

Sustainable human security is an expanded framework taken from the concept of human security. **9** The "sustainable" perspective for human security offers a more comprehensive vision for human survival, human development, human dignity, and environmental security in peace, economic, social, and sustainability leadership. At its core, this concept moves beyond traditional frameworks largely centered on state and military-centric security (national security). Instead, it focuses on a more holistic, people-centered approach, with four essential freedoms: freedom from fear, freedom from want, freedom from shame, and freedom from vulnerability. This novel perspective is crucial for understanding and addressing the intricate challenges our globalized societies face, many of which blur the lines between old threats and new, cross-cutting concerns.

1. **Freedom from Fear** *(Human Survival):* This element protects and promotes human survival. In the context of leadership, it implies that leaders should prioritize the safety and well-being of the people, ensuring that they live without the constant dread of conflict, violence, or persecution. Addressing root causes of fear, such as the outbreak of violence, wars, and internal conflicts, requires leaders to adopt strategies that promote peace, stability, and understanding among diverse groups.

2. **Freedom from Want** *(Human Development):* Highlighting human development, this aspect underscores the importance of fulfilling every person's basic needs and aspirations. Leaders practicing sustainability must address systemic challenges like chronic poverty, extreme inequalities, and recurring famines. The focus should be on long-term

solutions that ensure access to resources, equitable distribution, and opportunities for growth and progress.

3. **Freedom from Shame** *(Human Dignity):* Centered on human dignity, this dimension advocates for a world where every individual's rights and worth are recognized and respected. For leaders, this translates into championing human rights, fighting against human trafficking, and eliminating practices or policies that degrade or dehumanize individuals. It also underscores the necessity for post-conflict reconstruction and addressing artificial humanitarian emergencies.

4. **Freedom from Vulnerability** *(Human Vulnerability):* This freedom, emphasizing human sustainability, pushes for proactive measures against potential threats. Whether they stem from climate-related disasters or pandemic diseases, leaders must be equipped to foresee, mitigate, and address vulnerabilities that can destabilize societies. It also highlights the environmental and systemic elements crucial for understanding and resolving contemporary and future human insecurities.

Embracing the sustainable human security model is more than just recognizing these freedoms; it's about integrating them into leadership strategies and policies. It's a call to leaders everywhere to understand that genuine security is not just the absence of threats but the presence of systems and conditions that uphold these fundamental freedoms. By embedding this understanding into their approach, sustainability leaders can pave the way for a more peaceful, just, and resilient world. **10**

Sustainability Leadership for Peacebuilding

The United Nations, recognizing the critical role of business in peacebuilding, established the "Business for Peace" initiative to foster collaborative endeavors that promote peace. As a platform of about 150 preeminent companies and business groups across 37 countries, the initiative urges businesses to align their practices with peacebuilding principles. This is the essence of holistic peacebuilding hat recognizes that true peace isn't just the silencing of guns but ddressing profound grievances, such as ensuring rights to land, esources, and political participation. **11**

ustainability leaders engaging in the Business for Peace initiative eceive several benefits, including aid in better identifying and nanaging potential business risks, ultimately reducing operational osts. Moreover, these networks enable companies to share ioneering practices and learn from their counterparts' experiences vhile engaging in principle-based practices promoting the UNGC's rinciples of human rights, labor rights, environmental rights, and nti-corruption. Participating in the initiative is about showcasing usiness leadership and being acknowledged for spearheading ractical peacebuilding solutions.

n addition, sustainability leaders for peacebuilding engage and ncourage restorative justice solutions. Instead of solely focusing on unishing wrongdoers, imagine a system that emphasizes healing, estitution, and the restoration of rights. This could manifest in truth nd reconciliation commissions prioritizing victims' stories, rights, nd dignity, fostering communal healing. Business leadership can play n important role in the implementation of SDG 16 by respecting nd supporting governments in efforts to advance peace, justice, and he proper functioning of effective, accountable, and inclusive nstitutions. These institutions, impartial and accessible to all, serve to phold the rule of law and ensuring that the rights of every individual re protected. **12**

Jltimately, the story of sustainability leadership for peace is about eshaping our understanding of peace itself. It's not merely the bsence of conflict but a dynamic state where each person's rights are ecognized on paper and lived and experienced daily. Such an pproach offers a more holistic, inclusive, and lasting roadmap to eace rooted firmly in the tenets of human rights.

he Human Rights Principles in Business

he Human Rights Council endorsed the UN Guiding Principles on 3usiness and Human Rights (UNGPs) in June 2011 and have since become a benchmark for businesses and governments globally in addressing the impacts of business operations on human rights. **13**

The UNGPs are based on three pillars, comprising 31 principles and practical implications for sustainability leadership:

1. **Protect** The state's duty to protect against human rights abuses by third parties, including business enterprises through appropriate policies, regulations, and adjudication Governments are responsible for creating and enforcing laws and regulations safeguarding human rights and holding businesses accountable for violations. This implies that sustainability leadership requires governments to establish legal and regulatory framework that promotes responsible business conduct and ensures the protection of human rights

2. **Respect**: The corporate responsibility is to respect human rights, which means to avoid infringing on the rights of others and to address any adverse impacts. Businesses are responsible for avoiding infringing on the human rights of individuals and addressing any adverse human rights impact that may arise from their operations. This includes conducting human rights due diligence to identify and mitigate potential risks and implement effective grievance mechanisms to address complaints and provide remedies to victims. For sustainability leadership, businesses must integrate human rights considerations into their strategies, policies, and practices. They should assess the potential human rights impacts of their operations, supply chains, and business relationships and take appropriate measures to prevent and address negative consequences. This includes engaging with stakeholders, conducting impact assessments and implementing robust monitoring and reporting mechanisms.

3. **Remedy**: The need for greater access to effective remedies for victims of business-related human rights abuses, both through judicial and non-judicial means. This implies that businesses should establish effective grievance mechanisms that allow individuals and communities affected by their operations to seek redress for any harm suffered

Sustainability leadership requires businesses to provide accessible and transparent avenues for remedy, ensuring that affected individuals have access to justice and can obtain appropriate compensation or restitution. **14** The UNGPs have provided a strong foundation for developing national action plans and corporate human rights policies and have influenced the inclusion of human rights considerations in other business-related standards and initiatives. They serve as a guiding framework for businesses and states, ensuring that business operations do not lead to human rights abuses and that remedies are available when abuses occur.

Overall, the UNGPs emphasize that while states have a primary duty to protect human rights, businesses have a responsibility to respect human rights, which means acting with due diligence to avoid infringing on the rights of others. For sustainability leadership, businesses must integrate human rights considerations into their strategies and operations, engage with stakeholders, conduct human rights due diligence, and establish effective grievance mechanisms. By adhering to these principles, businesses can demonstrate their commitment to ethical and sustainable practices and contribute to promoting and protecting human rights.

The UNGPs and the SDGs

The link between the UNGPs and the 2030 Agenda for Sustainable Development, which includes the SDGs, is unmistakable. Both frameworks converge on the shared objective of realizing human rights and sustainable development, making businesses essential actors in this collective endeavor. Here's how the UNGPs serve as a roadmap for businesses in contributing to the SDGs:

1. **Shared Foundations**: The UNGPs and the SDGs are grounded in universal human rights principles. Businesses adhering to the UNGPs can be confident that they indirectly contribute to multiple SDGs by ensuring they do not infringe on human rights.

2. **Direct Alignments**: Several SDGs have explicit targets related to human rights. For instance, SDG 8 promotes

"decent work, "aligning with the UNGPs' emphasis on labor rights. Similarly, SDG 16 on "peace, justice, and strong institutions" aligns with the UNGPs' third pillar on remedies for human rights abuses.

3. **Risk Management and Positive Contributions**: The due diligence processes prescribed by the UNGPs help businesses identify risks and opportunities for positive impact. By addressing these risks and leveraging opportunities, businesses can advance several SDGs.

4. **Stakeholder Engagement and Partnerships**: The UNGPs stress meaningful engagement with stakeholders, which promotes collaborations and partnerships, directly supporting SDG 17 to revitalize global partnerships for sustainable development.

5. **Promoting Sustainability**: By encouraging businesses to respect human rights across their value chains, the UNGPs help them to adopt sustainable practices. For instance, ensuring the rights of Indigenous people (as outlined in the UNGPs) can also contribute to SDG 15 related to life on land, emphasizing sustainable use of terrestrial ecosystems.

6. **Transparency and Reporting**: The emphasis the UNGPs place on reporting human rights practices aligns with SDG 12, which calls for responsible consumption and production patterns, including transparency.

7. **Empowering Marginalized Groups**: Both frameworks stress the importance of leaving no one behind. Adhering to the UNGPs can help businesses contribute to SDGs focused on marginalized groups, such as SDG 5 on gender equality and SDG 10 on reducing inequalities.

In essence, the UNGPs, by pushing businesses towards respect for human rights and responsible conduct, ensure they operate in a way that not only prevents harm but also contributes to broader societal goals encapsulated in the SDGs. This integrated approach is vital to building sustainable and inclusive economies and societies.

Leadership Practices for Human Rights

The United Nations Global Compact (UNGC) leads businesses worldwide, inspiring them to adopt sustainable and responsible policies and champion human rights. Human rights principles are at the heart of this initiative.

The 10 principles of the UNGC focus on human rights and ESG paradigms closely connected to the SDGs sustainability agenda. Principles 1 and 2 specifically address human rights:

> **Principle 1**: Businesses should support and respect the protection of internationally proclaimed human rights. This principle underscores the responsibility of businesses to ensure they are not complicit in human rights abuses. This encompasses a broad range of rights, from civil and political rights, like freedom of expression and association, to economic, social, and cultural rights, like the right to work, education, and health.

> **Principle 2**: Businesses should ensure they are not complicit in human rights abuses. Complicity means being implicated in a human rights abuse that another party commits. This can arise in various scenarios – directly (through a company's activities), via a business relationship (suppliers, joint venture partners), or by providing products or services misused by others.

While the first two principles specifically mention human rights, other principles in the UNGC touch upon topics intrinsically linked to human rights. The UNGC also pulls businesses away from the shadows of unethical labor practices. It vehemently opposes all forms of forced and compulsory labor, underlining that work should always be a matter of choice, not coercion. Similarly, it underscores the importance of protecting our most vulnerable: children. Through its principles, the UNGC fervently appeals to businesses to eradicate child labor. Simultaneously, it champions the cause of creating workplaces free from discrimination, ensuring that opportunities are available to all, irrespective of their background or identity.

Principle 3: Businesses should uphold the freedom of association and effectively recognize the right to collective bargaining.

Principle 4: Businesses should eliminate all forms of forced and compulsory labor.

Principle 5: Businesses should uphold the effective abolition of child labor.

Principle 6: Businesses should eliminate discrimination concerning employment and occupation. **15**

These labor principles are closely connected to human rights, focusing on workers' rights, and ensuring fair and equitable treatment for all. Additionally, the UNGC encourages businesses to take broader actions on other human rights-related topics. **16** Here is a list of specific human rights topics that are relevant to sustainability leadership and business responsibility for human rights:

- **Women's empowerment and gender equality**: The UNGC emphasizes the pivotal role of women in shaping a sustainable future. Women's empowerment isn't merely about addressing social injustices; it's an essential catalyst for growth, innovation, and prosperity. For sustainability leaders, this means creating workplaces that actively challenge gender biases, provide equal opportunities, and uplift women to leadership roles. This could translate to policies ensuring equal pay, mentorship programs for aspiring female leaders, and gender-sensitive training modules that debunk stereotypes. There are specific frameworks that can be used to advance women's rights, such as the Universal Declaration of Human Rights, the International Covenant on Economic, Social, and Cultural Rights, and the Convention on the Elimination of All Forms of Discrimination Against Women (CEDAW) and the Women's Empowerment Principles (WEPs). **17**

- **Indigenous peoples' rights**: The rights of Indigenous peoples, as championed by the UNGC, underscore their unique connection to their ancestral lands, cultures, and traditions. Sustainability leaders must recognize that industrial and developmental projects can severely disrupt these connections. This means due diligence is needed before any project initiation, ensuring Indigenous communities are consulted, and their rights are respected. In essence, Indigenous communities' traditional knowledge isn't just to be acknowledged but can be incorporated into sustainable practices, offering valuable insights. Protecting the rights of Indigenous peoples in development projects is both a moral and legal imperative. Indigenous peoples have unique connections to their lands and environments, which are intertwined with their cultural, spiritual, economic, and social identities. Disregarding these connections can lead to not only loss of heritage but also breaches of internationally recognized human rights. The Free Prior and Informed Consent (FPIC) is a critical principle established in international frameworks like the ILO Convention 169 and the UN Declaration on the Rights of Indigenous Peoples (UNDRIP) that protect those rights through a specific process. **18**

- **Children's rights**: Children, the guardians of our future, hold particular importance in the UNGC's vision. Their well-being today directly affects the world of tomorrow. For sustainability leaders, this means understanding the broad spectrum of children's rights, from safeguarding them against labor and exploitation to ensuring access to necessities like education and health. It also means businesses must consider how their operations, even indirectly, impact children's well-being and be proactive in creating child-friendly policies. These rights are detailed in the Children's Rights and Business Principles developed jointly by UNICEF, the UNGC, and Save the Children. **19**

- **Migrant workers' rights**: Migrant workers often find themselves in vulnerable situations, facing discrimination, exploitation, and a lack of basic rights. The UNGC calls for their protection and equal treatment. Sustainability leaders should ensure migrant workers receive the same rights, protections, and benefits. This includes fair wages, safe working conditions, and freedom from coercion. Companies should also look at the bigger picture, recognizing the societal and economic value migrants bring and advocating for their rights on broader platforms. Besides the legal framework that protects the rights of displaced people, as in the 1951 Refugee Convention and its 1967 Protocol, several international legal frameworks are dedicated to the protection of migrant worker's rights. Among them, it is important to remember International Labour Organization (ILO) Convention (97/1945; 143/1975; 181/1997) and the International Convention on the Protection of the Rights of All Migrant Workers and Members of Their Families (ICRMW) (1990).

- **The Rights of Individuals Belonging to Vulnerable Groups:** Every individual, irrespective of their background has the right to live with dignity, respect, and freedom. The UNGC recognizes that certain groups, owing to various socio-political factors, are more susceptible to discrimination and rights violations. Sustainability leaders must adopt holistic approach, ensuring their policies and practices are inclusive. This could involve targeted community upliftment programs, partnerships with NGOs working with vulnerable groups, and ensuring representation of these groups in decision-making processes. The rights of vulnerable migrant groups, including women, children, persons with disabilities older adults, and victims of trafficking, among others, are encompassed by many international legal instruments Relevant here is the Convention on the Rights of Persons with Disabilities (CRPD), as persons with disabilities who are also migrants can face compounded vulnerabilities. The CRPD ensures their full and equal enjoyment of all human rights and fundamental freedoms. **20**

The UNGC isn't just about principles on paper. It's a clarion call inspiring businesses to build a world anchored in equality, justice, and human dignity.

The UNGC has shed light on specific areas of concern, from rights of migrants to the empowerment of women. These rights element underscore that businesses have a wide range of concerns and responsibilities to integrate, recognize, and respect. It's no longer adequate to remain passive or neutral; leaders must actively champion these rights, integrating them into the core of their strategies and operations. The UNGC principle-based approach paves a clear pathway and underscores the paramount importance of businesses in peacebuilding. Businesses, however, must interpret peace not just in its conventional sense but through the lens of sustainable human security. This means addressing the multiple dimensions of fear— whether it be from violence, deprivation, indignity, or vulnerability— and ensuring that every individual can lead a life marked by safety, dignity, and opportunity.

However, building peaceful, rights-respecting societies isn't a burden that businesses bear alone. It's a responsibility shared with governments, civil society, and other stakeholders. Sustainable human security and human rights-based well-being aren't mere buzzwords but capture the shared aspirations of humanity. In this shared vision, businesses play a pivotal role, leveraging their influence, resources, and networks to build bridges, foster understanding, and drive meaningful change.

In closing, it's evident that the mandate for sustainability leaders has evolved. Their responsibility transcends the immediate welfare of their communities. In today's interconnected world, sustainability leadership is about a broader commitment to sustainable human security, human rights, and peace. It's a call to action—a beckoning to reimagine businesses as potent forces for good, shaping a world marked by fairness, respect, and enduring peace.

Key Takeaways: Peace-Security Practices

1. **Holistic Conception of Peace**: Peace is not just the cessation of hostilities; it is creating an environment where sustainable human security and human dignity flourish. Businesses and leaders must recognize their role in promoting holistic peace, which entails addressing the underlying causes of conflict and ensuring the well-being of all.

2. **Human Rights-Based Approach**: The human rights-based approach is central to peace and security, emphasizing every individual's intrinsic value and rights. Businesses are urged to

place human rights at the forefront of their operations, ensuring that their actions uphold, respect, and further these rights in all contexts.

3. **Sustainable Human Security**: The evolving concept of sustainable human security encompasses freedoms from fear, want, shame, and vulnerability. It underscores the persistent, interdependent, and universal nature of these freedoms. For businesses, this means considering the immediate and long-term implications of their actions on the comprehensive well-being of individuals and communities.

4. **UN's Human Rights Principle for Businesses**: The United Nations Global Compact outlines a clear framework for businesses, emphasizing the protection and promotion of human rights. Beyond mere compliance, businesses have the opportunity and responsibility to be proactive champions of these rights, setting standards and leading by example.

5. **Collaborative Responsibility for Peace**: Peace and security are a collective responsibility. Beyond governments, businesses, civil societies, and other stakeholders share the duty of fostering a peaceful environment. This shared mission requires collaboration, leveraging each entity's unique strengths and capabilities to build rights-respecting, peaceful, and inclusive societies.

CHAPTER 10

PROSPERITY: CARING FOR GOOD BUSINESS

DOING GOOD AND DOING WELL

Overview

Good business isn't solely about profits; it's about creating value that benefits all stakeholders. This chapter delves into the principles of ethical business practices that promote prosperity while ensuring fairness, equity, and sustainability. It reviews various solutions for ESG and sustainability practices. It makes a case for business engagement for global social responsibility and for leadership that promotes global sustainability and prosperity. It also explores the future of technology advancements that need orientation by a "humane technology" paradigm and "value" and "ethical" sustainability leaders.

Prosperity is More Than Profit

The true essence of prosperity goes beyond simple economic growth. As stated in Chapter 3, well-being and prosperity are inextricably linked. In the context of well-being, prosperity becomes more than an economic goal; it's a bedrock for societal stability and peace. The intertwined nature of prosperity and human security cannot be overstated, especially in a world where socioeconomic disparities can swiftly escalate into larger conflicts. **1**

But the journey to genuine prosperity isn't solely about economic milestones. Sustainability leadership recognizes the multifaceted nature of development. True prosperity embraces the economic dimension along the social and environmental facets, creating a trinity essential for sustainable progress. While short-term economic gains might seem appealing, focusing solely on profit risks overshadows a community's holistic well-being. As we reviewed in Chapter 7 (People), businesses are not isolated entities; they're woven into the very fabric of society, influenced by, and impacting both human communities and the natural environment. A business model that caters only to "shareholders," sidelining the broader "stakeholders," presents a narrow, potentially perilous view.

Sustainability leadership practices urge a shift in this perspective. Such leadership acknowledges prosperity as a financial measure and a comprehensive gauge of societal health, environmental balance, and economic vitality. This chapter explores how these leadership practices, rooted in a balanced and holistic view of prosperity, can drive businesses to contribute positively to a sustainable and harmonious global future. We will investigate contemporary economic and business practices that are more likely to promote prosperity and advance the collective and long-term values associated with sustainability leadership.

Prosperity in Leadership Practices

Sustainability leadership in business requires understanding and investing in practices that are more likely to generate a shared (common) benefit for prosperity (economic), people (social), and planet (environmental) dimensions. This not only addresses present needs but also ensures the conditions for long-term development and shared prosperity. Here, we analyze some of the most promising economic practices for sustainability leadership with some examples and implications for business and corporate performance:

1. **Circular Economy:** A circular economy aims to reduce waste and maximize resources. This involves designing products for longevity, promoting recycling and reusability, and reducing resource extraction and waste. The circular economy, grounded in resource optimization and waste

minimization tenets, offers businesses a transformative roadmap for enduring value creation. By internalizing circular principles, businesses can save significantly from reduced resource consumption and waste management costs while identifying novel revenue opportunities. Besides known examples of companies like Apple and Ikea that have integrated the circular economy into their planning and operations, other innovative examples are worth mentioning. For example, Echogen Power Systems, an Ohio-based company, harnesses waste heat from various sources to produce electricity, transforming what was once waste into valuable energy. **2**

Another innovative example is Mud Jeans, a Dutch company that leases jeans to customers and then recycles worn-out pairs to produce new ones, encapsulating the essence of a circular product lifecycle. From the vantage point of sustainability leadership, embracing the circular economy translates into moving away from temporary, linear strategies to a more integrated, enduring approach. It compels leaders to reimagine product lifecycles, recalibrate supply chain strategies, and engage with consumers in novel ways, ensuring their businesses remain adaptable and relevant in a world pivoting towards sustainable paradigms.

2. **Sustainable Supply Chain Management (SSCM):** All key elements are adopting responsible sourcing practices, ensuring suppliers maintain social and environmental standards, and reducing transportation emissions. By integrating SSCM principles, businesses can mitigate risks, enhance brand reputation, and potentially realize cost savings. Consider the case of Fairphone, a Dutch electronics manufacturing company focusing on sourcing conflict-free minerals for their devices. Doing so ensures ethical production and appeals to a growing base of socially conscious consumers. Another example is Dr. Bronner's, a soap manufacturer, prioritizes sourcing its organic ingredients from regenerative organic certified farms, setting new benchmarks in sustainable sourcing. **3**

For sustainability leaders, the implications of SSCM are vast. Adopting SSCM signifies a move from isolated corporate responsibility to a holistic, integrated approach encompassing a product's lifecycle. It challenges leaders to rethink supplier relationships, innovate logistics to reduce emissions, and foster transparency at every step. In doing so, companies can position themselves as frontrunners in responsible business practices, laying a strong foundation for long-term success in a market where sustainability is becoming a defining criterion.

3. **Green Financing:** Investment in green bonds, sustainable projects, and other financial tools can generate profits while addressing environmental issues. Green financing stands at the nexus of economic growth and environmental stewardship, offering an innovative avenue for businesses to access capital while driving positive environmental outcomes. Large financial institutions such as Bank of America and HSBC have embraced the potential of green bonds, investing heavily in sustainable infrastructure and renewable energy projects. On the other end of the spectrum, lesser-known entities like Triodos Bank have carved a niche for themselves by exclusively financing projects with social and environmental benefits. Another interesting case is the M-KOPA Solar in Africa, which, using a pay-as-you-go model, provides affordable solar energy systems to households, funded in part through green finance mechanisms. **4**

For sustainability leaders, green financing isn't just a trend but a testament to the evolving priorities of the global financial system. Engaging with green finance compels companies to align their business strategies with broader environmental objectives. This taps into the growing pool of sustainability-driven capital and signifies a proactive approach to the global challenges of climate change and resource scarcity. Through green financing, businesses can showcase their commitment to sustainable growth while positioning themselves as pioneers in a future-oriented economic landscape.

4. **Triple Bottom Line (TBL) Accounting:** The TBL approach transcends traditional profit metrics to incorporate

the three Ps: People, Planet, and Profit. Interface, a global commercial flooring leader, is an example. The company has been unwavering in its mission to have zero negative environmental impact by 2020, addressing carbon footprint, waste, and fair labor in its supply chain while remaining profitable. A less frequently cited yet impactful example is Novo Nordisk, a pharmaceutical company that incorporates TBL by addressing the global diabetes epidemic (people), maintaining a commitment to environmental responsibility (planet), and ensuring a steady financial performance (profit). **5**

Other inspiring examples are Patagonia and Eileen Fisher clothing brands with fully integrated TBL principles emphasizing sustainable materials, ethical production, and community engagement. For sustainability leaders, the TBL approach signifies a broader perspective on what truly constitutes business success. It underscores an organization's need to align their operational strategies with global sustainability objectives and promote a more encompassing sense of corporate responsibility.

5. **Stakeholder Engagement:** Modern businesses thrive in interconnected ecosystems, making it imperative to acknowledge and engage with diverse stakeholders. Engaging with a wider group of stakeholders (like local communities, NGOs, and employees) ensures a broader perspective and a more sustainable approach. Renowned companies like Starbucks have actively engaged with coffee farmers (ensuring fair trade practices) and local communities, emphasizing shared growth. A lesser known but impactful and inspiring example is the Seventh Generation. This green cleaning products company maintains transparent dialogues with its customers, suppliers, and competitors to elevate industry sustainability standards. **6**

For sustainability leaders, embracing stakeholder engagement is more than just a best practice—it's foundational to enduring business success. This approach ensures a broad-based buy-in, fosters innovation through diverse inputs, and builds resilience against socio-environmental disruptions. The leaders championing stakeholder engagement are safeguarding their businesses and setting the bar for what responsible, future-focused enterprises should embody.

6. **Eco-efficiency:** Eco-efficiency embodies the fusion of economic and ecological efficiency in business operations. At its core, it involves optimizing processes to achieve more with fewer resources, curtailing costs, and lessening environmental impact. This practice encompasses various facets, from energy conservation, where businesses might retrofit operations with LED lighting or implement renewable energy sources, water preservation through reclamation and recycling systems, and waste reduction via recyclable material usage or lean manufacturing methods. Notable companies like Toyota have made strides in this realm, committed to reducing waste through the Toyota Production System. Similarly, Siemens has been at the forefront of energy efficiency, offering green building solutions that save energy and reduce costs. **7**

For sustainability leaders, embracing eco-efficiency is both a strategic and ethical imperative. It positions a company as a responsible steward of the planet's limited resources and translates to tangible economic advantages, enhancing long-term business viability. As consumer consciousness grows and regulatory landscapes evolve, businesses championing eco-efficiency will likely find themselves better equipped to navigate future challenges and capitalize on emerging opportunities.

7. **Clean Technology:** Clean technology, often called "cleantech," encapsulates diverse products, services, and processes primarily designed to mitigate environmental harm while delivering equivalent or superior performance to their conventional counterparts. This field spans several industries, from renewable energy sources such as wind, solar, and biofuels to water purification systems and green transportation solutions. Companies like Tesla have revolutionized the automobile sector with electric vehicles, diminishing greenhouse gas emissions and propelling

advancements in battery technology. On a less mainstream front, Bloom Energy, with its solid oxide fuel cells, aims to provide cleaner, more reliable, and more resilient energy solutions, marking a shift from conventional power generation methods. **8**

For those in sustainability leadership roles, adopting and promoting clean technology represents a forward-thinking approach to business. Such investments underline a company's commitment to environmental responsibility and position it at the vanguard of innovation. As global demands shift towards sustainability and regulatory environments tighten, businesses anchored in clean technology principles will likely reap both the tangible benefits of operational efficiencies and the intangible benefits of enhanced brand reputation and stakeholder trust.

8. **Green Marketing:** Green marketing, often synonymous with eco-marketing or sustainable marketing, highlights the environmental attributes of products or services in promotional efforts. It taps into an emerging market segment of consumers prioritizing environmental considerations in their purchasing decisions. This marketing approach spans a range of sectors, from organic foods to eco-friendly household products and sustainable fashion. Method, a company specializing in biodegradable cleaning products, effectively markets its offerings, emphasizing both efficacy and environmental responsibility. Another brand, Allbirds, has carved a niche in the footwear industry, promoting shoes made of sustainable materials like wool and recycled plastics, directly appealing to eco-conscious consumers. **9**

For sustainability leaders, green marketing isn't merely a tactic—it's a testament to a company's genuine commitment to environmental stewardship. But it carries a responsibility: to ensure that marketing claims are backed by real, tangible, environmentally friendly practices, avoiding the pitfall of "greenwashing." As the global consumer base becomes more informed and discerning, businesses that authentically embed sustainability into their products and communicate these efforts transparently will likely forge deeper connections with their customers, solidifying trust and brand loyalty in an increasingly green-centric market landscape.

9. **Innovative Business Models:** Today, innovative business models are emerging as powerful tools to address sustainability challenges while meeting evolving consumer demands. One prominent example is the sharing economy, where platforms enable individuals to rent or share assets instead of purchasing them outright. Companies like Airbnb and Zipcar exemplify this, allowing users to rent homes for short stays or vehicles for specific trips, reducing the need for hotel constructions or car ownership. Another paradigm is the service-based or "product-as-a-service" model. Philips, for instance, has introduced "lighting as a service," where customers purchase the light they use rather than the light fixtures or bulbs, encouraging the company to design longer-lasting, more efficient products. **10**

For sustainability leaders, such innovative business models are disruptive strategies and conscious responses to global resource constraints and shifting consumer values. By promoting access over ownership or service over product, businesses can significantly mitigate the environmental impact of production and waste, fostering a circular economy. Embracing these models signals a company's commitment to sustainability, resilience, and forward-thinking, setting it apart in an increasingly conscious market and paving the way for a more sustainable and resource-efficient future.

10. **Integrated Reporting:** Integrated reporting represents a paradigm shift in corporate communication, blending traditional financial reporting with non-financial metrics to offer a more holistic view of an organization's performance. This approach recognizes that its financial metrics do not solely determine a company's value but are linked to its environmental, social, and governance (ESG) practices. **11** Firms such as Unilever and Nestlé have been pioneers in this space, presenting integrated reports that transparently convey their economic impact, sustainability initiatives, and societal

contributions. Another trailblazer, the Dutch bank ING, has been keen on providing integrated insights, reflecting the interconnectedness of its financial outcomes with its broader societal and environmental commitments. **12**

For those spearheading sustainability initiatives, integrated reporting is more than a communication tool—it reflects an evolved business mindset. It acknowledges the interdependence between financial success and responsible corporate citizenship. By offering a consolidated view of their performance across multiple dimensions, companies cater to an informed and conscious stakeholder base and drive internal alignment toward a broader, purpose-driven vision. This approach reinforces transparency, fosters trust, and underscores the imperative for businesses to be profitable and socially responsible in today's interconnected world.

11. **Sustainable Investments:** Sustainable investments, often underpinned by ESG criteria, have ushered in a transformative approach to investing, transcending traditional financial analysis. ESG investing evaluates potential investments on their expected financial returns and their performance on a trio of critical criteria: environmental responsibility, social practices, and governance structures. BlackRock, one of the world's largest asset managers, has been a vocal advocate for integrating ESG principles into investment strategies, emphasizing the long-term value creation that responsible investing can yield. Similarly, Nordea Bank, a European financial heavyweight, has channeled significant assets into ESG-focused funds, reflecting the growing appetite among investors for ethically grounded and sustainable investment opportunities. **13**

For leaders in the realm of sustainability, ESG investing isn't a mere trend—it's a testament to the inextricable link between financial performance and responsible business conduct. It underscores the belief that companies prioritizing environmental stewardship, social equity, and robust governance are better poised for long-term success and resilience. As more investors pivot towards sustainable investment strategies, it sends a potent signal to the market about the significance of corporate responsibility Consequently, businesses are motivated to deepen their commitment to sustainable practices, ensuring they remain attractive to this burgeoning segment of conscious investors.

12. **Responsible Consumption and Production:** Businesses can promote sustainable practices, like reducing packaging or promoting local produce, to ensure resources are used efficiently. Responsible consumption and production emerge as critical tenets at the crossroads of sustainability and commerce, calling businesses to reassess and refine their operational and consumer-facing practices. This ethos champions the judicious use of resources throughout production and encourages consumers to make informed, sustainable choices. Lush Cosmetics exemplifies this approach, creating package-free or minimal packaging products and drastically reducing plastic waste. Similarly, Patagonia, the outdoor apparel brand, promotes repairing and reusing its products, fostering a longevity culture, and reducing consumerism. On the food frontier, companies like Farmdrop bridge consumers with local farmers, ensuring fresh, locally sourced produce that minimizes transportation emissions and supports community agriculture. **14**

For sustainability pioneers, promoting responsible consumption and production is a dual mandate: internally optimizing resources and externally influencing consumer behavior. This approach signifies a departure from the linear "make, use, dispose" model, inching closer to a circular economy that values resource optimization and waste reduction. By actively embedding these practices, businesses fortify their brand identity in the eyes of environmentally conscious consumers and position themselves for long-term resilience in an era of finite resources and increasing environmental challenges.

13. **Training and Education:** An integral component of a company's sustainability journey is the education and training of its workforce. By equipping employees with knowledge

and tools, businesses can foster a culture where sustainability is not just an external commitment but an internalized value. Accenture, for instance, has invested heavily in training programs that ensure its global workforce is aligned with its ambitious sustainability objectives. Another significant stride in this space is the Principles for Responsible Management Education (PRME), an initiative backed by the United Nations to elevate sustainability in business school curricula worldwide. Institutions adhering to PRME are committed to producing future business leaders who understand the intricacies of profit and the imperatives of responsible management. **15**

Training and education are not mere add-ons but foundational investments for those leading sustainability initiatives. A workforce educated in sustainability principles is better equipped to identify opportunities for innovation, streamline operations, and engage with stakeholders on pressing environmental and social challenges. Furthermore, as companies vie for top talent, demonstrating a commitment to sustainability education can serve as a competitive differentiator, attracting individuals motivated by purpose as much as profit. Through consistent education and training, businesses can seamlessly weave sustainability into the fabric of their organizational culture.

14. **Partnerships for Goals:** Our time's complex global and sustainability challenges require us to join our strengths and collaborate across organizations, sectors, and nations. No matter how impactful, isolated efforts are often needed to achieve systemic change. Recognizing this, many forward-thinking businesses have turned to partnerships as a strategic lever to amplify their sustainability impact. These collaborations, spanning governments, NGOs, and even erstwhile competitors, harness collective expertise and resources to tackle global challenges. Unilever's collaboration with the World Food Programme to combat child malnutrition is a testament to the transformative power of such partnerships. Central to this collaborative ethos is the

United Nations' SDG 17, which emphasizes the role of partnerships in achieving a sustainable future. **16**

For sustainability leaders, embracing the "Partnerships for Goals" principle is a strategic imperative. Such collaborations magnify the scale of impact and bring diverse perspectives to the table, enriching solutions and strategies. More than just a means to an end, partnerships reflect a recognition that the challenges of the 21st century are too vast and complicated for any single entity to tackle alone. As businesses pivot towards a more sustainable future, forging and nurturing these alliances will be central to their strategy, signaling their commitment to global goals and recognition of the interconnectedness of today's global challenges.

15. **Scenario Planning and Risk Management:** In a VUCA era of unprecedented volatility and change, foresight is no longer a luxury but a critical business tool. In this context, scenario planning and risk management align with a structured approach to anticipate, prepare for, and navigate potential future challenges. Shell, one of the world's largest oil companies, has long been recognized for its sophisticated scenario planning, allowing it to envision and prepare for multiple possible futures, including shifts in energy demand and the impact of climate change. Meanwhile, Swiss Re, a global reinsurance and insurance company, employs extensive risk management strategies, quantifying and strategizing around climate-related risks to safeguard their portfolio and guide clients. **17**

For sustainability champions, this forward-looking approach is a game changer. It's not just about navigating challenges but about turning potential threats into opportunities for innovation and transformation. By systematically considering potential future challenges, from environmental shifts to regulatory changes, businesses can make more informed decisions today that ensure their resilience and prosperity in the years to come. Moreover, as sustainability-related risks increasingly intersect with core business operations, an integrated approach to scenario planning and risk management becomes a cornerstone of corporate responsibility and strategic agility. It's about future-proofing businesses in a world where change is the only constant.

16. **Transparency and Accountability:** Companies that are transparent about their sustainability practices and are held accountable are more likely to build trust with their stakeholders. In today's highly informed modern business landscape, where stakeholders are more informed and demanding than ever, transparency and accountability have evolved from mere buzzwords to mainstays of corporate integrity. Companies that candidly share their sustainability practices, successes, and challenges invariably engender trust among consumers, investors, and broader communities. Everlane is an example here. As a clothing company, it made waves in the fashion industry with its "radical transparency" approach. Everlane breaks down the cost of each product for the consumer, detailing materials, labor, duties, and transport. **18**

Furthermore, they provide information about the factories where their products are made, ensuring ethical production practices. Similarly, Buffer, a social media management platform, is known for its commitment to transparency in the tech sector. The company openly shares employee details, equity breakdowns, and revenue details. Transparency has taken steps to ensure stakeholders have insight into their operations and financials. Both these companies underscore that transparency is not just a strategy but a core value that can differentiate a brand in competitive markets.

For sustainability leaders, emphasizing transparency and accountability is both a challenge and an opportunity. It necessitates an unwavering commitment to honesty, even when the news isn't all positive. However, in doing so, businesses solidify stakeholder trust and position themselves to receive constructive feedback that can further refine their sustainability efforts. In a digital age where information flows freely, being transparent and accountable is not just about meeting stakeholder expectations—it's about setting the standard for ethical business practices and leading by example in a world increasingly attuned to corporate responsibility.

Adopting these practices contributes to global sustainability, offers businesses competitive advantages, opens new markets, and fosters innovation. It's a blend of doing good for the planet and securing long-term economic prosperity. However, implementing sustainable business practices requires more than a list. At the heart of sustainable leadership lies an intricate dance between the macro and micro, the global and local, and the policy and practice. It's not merely about implementing best practices but shaping a holistic movement that transcends traditional boundaries.

Good Business is Globally Responsible and Sustainable

Today's global sustainability challenges require businesses to do more. The boundaries of corporate responsibility have expanded, and CSR side activities are no longer sufficient to meet the stakes of these times. Businesses must fully integrate a "sustainability" DNA where global social responsibility is their modus operandi. While once "good business" meant simply not engaging in harmful practices (business ethics of "do-no-harm'"), the modern business landscape requires corporations to actively seek opportunities for global sustainability and well-being for all (business ethics as "doing good" sustainably and systemically). This reflects a more advanced understanding of business ethics. Look at these components to better understand how prosperity springs from caring for good business as sustainability agents and globally responsible actors.

1. **The Good Business Paradigm:** Historically, a "good business" was one that made profits and complied with the law. In modern contexts, it refers to enterprises that generate profits and consider their impact on the environment, society, and the global community. This encompasses their direct actions, supply chain, influence on communities, and the overall footprint of their products or services. Good business now embodies practices prioritizing environmental health, societal well-being, and economic prosperity. **19**

2. **The Sustainability Paradigm:** Sustainability, in a business context, means meeting the needs of the present without compromising the ability of future generations to meet their own needs. This definition originates from the United Nations World Commission on Environment and Development's 1987 Brundtland Report. For businesses, sustainability involves promoting long-term ecological balance, reducing resource depletion, and preventing environmental degradation. This requires a multi-dimensional approach that looks beyond profits, incorporating social and environmental dimensions into core business strategies. Today, this paradigm is defined by specific practices along the economic, environmental, social, and governance (E-ESG) priorities. [20]

3. **The Globally Responsible Business Paradigm:** As the United Nations Global Compact suggested, a globally responsible business operates with principles that align with broader societal goals. The UN Global Compact proposes a set of principles in areas of human rights, labor, environment, and anti-corruption. For businesses to be considered globally responsible, they need to comply with their principles and go beyond them, engaging in the global agenda for sustainable outcomes. The cluster of principles includes these areas:

- **Human Rights:** Businesses should support and respect the protection of internationally proclaimed human rights and ensure they are not complicit in human rights abuses.

- **Labor Rights:** This encompasses principles like upholding the freedom of association and recognizing the right to collective bargaining. It also means eliminating all forms of forced and compulsory labor, child labor, and discrimination in employment and occupation.

- **Environmental Rights:** Companies should adopt a precautionary approach to environmental challenges, undertake initiatives to promote environmental responsibility, and encourage the development and diffusion of environmentally friendly technologies.

- **Anti-Corruption:** Businesses should work against corruption, including extortion and bribery.

To conclude, while businesses have traditionally focused on profitability and compliance, the global landscape now demands that they proactively engage in sustainability initiatives. The United Nations Global Compact offers a comprehensive model that aligns business operations with global responsibilities, ensuring that enterprises are profitable and beneficial to society and the environment. It also offers business leaders the opportunity to engage in the global call for making the world a better place through principle-based practices for sustainable, inclusive, and prosperous opportunities for all.

Leadership for Global Sustainable Prosperity

The concept of global sustainable prosperity presents a challenging but necessary direction for our common future. It means investing in sustainable economic solutions for the societal well-being of the planet. Safeguarding our planet's environmental and social limits is the difference between a profit-only economy of growth at all costs and only for a few and a coordinated international effort for ESG investments and circular economic solutions for global prosperity.

Global Sustainable Prosperity (GSP) is the overarching objective where people and economies worldwide thrive and prosper. This prosperity ensures a high quality of life and resilience against unforeseen shocks and remains acutely conscious of the planet's boundaries. It involves the judicious use and management of the world's diverse resources—from human talents and natural reserves to technological systems and food sources—ensuring they are used to guarantee their availability for current and future generations. **21**

The Preamble for the 2030 Agenda expresses this global aspiration and common plan for GSP. It states, "This Agenda is a plan of action for people, planet, and prosperity. It also seeks to strengthen universal peace in larger freedom. We recognize that eradicating poverty in all its forms and dimensions, including extreme poverty, is the greatest global challenge and an indispensable requirement for sustainable development." **22**

The traditional concept of "international development," primarily focusing on economic growth and poverty alleviation, is increasingly recognized as inadequate for achieving genuine global sustainability. Its inherent limitation lies in its reluctance to challenge the established economic growth paradigms. By merely repackaging the same old economic and social models under the umbrella of SDGs, we miss the opportunity to explore transformative paths toward true sustainability. **23**

Instead, the spotlight should shift to "global prosperity," a paradigm emphasizing holistic well-being, moving beyond mere economic metrics. Such a shift underscores the necessity of political and social innovations that can harness individual potential within the constraints of limited resources. Given socio-ecological system's intricate and ever-shifting nature, a universal, one-size-fits-all approach needs to be revised. The journey to prosperity requires recognizing diverse objectives with no singular, prescriptive path. Taking cues from initiatives in the Global South, like agroecology, can offer invaluable insights into this paradigm shift, highlighting the richness of diverse routes to prosperity in contrast to the narrow lane of conventional development. **24**

The World Bank defines and annually measures "shared prosperity," a closely connected indicator to global sustainability prosperity. It states, "Shared prosperity measures the extent to which economic growth is inclusive by focusing on household consumption or income growth among the poorest population relative to the population as a whole." **25**

To address the modern demands of Global Sustainability Prosperity (GSP), leadership must make a new path, particularly reflecting the priorities set out in the ESG (Environmental, Social, Governance) model. Such leadership is more than strategic; it's visionary, responsive, transformative, shaping pathways for holistic and shared prosperity.

1. **Direction and Vision:** GSP leadership starts with a vision at its core. These leaders understand that achieving sustainable prosperity is an evolution from profit-centric approaches, taking a longer view that balances profits with planetary well-being. Setting an unambiguous course for this transformation,

they engage and rally stakeholders to a common and enduring vision.

2. **Decision-making:** GSP leaders are not just decision-makers; they are courageous pioneers. The path to sustainability often strays from immediate profitability or challenge deep-rooted practices. Yet, these leaders dare to take the road less traveled, valuing our collective long-term future over fleeting advantages.

3. **Balancing Stakeholder Interests:** Embracing the "Social" in ESG, GSP leaders adeptly navigate the complex interplay of stakeholder expectations – from customers and investors to governments and civil societies. Their expertise ensures the quest for prosperity is congruent without compromising societal or environmental imperatives.

4. **Innovation Catalysts:** Recognizing the "Environmental" pillar of ESG, these leaders champion green innovation. They recognize that today's challenges require groundbreaking solutions, promoting a culture of discovery, and harnessing technological advancements that embed sustainability at their core.

5. **Architects of Resilience:** In our dynamic global landscape, rife with uncertainties, GSP leaders fortify their domains against potential shocks. Their governance strategy, reflecting the "G" in ESG, is about building adaptive, robust systems and infrastructure that can weather tumultuous times.

Central to GSP leadership is the dual role of an educator and advocate. Such leaders grasp the essence that sustainable prosperity is a collective endeavor. They leverage their influence, shaping dialogues, fostering understanding, and promoting actionable steps toward sustainability across diverse platforms.

Moreover, genuine leadership transcends words and is reflected in actions and personal choices. GSP leaders personify the ethos of sustainable prosperity, serving as living testaments to its feasibility and worth. Their daily actions, both in boardrooms and beyond, inspire and guide, making sustainability a lived experience.

This leadership journey is resource-intensive, demanding time, expertise, and capital. Yet, GSP leaders are strategic orchestrators, pulling together these resources from their entities and fostering synergies across sectors and geographies.

In conclusion, as the world stands at the cusp of a sustainable future, the GSP leaders, reflecting the ESG model, will be the forerunners. Their vision, resilience, and commitment will define our collective trajectory, ensuring that the planet and its inhabitants prosper in tandem for generations to come.

Technology Innovations and Prosperity Leadership

As technology innovations accelerate at an incredible rate, we need to re-evaluate the direction and benefits of these trends concerning sustainability values like prosperity and well-being. We also need to consider the role of value leadership and ethics for decision-making and policy design, defining the intended purpose, process, and outcomes. Areas like artificial intelligence (AI), satellite information, biotechnology, and nanotechnology, are becoming increasingly intertwined with the trajectory of human evolution. These technologies have unprecedented potential to reshape economies, social structures, and even the very nature of human experience. However, to ensure that these innovations lead us to a brighter future rather than dystopia, there is a pressing need to embed humaneness into these tech advancements—transforming them into tools that prioritize "doing good" and "benefit all people" for global sustainable prosperity. **26**

A fundamental reorientation is essential in harmonizing technology with our human essence and sustainability vision. Leadership that embodies values, ethics, and purpose is paramount. The trajectory of our future shouldn't be merely determined by rushed AI innovations based on algorithms or big data-driven outcomes. **27** Even as technology and data become deeply ingrained into our daily lives and choices, the essence of leadership must transcend the merely "apparent" and "essential", guiding us towards a future that is both "aspiring" and "compassionate". **28**

Humane Intelligence: A Paradigm Shift

The term "artificial intelligence" has historically focused on the quest to replicate human cognition and reasoning. But as AI evolves, it's becoming apparent that mere replication isn't the end goal. Instead, we need "humane" intelligence. **29** This means technology should:

1. **Uphold Human Dignity:** Every technological solution should respect human rights, individual differences, and the inherent value of every person. Discriminatory AI or intrusive satellite surveillance, for example, should be strictly avoided.

2. **Promote Sustainable Prosperity:** Innovations should cater to long-term global prosperity rather than short-term gains. For instance, while AI can optimize profit margins by replacing human jobs, humane intelligence would ensure people are retrained, or new avenues of employment are created.

3. **Preserve and Enhance Human Well-being:** Like the first law of robotics, which states a robot may not harm a human being, AI systems should prioritize the physical, psychological, and emotional well-being of humans.

The Imperative Role of Value Leaders

In steering technology towards humane ends, a new breed of leaders—value leaders—become crucial. These individuals understand both the technical aspects of their fields and the larger ethical implications. They are the forbearers ensuring that technological advancements are harmonized with human-centric values. **30** Their roles encompass:

1. **Ethical Oversight:** Establishing ethical committees or boards that regularly review the implications and applications of new technologies. These bodies can set guidelines, best practices, and even intervene when certain applications of technology overstep moral bounds.

2. **Education and Training:** Technology developers need constant training not just in the latest coding languages or satellite technologies but also in ethics, sociology, and even

philosophy. A holistic education ensures that they create solutions that are beneficial for humanity.

3. **Public Engagement:** Value leaders should engage with the public, listening to concerns, educating them about the potential and pitfalls of new technologies, and making sure that the direction of tech innovation is democratically influenced.

4. **Interdisciplinary Collaboration:** Collaboration between technologists, ethicists, psychologists, sociologists, and other specialists can lead to more comprehensive and humane technological solutions. Value leaders can bridge these domains.

5. **Global Perspective:** The effects of technology are not confined by borders. As such, value leaders should champion international standards and cooperation to ensure that innovations benefit all of humanity, not just privileged segments.

A fundamental reorientation is essential in balancing technology with our human essence a sustainability vision. Leadership that embodies values, ethics, and purpose is paramount. Algorithms or data-driven outcomes shouldn't merely determine the trajectory of our futures. As we stand at the nexus of profound environmental, economic, and social changes, the implications of this paradigm shift extend far beyond individual benefits. The coordination of technology and sustainability holds the promise of mitigating climate change, promoting equitable growth, preserving biodiversity, and ensuring resource availability for future generations.

Even as technology and data become deeply ingrained in our daily lives and choices, the essence of leadership must transcend the merely "apparent" and "essential". Guiding us towards a future that is both "aspiring" and "compassionate", this kind of leadership not only uplifts individual lives but also paves the way for global sustainable prosperity, ensuring that every corner of our planet thrives in synergy.

Key Takeaways: Prosperity-Business Practices

1. **Beyond Financial Metrics**: Prosperity is fundamentally about enhancing well-being, encompassing not just financial growth but also societal, emotional, and environmental health.

2. **ESG as the North Star**: For sustainable economic solutions to be effective and relevant, they must prioritize and operate within the Environmental, Social, and Governance (ESG) paradigms, balancing profit with responsibility.

3. **Shifting the Paradigm**: The traditional concept of sustainable development is limited. Instead, the focus should be sustainable prosperity, emphasizing growth and well-being within planetary boundaries.

4. **Global Responsibility**: Good business isn't confined to local or national considerations. A truly prosperous business acknowledges and acts upon its global responsibilities in our interconnected world.

5. **Humane Technology**: Technology advancements need to be with human values and ethical principles as true progress isn't just about advanced algorithms or cutting-edge innovations but advancing well-being, contributing to global sustainable prosperity, and protecting our planet for future generations.

CONCLUSION

As we conclude this book, we reflect on a pivotal inquiry: What does it take to be a true leader in sustainability? This journey has shown core theories and practical approaches to sustainability and leadership. However, the crucial question persists: How can we enhance our careers and efficacy in this critical field?

For those already recognized as sustainability leaders, the journey is about continual self-development, mindset evolution, and competency building. This book has equipped you with the foundational elements essential for effective sustainability leadership.

For others, still navigating the path to becoming sustainability leaders, it's vital not to depend solely on formal education. Instead, embrace a continuous quest for knowledge, incorporating critical thinking, interdisciplinary exploration, global engagement, and the integration of theory with practice.

Witnessing the dynamic growth in sustainability leadership is exhilarating. From CSOs mastering sustainability reporting to CEOs prioritizing sustainable practices, the landscape is ever-changing. Seeing passionate social entrepreneurs and ecopreneurs blend innovative ideas with business acumen to make a tangible impact. Despite challenges, this era is ripe with opportunity and excitement.

Reflecting on my career spanning over three decades in technology, community organizations, academia, and the United Nations, one lesson has been paramount: the critical role of principled actions. I've learned from the value of principles from the emergence of sustainable management education at the United Nations to exploring Indigenous rights and teaching business ethics.

Here are four interconnected principles recommended for your growth as a sustainability leader:

1. **The Synchronicity Principle**: Aligning personal values with a deeper purpose, focusing on integrity, empathy, and respect for the environment.

2. **The Solidarity Principle**: Addressing societal inequalities and committing to structural change.

3. **The Subsidiarity Principle**: Empowering others and fostering inclusive leadership.

4. **The Sustainability Principle**: Making decisions that positively affect current and future generations, balancing economic, social, and environmental considerations. 1

View your journey in sustainability leadership as navigating uncharted waters, with these principles as your guide. They form the foundation of curricula in leading management schools and symbolize the ethos of the next generation of value-driven leaders.

These principles aren't mere ideals; they are the bedrock for building a more equitable, sustainable, and compassionate world. Embrace them in your life and career, letting them guide you through the complexities of leadership in a rapidly changing world. Together, we can make a lasting impact on society and the planet.

The future for new generations of leaders aspiring to promote sustainability is simultaneously more challenging and more exhilarating. As awareness about environmental issues and the need for sustainable practices grows, these leaders are faced with complex challenges that require innovative solutions. However, this increased awareness also means that they have more support and resources at their disposal, along with a collective effort from various sectors of society. This creates an exciting opportunity for these leaders to make significant impacts in the field of sustainability, leveraging collaboration and advanced technology to address pressing environmental concerns. Their journey, though fraught with obstacles, is enriched by the growing global commitment to a sustainable future.

Building upon the momentum of the 2030 and 2050 sustainability targets, a new wave of opportunities for sustainability leadership is poised to emerge. The development of the New Sustainability Agenda post-2030 will open doors for innovative strategies and collaborations, allowing leaders to navigate and shape a rapidly evolving landscape. This agenda will likely emphasize not only ecological and economic sustainability but also social and cultural aspects, broadening the scope of impact for leaders in this field. **2**

Moreover, tools and frameworks that align personal and professional goals with sustainability objectives will become increasingly important. The Inner Development Goals (IDGs) framework is a prime example of this trend. It offers a comprehensive path for leadership growth and development, integrating personal values and ethics with professional responsibilities and goals. This approach will enable leaders to foster a more holistic and effective form of sustainability leadership, one that resonates deeply with both individuals and organizations, driving meaningful change and progress towards a sustainable future. **3**

This book has covered the core values observed in diverse organizations worldwide, going beyond mere analysis to going deeper in meaning and action. It has not only presented theories and paradigms of leadership and sustainability but also emphasized the need for ongoing learning and adaptation in this field. As we embrace global collaboration and partnerships, we recognize the importance of a purpose-driven approach, transcending transactional objectives for the greater good.

In closing, I invite you to embrace and innovate these values and principles, shaping them to fit your vision. Equip yourself with forward-thinking tools and theories that prioritize holistic well-being and sustainable change. Be a leader who aims for growth and also champions resilience and regeneration for future generations.

ENDNOTES

FOREWORD

1 Dr. Sfeir Younis, a Chilean economist and spiritual leader, worked for almost thirty years at the World Bank. He is a renowned authority in sustainable development, shared governance, and international relations.

INTRODUCTION

1 Stewardship is a concept that can be instrumental in achieving the 2030 Agenda and the SDGs. See Kuenkel, Petra. *Stewarding Sustainability Transformations: An Emerging Theory and Practice of SDG Implementation.* Germany: Springer International Publishing, 2018.

2 There are many studies that combine theories and practices applied to leadership or to sustainability, but very few have attempted to consider the theoretical and practical implications of the combined concept of 'sustainability leadership.' For leadership studies in theories and practices see Northouse, Peter G. *Leadership: Theory and Practice.* United States: SAGE Publications, 2018. For theories and practices reviews of sustainable development in higher education see Julie Newman, Luciana Brandli, Paula Castro, Walter Leal Filho. *Handbook of Theory and Practice of Sustainable Development in Higher Education: Volume 1.* Germany: Springer International Publishing, 2016. For corporate social responsibility in theories and practices see: Celine Louche, Samuel O. Idowu. *Theory and Practice of Corporate Social Responsibility.* Germany: Springer, 2011.

3 Various system-thinking studies present it as a fundamental "mindset" and "competency" for dealing with "wicked" (complex) problems. See Meadows, Donella H. *Thinking in Systems: A Primer.* United Kingdom: Chelsea

Green Publishing, 2008. Hester, Patrick T.., Adams, Kevin MacG. *Systemic Thinking: Fundamentals for Understanding Problems and Messes.* Germany: Springer International Publishing, 2014.

4 The connection between complexity and sustainability is less well known than "system-thinking" but not less important. There are a few important studies that explored these connections of complex-thinking and sustainability. See these to know more: Norberg, Jon, and Graeme Cumming. *Complexity theory for a sustainable future.* Columbia University Press, 2008; Wells, Jennifer. *Complexity and Sustainability.* United Kingdom: Routledge, 2013; See also: Espinosa, Angela., Walker, Jon. *Complexity Approach to Sustainability, A: Theory and Application* (Second Edition). Singapore: World Scientific Publishing Company, 2017.

5 Eco-thinking offers emerging innovative approaches from environmental learning and environmental design thinking applied to architecture and visionary designs. See David Zandvliet, *Eco-Thinking: A Compendium of Research on Environmental Learning.* United States: DIO Press Incorporated, 2021. See also Mitra Kanaani, *The Routledge Companion to Ecological Design Thinking: Healthful Ecotopian Visions for Architecture and Urbanism.* United Kingdom: Taylor & Francis, 2022.

6 To further explore this notion of "future thinking" in relation to organizational leadership and management, see Schreiber, Deborah A., and Zane L. Berge. *Futures thinking and organizational policy.* Springer, 2019.

7 There are many studies that explore this connection of "executive leadership" with organizational sustainability practices. See for example: Tideman, Sander. *Triple Value Leadership: Creating Sustainable Value for Your Business, Your Customers and Society.* United States: Taylor & Francis, 2022. See also: Stanwick, Peter A.., Stanwick, Sarah D. *Corporate Sustainability Leadership.* United Kingdom: Taylor & Francis, 2020.

8 The rapid advancement of technological solutions represents for the sustainability leader opportunities to transform "agile" and "innovative" thinking into possible win-win outcomes. See: Rushi, Bella. *The Innovative Executive: Leading Intelligently in the Age of Disruption.* United States: Forefront Books, 2022.

9 See Sunter, Clem., Ilbury, Mitch. *Thinking the Future: New Perspectives from the Shoulders of Giants.* United Kingdom: Penguin Random House South Africa, 2021. It will be important to observe how Generative AI will offer transformative potential for future thinking when leveraged by designers, futurists, and strategists. See Groth, Olaf., Nitzberg, Mark. *The AI Generation: Shaping Our Global Future with Thinking Machines.* United States: Pegasus Books, 2018.

10 We will explore "regenerative" leadership dimensions throughout the book and consider in its implications in the conclusion. For an overview of regenerative leadership paradigms read: Hutchins, Giles and Storm, Laura. *Regenerative leadership.* eBook Partnership, 2019. See also: Aoustin, Emmanuelle. "Regenerative Leadership: What It Takes to Transform Business into a Force for Good." *Field Actions Science Reports. The Journal of Field Actions,* no. Special Issue 25 (November 10, 2023): 92–97. http://journals.openedition.org/factsreports/7359.

CHAPTER 1: SHARED VALUES

1 The scholarship on "value leadership" indicates a similar approach suggesting "value contributions" across sectors. See Cohan, Peter S., *Value Leadership: The 7 Principles that Drive Corporate Value in Any Economy* (Germany: Wiley, 2004). See also Jessica Lange, *Value-Oriented Leadership in Theory and Practice: Concepts - Study Results - Practical Insight*s (Germany: Springer Berlin Heidelberg, 2023).

2 We purposely use the term "shared values' to not restrictively interpret these diverse value contributions to the context of corporate business strategy. This is not to be confused with the alternative term "shared value" introduced by Michael E. Porter and Mark R. Kramer in their idea of "Creating Shared Value" for companies that can enhance their competitiveness while simultaneously advancing social and economic conditions in the communities where they operate. Porter, Michael E., and Mark R. Kramer. "Creating shared value: Redefining capitalism and the corporation's role in society." *Harvard Business Review* 89, no. 1/2 (2011): 62-77.

3 There are several studies that review the evolution and value-contributions of various leadership theories. For an overview see: Melissa Horner, "Leadership theory: past, present and future." *Team Performance Management: An International Journal* 3, no. 4 (1997): 270-287. For a recent study overviewing the value contributions in organizational leadership see: Jessica Lange, *Value-Oriented Leadership in Theory and Practice: Concepts - Study Results - Practical Insights* (Germany: Springer Berlin Heidelberg, 2023).

4 For an exploration of the main leadership theories see: Northouse, Peter G. *Leadership: Theory and Practice.* United Kingdom: SAGE Publications, 2015.

5 Carlyle, Thomas. *On Heroes, Hero-worship, and the Heroic in History: Six Lectures, Reported, with Emendations and Additions.* United Kingdom: Chapman and Hall, 1852. For a more critical review of this theory see: Harrison, Christian. *Leadership Theory and Research: A Critical Approach to New and Existing Paradigms.* Germany: Springer International Publishing, 2017.

6 Katz, Robert L. "Skills of an effective administrator." *Harvard business review* 33 (1955): 33-42.

7 Read the original work Blake, Robert Rogers., McCanse, Anne Adams. *Leadership Dilemmas--Grid Solutions.* United States: Gulf Publishing Company, 1991.

8 Read more in Gill, Roger. *Theory and Practice of Leadership*. United Kingdom: SAGE Publications, 2011.

9 For a good study on leadership on organizational sustainability as CSR complexity, see Metcalf, Louise, and Sue Benn. "Leadership for sustainability: An evolution of leadership ability." *Journal of Business Ethics* 112 (2013): 369-384.

10 For an overview and reflection on the evolution of the situational leadership approach see: Blanchard, Kenneth H., Drea Zigarmi, and Robert B. Nelson. "Situational Leadership® after 25 years: A retrospective." *Journal of Leadership Studies* 1, no. 1 (1993): 21-36.

11 For a literature overview of "contingency" implications for leadership see: Kerr, Steven, Chester A. Schriesheim, Charles J. Murphy, and Ralph M. Stogdill. "Toward a contingency theory of leadership based upon the consideration and initiating structure literature." *Organizational behavior and human performance* 12, no. 1 (1974): 62-82.

12 Worthy to notice that some interpret the Path-Goal Theory in the realm of "transactional" leadership as they associate with it "a carrots-and-sticks approach to leadership in which the leader offers either rewards (carrots) or punishments (sticks) characterize one of two popular models of leadership." Mark Peterson, *Sustainable Enterprise: A Macromarketing Approach* (United States: SAGE Publications, 2012), 244.

13 For a more comprehensive overview of LMX theory's values and weaknesses and for current and future developments see Aharon Tziner and Erich Christian Fein, *The Future of the Leader-Member Exchange Theory* (N.p.: Frontiers Media SA, 2021).

14 An excellent and comprehensive overview of LMX theory is given by Berrin Erdogan, Talya N. Bauer. *The Oxford Handbook of Leader-Member Exchange*. United States: Oxford University Press, 2015. More specifically to the contexts of sustainability see: Godwell Nhamo, Kaitano Dube, and Muchaiteyi Togo, *Sustainable Development Goals for Society Vol. 1: Selected Topics of Global Relevance* (Germany, Springer International Publishing, 2021), 97-106.

15 For a modern interpretation of these dynamics into power and influence in organizations see Barbara Wisse, Dean Tjosvold. *Power and Interdependence in Organizations*. United Kingdom: Cambridge University Press, 2009.

16 For a critical overview of SCT see: Shenkar, Oded, and Shmuel Ellis. "The rise and fall of structural contingency theory: A theory's 'autopsy'." *Journal of Management Studies* 59, no. 3 (2022): 782-818.

17 An excellent exploration of transformational values in relation to sustainability mindsets is given by Aixa A. Ritz and Isabel Rimanoczy, *Sustainability Mindset and Transformative Leadership: A Multidisciplinary Perspective* (Switzerland: Springer International Publishing, 2021). Chapter 12 in this edited volume (Marco Tavanti and Elizabeth A. Wilp, *Common Good Mindset: The Public Dimensions of Sustainability*) explores the values and dimensions of 'care' for the 'common good' and the global/social responsibility toward the commons.

18 Shields, Christopher M. "Transformative Leadership: Working for Equity in Diverse Contexts." *Harvard University*, 2010.

19 To further explore the "transformative" and "transformational" leadership practices in relation to sustainability see: "Transformational Leadership for Sustainability: A Review and Research Agenda" (2021) by Joost Bolderdijk, Sarah Mehmood, and Jeroen C.J.M. van den Enden. See also: "Sustainable Transformational Leadership: A Multi-Level Model for Organizational Sustainability" (2020) by Robert J. Russell, Jeroen C.J.M. van den Enden, and Peter J. Cowling. See also: "Transformative Leadership and Corporate Sustainability: Exploring the Mediating Role of Employee Green Behaviors" (2019) by David S. Steingard and Robert J. Russell.

20 To explore the vast scholarship on servant leadership, see Gary E. Roberts and Satinder K. Dhiman, *The Palgrave Handbook of Servant Leadership* (Germany: Springer International Publishing, 2023).

21 A useful reference book that explores these connections of leadership with "service" and "stewardship" for environmental sustainability is offered by Deborah Rigling Gallagher, *Environmental Leadership: A Reference Handbook* (United Kingdom: SAGE Publications, 2012).

22 Hoshmand, A. R., Chung, P. (2021). *Service Leadership: Leading with Competence, Character and Care in the Service Economy*. United Kingdom: Taylor & Francis.

23 Read more in Russell, Robert J., et al. "The Impact of Environmentally Specific Servant Leadership on Organizational Green Performance: The Mediating Role of Green Creativity." *Sustainability*, vol. 13, no. 17, 2021, pp. 9874. See also: Steingard, David S., et al. "The Influence of Servant Leadership on Corporate Social Performance." *Journal of Business Ethics*, vol. 124, no. 4, 2014, pp. 677-690.

24 Read Bill George's pioneering book and its Foreword by Warren Bennis, considered one of the most prominent scholars in modern studies of leadership. George, Bill. *Authentic Leadership: Rediscovering the Secrets to Creating Lasting Value* (Germany: Wiley, 2003).

25 There are many studies that center on ethical leadership. Among the numerous ones, check these: Joanne Ciulla, Mary Uhl-Biel, and Patricia J. Werhane, *Leadership*

Ethics. 3 Volumes (Los Angeles, CA: SAGE). McQuade, Aidan. *Ethical Leadership: Moral Decision-making Under Pressure* (Germany: De Gruyter, 2022) and Leigh, Andrew. *Ethical Leadership: Creating and Sustaining an Ethical Business Culture* (India: Kogan Page, 2013). Also, this edited volume by Rune Todnem, Bernard Burnes, and Mark Hughes, *Organizational Change, Leadership and Ethics.* (United Kingdom: Taylor & Francis, 2023).

26 There is a long tradition of studying "virtues" in the context of leadership starting with Marcus Aurelio's *Meditations* (Dover Publications, 2021) suggesting a Stoic ideal for virtuous practices of leadership. See other scholarly works like Kirkeby, Ole Fogh. *The Virtue of Leadership* (United States: Copenhagen Business School Press, 2008).

27 For a more in-depth exploration of the leadership and ethical-related issues of the emerging field called EVE (Environmental Virtue Ethics) see Philip Cafaro and Ronald D. Sandler, *Environmental Virtue Ethics.* United Kingdom: Rowman & Littlefield Publishers, 2005. See also Philip Cafaro and Ronald Sandler, *Virtue Ethics and the Environment.* Netherlands: Springer Netherlands, 2014.

28 The psychodynamic leadership theory is rooted in the contributions of both Freud and Jung. Abraham Zeleznik, a renowned Professor of Management at Harvard Business School, was its most notable proponent. Zaleznik, Abraham. *Learning Leadership: The Abuse of Power in Organizations.* United States: Beard Books, Incorporated, 1993.

29 See for example: Manfred F.R. Kets de Vries, et al. *Coach and Couch 2nd Edition: The Psychology of Making Better Leaders* (United Kingdom: Palgrave Macmillan, 2015) and also Brent Davies, *Developing Sustainable Leadership* (United Kingdom: SAGE Publications, 2007).

30 See Škerlavaj, Miha, *Post-Heroic Leadership: Context, Process and Outcomes* (Switzerland: Springer International Publishing, 2022).

31 Heifetz, Ronald Abadian., Grashow, Alexander., Linsky, Martin. *The Practice of Adaptive Leadership: Tools and Tactics for Changing Your Organization and the World.* (United States: Harvard Business Press, 2009).

32 Craig Pearce and Jay Conger, *Shared Leadership: Reframing the Hows and Whys of Leadership* (United Kingdom: SAGE Publications, 2002).

33 Among the numerous scholarly contributions exploring the interconnections of complexity with leadership and system see Benyamin B. Lichtenstein, James K. Hazy, Jeffrey A. Goldstein, *Complex Systems Leadership Theory: New Perspectives from Complexity Science on Social and Organizational Effectiveness* (United States: ISCE Publishing, 2007). For an overview of leadership and organizational change implications in complex systems see: Varney, Sharon, *Leadership in Complexity and Change: For a World in Constant Motion*. (Germany: De Gruyter, 2021).

34 See Googins, Bradley K.., Mirvis, Philip H.., Rochlin, Steven A. *Beyond Good Company: Next Generation Corporate Citizenship*. Switzerland: Palgrave Macmillan, 2007.

35 Amanda Lange Salvia, Anabela Marisa Azul, Luciana Brandli, Tony Wall, Walter Leal Filho. *Partnerships for the Goals*. Switzerland: Springer International Publishing, 2021.

36 Among the fast-growing literature on diversity and inclusive leadership see these works that best highlight the implications for sustainability values: Joan Marques, *The Routledge Companion to Inclusive Leadership*. United Kingdom: Taylor & Francis, 2020. Formanek, Kay. *Beyond D&I: Leading Diversity with Purpose and Inclusiveness* (Switzerland: Springer International Publishing, 2021). Eduardo Luis Soares Tomé, José Baptista, Paula Cristina Nunes Figueiredo, Sónia Gonçalves. *Developing Diversity, Equity, and Inclusion Policies for Promoting Employee Sustainability and Well-Being*. (United States: IGI Global, 2023).

37 There are many works on cross-cultural and CQ leadership. Among them is worth motioning is Salih, Ahmad M. *Cross-Cultural Leadership: Being Effective in an Era of Globalization, Digital Transformation and Disruptive Innovation*. United Kingdom: Taylor & Francis, 2020.

38 Western, Simon. *Leadership: A Critical Text*. United Kingdom: SAGE Publications, 2019.

39 Western, Simon. "Eco-leadership: Towards the development of a new paradigm." In *Leadership for environmental sustainability*, pp. 50-68. Routledge, 2010.

40 Hawken, Paul. *Regeneration: Ending the Climate Crisis in One Generation*. United Kingdom: Penguin Publishing Group, 2021.

41 Hutchins, Giles. *Regenerative Leadership*. United Kingdom: Wordzworth Publishing, 2019.

42 On the Quantum Leadership paradigm read more in Tsao, Frederick Chavalit, and Chris Laszlo. *Quantum leadership: New consciousness in business*. Stanford University Press, 2020. On the consciousness leadership paradigm in relation to sustainability see Alfredo Sfeir-Younis and Marco Tavanti. *Conscious sustainability leadership: A new paradigm for next generation leaders*. (Planet Healing Press, 2020).

ENDNOTES

CHAPTER 2: CONSCIOUSNESS PARADIGM

1 See the pioneering work on sustainability mindsets by Isabel Rimanoczy. In particular, Rimanoczy, Isabel. *The Sustainability Mindset Principles: A Guide to Developing a Mindset for a Better World.* United Kingdom: Taylor & Francis, 2020. See the definition of sustainability mindset in Rimanoczy, Isabel. *Big Bang Being: Developing the Sustainability Mindset.* 2018: Taylor & Francis, p. 7. The dimensions of a sustainability mindset were illustrated in Kassel, K., Rimanoczy, I., & Mitchell, S. F. (2018). A sustainability mindset model for management education. In K. Kassel & I. Rimanoczy. (Eds.), *Developing a sustainability mindset in management education,* (3–37). London: Routledge.

2 Mackey, J., Mcintosh, S., Phipps, C. (2020). *Conscious Leadership: Elevating Humanity Through Business.* United States: Penguin Publishing Group. This volume on "Conscious Leadership" completes his earlier publication on "Conscious Capitalism." Mackey, J., Sisodia, R. (2014). *Conscious Capitalism: Liberating the Heroic Spirit of Business.* United Kingdom: Harvard Business Review Press.

3 Deckman, Jeffrey S. (2019). *Developing the Conscious Leadership Mindset for the 21st Century: Insight for Leading Change, Improving Employee Engagement, and Achieving Extraordinary Results (Conscious Leadership Series).* Capability Accelerators, Inc.

4 Deckman, J. (2021, October 27). Council Post: Five Aspects of Conscious Leadership In Action. *Forbes.* https://www.forbes.com/sites/forbescoachescouncil/2021/10/27/five-aspects-of-conscious-leadership-in-action/?sh=517c0fc923e3

5 Kirilyuk, A. P. (2014). *Complex-Dynamic Origin of Consciousness and Sustainability Transition.* Germany: Lap Lambert Academic Publishing GmbH KG.

6 Chapman, Diana., Dethmer, Jim., Klemp, Kaley. *The 15 Commitments of Conscious Leadership: A New Paradigm for Sustainable Success.* United States: Conscious Leadership Group, 2015.

7 Reciniello, Shelley. *The Conscious Leader: 9 Principles and Practices to Create a Wide-awake and Productive Workplace.* Spain: LID Publishing Incorporated, 2014.

8 Tavanti, Marco., Sfeir-Younis, Alfredo. *Conscious Sustainability Leadership: A New Paradigm for Next Generation Leaders.* Planet Healing Press, 2020.

9 Benioff, Marc., Langley, Monica. *Trailblazer: The Power of Business as the Greatest Platform for Change.* United States: Crown, 2019.

10 Colby, L. (2015). *Road to Power: How GM's Mary Barra Shattered the Glass Ceiling.* John Wiley & Sons.

11 Smit, J. (2023). *The Lonely Quest of Unilever's CEO Paul Polman*. Anthem Press.

12 Nooyi, I. (2021). *My Life in Full: Work, Family and Our Future*. United Kingdom: Little, Brown Book Group.

13 Nadella, S. (2018). *Hit refresh*. Bentang Pustaka.

14 Blackburn, Richard. *Sustainable Apparel: Production, Processing and Recycling*. (2015). Netherlands: Elsevier Science.

15 Chouinard, Y. (2006). *Let My People Go Surfing: The Education of a Reluctant Businessman*. United Kingdom: Penguin Books.

16 Simões-Coelho, M., Figueira, A. R., & Russo, E. (2023). Motivations for a sustainable ethos: evidence from the globally present Brazilian multinational Natura &Co. *Environment Systems and Decisions*, 1-16.

17 Orange, E., & Cohen, A. M. (2010). From eco-friendly to eco-intelligent. *The Futurist, 44*(5), 28.

18 Maathai, W. (2003). *The Green Belt Movement: Sharing the approach and the experience*. Lantern Books.

19 Yousafzai, M., & McCormick, P. (2014). *I Am Malala: How One Girl Stood Up for Education and Changed the World; Teen Edition Retold by Malala for her Own Generation*. Hachette UK.

20 Satyarthi, Kailash. *Every Child Matters*. Prabhat Prakashan, 2018.

21 Chapman, M. (2020). *Jacinda Ardern: A new kind of leader*. Black Inc..

22 Khan, S. (2023). Breathe: Seven Ways to Win a Greener World. United Kingdom: Cornerstone.

23 Read more at https://en.wikipedia.org/wiki/Carlos_Alvarado_Quesada

24 Solberg, E. (2015). From mdgs to sdgs the political value of common global goals. *Harvard International Review, 37*(1), 58.

25 Sfeir-Younis, A., & Tavanti, M. (2020). *Conscious sustainability leadership: A new paradigm for next generation leaders*. Planet Healing Press.

CHAPTER 3: WELL-BEING DIMENSIONS

1 Ruggeri, Kai, Eduardo Garcia-Garzon, Áine Maguire, Sandra Matz, and Felicia A. Huppert. "Well-being is more than happiness and life satisfaction: a multidimensional analysis of 21 countries." *Health and Quality of Life Outcomes* 18, no. 1 (2020): 1-16.

2 WHO. "Promoting Well-Being," Who.int. 2023. https://www.who.int/activities/promoting-well-being

3 WHO. Health Promotion Glossary of Terms 2021. https://www.who.int/publications/i/item/9789240038349

4 Diener, Ed, Sarah D. Pressman, John Hunter, and Desiree Delgadillo-Chase. "If, why, and when subjective well-being influences health, and future needed research." *Applied Psychology: Health and Well-Being* 9, no. 2 (2017): 133-167

5 For an overview of the interconnections between sustainability and happiness in relation to well-being see Cloutier, Scott, Sara El-Sayed, Allison Ross, and Melanie Weaver. *Linking Sustainability and Happiness.* Springer International Publishing, 2022.

6 Some studies trace the definition of 'sustainability leadership' in relation to the principles of sustainable well-being of people and ecosystems like Tideman, Sander G., Muriel C. Arts, and Danielle P. Zandee. "Sustainable leadership: Towards a workable definition." *Journal of Corporate Citizenship* 49 (2013): 17-33.

7 Aristotle. (2019). *Nicomachean Ethics.* Sde Classics. See also: Fretcher, G. (2015). *The Routledge Handbook of Philosophy of Well-Being.* Taylor & Francis.

8 See this study that explore the role of arete in relation to sustainability education and academic excellence: Aaltola, E. (2021). Cultivating arete for flourishing: A virtue ethical approach to sustainability education. *Journal of Moral Education,* 50(4), 469-484. See also: D'Ambrosio, C. A., & Boler, M. (2021). Arete, expertise, and leadership in a time of climate change. *Journal of Leadership & Organizational Studies,* 28(4), 330-341.

9 For an exploration of the role that phronesis plays in applying virtue ethics to sustainability challenges see: Hursthouse, R. (2020). Virtue ethics and sustainability: A fruitful partnership? *Journal of Global Ethics,* 16(2), 127-144.

10 There are many studies that explore Aristotle's notion of eudaimonia in relation to well-being and sustainability. See: Ben-Porat, A. (2022). Aristotle's eudaimonia and the search for well-being in the 21st century: A critical appraisal. *Journal of Happiness Studies,* 23(1), 33-55. See also: Cooper, J. (2023). Aristotle and the environment: Virtue ethics and the pursuit of sustainability. *Environmental Values,* 32(2), 169-185. See also in relation to ethics: Van den Enden, J. C. J. M., & Bolderdijk, J. (2021). A virtue ethics perspective on corporate social responsibility: Promoting the flourishing of stakeholders. *Journal of Business Ethics,* 174(1), 151-166.

11 In accordance with these 9 domains, Bhutan has developed 38 sub-indexes, 72 indicators, and 151 variables that are used to define and analyze the happiness of the Bhutanese people. Read more at https://www.gnhcentrebhutan.org/

12 Read Tideman's Buddhist's analysis of GNH leadership in Tideman, Sander, "Gross National Happiness: lessons for sustainability leadership" *South Asian Journal of Global Business Research*, 2016, 5(2):190-213.

13 To explore well-being across cultures, see Annamaria Di Fabio, *Cross-cultural Perspectives on Well-Being and Sustainability in Organizations*. Springer International Publishing, 2022.

14 For an overview and alternative measurements of GDP, including the GNH, see Hoekstra, Rutger. *Replacing GDP by 2030: Towards a Common Language for the Well-being and Sustainability Community*. United Kingdom: Cambridge University Press, 2019.

15 For an excellent overview of the leadership implications of integrating these approaches represented in the sustainability agenda, see the edited volume by Jamie Rezmovits, Seana Lowe Steffen, Shana Rappaport, Shanah Trevenna, *Evolving Leadership for Collective Wellbeing: Lessons for Implementing the United Nations Sustainable Development Goals*. United Kingdom: Emerald Publishing Limited, 2018.

16 Parkin, S. (2010). *The positive deviant: Sustainability leadership in a perverse world*. Routledge.

17 Gimenes, T. C., Machado, M. K., & Vernalha, E. B. R. (2019). Empowerment in sustainability. *Encyclopedia of Sustainability in Higher Education*, 482-488.

18 Ngunjiri, F. W. (2014). "I Will Be a Hummingbird": Lessons in Radical Transformative Leadership from Professor Wangari Maathai. In *Leadership in postcolonial Africa: Trends transformed by independence* (pp. 123-141). New York: Palgrave Macmillan US.

CHAPTER 4: RESILIENT ADAPTATIONS

1 VUCA has become a known term, especially after the "volatility, uncertainty, complexity, and ambiguity" situations exasperated by the COVID-19 pandemic and perpetrated in our times' environmental, social, economic, and cultural crises. For an overview of this concept of sustainability leadership, see Ducheyne, David. *Sustainable Leadership: How to Lead in a VUCA World*. Belgium: Die Keure Publishing, 2017. See also Worley, Christopher G., and Claudy Jules. "COVID-19's uncomfortable revelations about agile and sustainable organizations in a VUCA world." *The Journal of Applied Behavioral Science* 56, no. 3 (2020): 279-283.

2 See for examples these studies: Redman, Charles L. "Should sustainability and resilience be combined or remain distinct pursuits?" *Ecology and Society* 19, no. 2 (2014); Meacham, Brian J. "Sustainability and resiliency objectives in performance building regulations." In *Building Governance and Climate Change*, pp. 8-23. Routledge, 2019.

3 For an excellent and analytical overview of sustainability and resilience, see Marchese, Dayton, Erin Reynolds, Matthew E. Bates, Heather Morgan, Susan S. Clark, and Igor Linkov. "Resilience and Sustainability: Similarities and Differences in Environmental Management Applications." *Science of The Total Environment 613-614*, (2018): 1275-1283.

4 Rifkin, Jeremy. *The Age of Resilience: Reimagining Existence on a Rewilding Earth.* United Kingdom: Swift Press, 2022.

5 Duggan, Bob., Theurer, Bridgette. *Resilient Leadership 2.0: Leading with Calm, Clarity, and Conviction in Anxious Times.* United States: CreateSpace Independent Publishing Platform, 2017.

6 Drath, Karsten. *Resilient Leadership: Beyond Myths and Misunderstandings.* United Kingdom: Taylor & Francis, 2016.

7 Everly, Dr. George S.., Athey, Amy B. *Leading Beyond Crisis: The Five Pillars of Transformative Resilient Leadership.* American Psychological Association, 2022.

8 While the values added by this model to contemporary "resilience" challenges and "sustainability" needs, there are also some criticisms. For example, several studies rely on traits that could be difficult to translate into leadership development and skills for leader effectiveness. Read more in Nelson, Tenneisha, and Vicki Squires. "Addressing complex challenges through adaptive leadership: A promising approach to collaborative problem solving." *Journal of Leadership Education* 16, no. 4 (2017).

9 As we consider in Chapter 1 (#14), adaptive leadership is a known paradigm with implications for resilience and sustainability leadership. For an overview of the adaptive leadership paradigm see Bradberry, T., Greaves, J. (2012). Leadership 2.0. United States: TalentSmart. See also Heifetz, Ronald A., Linsky, Marty. Adaptive Leadership: The Heifetz Collection (3 Items). United States: Harvard Business Review Press, 2014.

10 Although less explored than other paradigms, leadership by cross boundaries is an important field for operating across systems and multisector partnerships. See for example the studies of: Linden, Russell M. *Leading Across Boundaries: Creating Collaborative Agencies in a Networked World.* United Kingdom: Wiley, 2010; WIlliams, Dean. *Leadership for a Fractured World: How to Cross Boundaries, Build Bridges, and Lead Change.* United States: Berrett-Koehler Publishers, 2015.

11 Cross-cultural studies for leaders are quite advanced drawing from seminal works on cultural dimensions and characteristics like Hofstede, Geert., Hofstede, Gert Jan., Minkov, Michael. *Cultures and Organizations: Software of the Mind,* Third Edition. Spain: McGraw Hill LLC, 2010 and the Globe study by Mansour Javidan, Paul J. Hanges, Peter W. Dorfman, Robert J. House, Vipin Gupta. *Culture, Leadership, and Organizations: The GLOBE Study of 62 Societies.* United States: SAGE Publications, 2004. For cross-cultural and cultural intelligence (CQ) studies on leadership see Livermore, David., ANG, Soon. *Leading with Cultural Intelligence: The Real Secret to Success.* United States: AMACOM, 2015.

12 For an overview of polymath leadership characteristics for innovation comparing Florence' Renaissance and Silicon Valley eco-innovations see my chapter Tavanti & Wilp (2020). Humanistic Renaissance for Good: Leadership Lessons from Florence to Silicon Valley. In Stachowicz-Stanusch, A., Lewis, A. and Stanusch, N. (Eds). *Humanistic Values from Academic Community Perspective* (pp. 221-240). Information Age Publishing (IAP). Also available in my author's collection at http://www.marcotavanti.com/publications.html

13 The "Zeitgeist" theory is often used to express the notions of the "situational" theory of leadership, and it is recognized as the backdrop of what later evolved as "contingency" theory. Explore more in David V. Day, John Antonakis. *The Nature of Leadership.* SAGE Publications, 2012; and in Murthy, Vikram., McKie, David. *Please Don't Stop the Music: An Ensemble Leadership Repertoire for Productive Sustainability, and Strategic Innovation in Uncertain Times.* United Kingdom: World Association for Sustainable Development, 2009.

14 For a good overview of "leadership contextualization" examples as local government's diverse responses to the COVID-19 crisis, see Carlos Nunes Silva. *Local Government and the COVID-19 Pandemic: A Global Perspective.* Switzerland: Springer International Publishing, 2022.

15 Explore these two articles and related studies by McKinsey and Company: Brende, Børge, and Bob Sternfels. "Resilience for Sustainable, Inclusive Growth." McKinsey & Company. McKinsey & Company, June 7, 2022. https://www.mckinsey.com/capabilities/risk-and-resilience/our-insights/resilience-for-sustainable-inclusive-growth and D'Auria, Gemma, and Aaron De Smet. "Leadership in a Crisis: Responding to the Coronavirus Outbreak and Future Challenges." McKinsey & Company. McKinsey & Company, March 16, 2020. https://www.mckinsey.com/capabilities/people-and-organizational-performance/our-insights/leadership-in-a-crisis-responding-to-the-coronavirus-outbreak-and-future-challenges.

16 Abrams, Zara. "Leadership in Times of Crisis: Psychologists' research and expertise can help leaders communicate clearly and support their communities through the pandemic." https://www.apa.org, 2020. https://www.apa.org/monitor/2020/07/leadership-crisis.

CHAPTER 5: STEWARDSHIP AS CARE

1 Block, Peter. *Stewardship: Choosing service over self-interest.* Berrett-Koehler Publishers, 1993. P. 18.

2 Block, Peter. *Stewardship: Choosing service over self-interest.* Berrett-Koehler Publishers, 1993. P. xx.

3 Block, Peter. *The empowered manager: Positive political skills at work.* John Wiley & Sons, 2016.

4 For exploring these religious interpretations and the overview of alternative environmental perspectives see Elvin Anderson, et al. *Environmental Stewardship: Critical Perspectives – Past and Present.* United Kingdom: Bloomsbury Academic, 2006.

5 See McIntyre-Mills, Janet J. "Stewardship: An Anthropocentric Misnomer? Rights, Responsibilities and Multispecies Relationships." *From Polarisation to Multispecies Relationships: Re-Generation of the Commons in the Era of Mass Extinctions* (2021): 119-139.

6 See the arguments in Welchman, Jennifer. "A defence of environmental stewardship." *Environmental Values* 21, no. 3 (2012): 297-316.

7 See for example the work of Bennett, Nathan J., Tara S. Whitty, Elena Finkbeiner, Jeremy Pittman, Hannah Bassett, Stefan Gelcich, and Edward H. Allison. "Environmental stewardship: a conceptual review and analytical framework." *Environmental management* 61 (2018): 597-614.

8 Rajeev Peshawaria. "From Governance to Steward Leadership – the Key to Meaningful Sustainability." *Forbes,* July 4, 2023. https://www.forbes.com/sites/rajeevpeshawaria/2023/07/02/from-governance-to-steward-leadership--the-key-to-meaningful-sustainability/?sh=564bc1e5732a.

9 Ostrom, Elinor. *Future of the Commons: Beyond Market Failure and Government Regulations.* United Kingdom: Institute of Economic Affairs, 2012. See also her pioneering book Ostrom, Elinor. *Governing the Commons: The Evolution of Institutions for Collective Action.* United Kingdom: Cambridge University Press, 2015.

10 Pope Francis (2015). *Encyclical Laudato Si' of The Holy Father Francis on Care For Our Common Home.* https://www.vatican.va/content/francesco/en/encyclicals/documents/papa-francesco_20150524_enciclica-laudato-si.html

11 See DeWitt, Calvin B. "III. Earth Stewardship and Laudato Sí." *The Quarterly Review of Biology* 91, no. 3 (2016): 271-284.

12 Read more in my book: Tavanti, Marco. *Sustainability Ethics: Common Good Values for a Better World.* Ethics International Press, Incorporated, 2023. Pp. 9-11.

13 For a more in-depth exploration of these levels of care in relation to the common good, sustainability mindset, and transformative leadership see Tavanti, Marco. & Wilp, A. Elizabeth. (2021). "A Common Good Mindset: An Integrated Model for Sustainability and Leadership Management Education." In Rimanoczy, I. & Ritz, A. (eds.), *Sustainability Mindset and Transformative Leadership: A Multidisciplinary Perspective* (pp. 241-266). Palgrave Macmillan.

14 See also Younger, Heather R. *The Art of Caring Leadership: How Leading with Heart Uplifts Teams and Organizations.* United States: Berrett-Koehler Publishers, 2021.

15 Joan F. Marques, Satinder K. Dhiman, eds. *Leadership After COVID-19: Working Together Toward a Sustainable Future.* Switzerland: Springer International Publishing, 2022. P. 214.

16 Lean Watson. Nursing. The philosophy and science of caring. Boulder, CO: University Press of Colorado. 2008, pp. 281-288. See also the Watson Caring Science Institute website at https://www.watsoncaringscience.org/jean-bio/caring-science-theory/10-caritas-processes/

17 Other studies have made these connections between caring principles and quantum-unitarian paradigms. See Watson, Jean, Sara Horton-Deutsch, and Kathy Malloch. "Quantum Caring Leadership: Integrating Quantum Leadership with Caring Science." *Nursing Science Quarterly*, (2018). Accessed September 5, 2023. https://doi.org/10.1177/0894318418774893.

18 For an overview of the life of Don Lorenzo Milani with his social justice pedagogy developed in Barbiana see Batini, Federico., Mayo, Peter., Surian, Alessio. *Lorenzo Milani, the School of Barbiana and the Struggle for Social Justice.* Austria: Peter Lang, 2014.

CHAPTER 6: PURPOSE AND PRINCIPLES

1 To further explore this notion of "higher purpose" in sustainability leadership practices of organizations across sectors see my publication Tavanti, Marco. *Developing Sustainability in Organizations: A Values-Based Approach.* Switzerland: Springer International Publishing, 2023.

2 See Gulati, Ranjay. *Deep Purpose: The Heart and Soul of High-Performance Companies.* United States: HarperCollins, 2022. See also Quinn, Robert

E.., Thakor, Anjan V. *The Economics of Higher Purpose: Eight Counterintuitive Steps for Creating a Purpose-Driven Organization.* United States: Berrett-Koehler Publishers, 2019.

3 For an overview of companies that go beyond CSR see Milenko Gudic, Patricia M. Flynn, Tay Keong Tan. *Beyond the Bottom Line: Integrating Sustainability into Business and Management Practice.* United Kingdom: Taylor & Francis, 2020. See also Alexander, Frederick H.., Alexander, Rick. *Benefit Corporation Law and Governance: Pursuing Profit with Purpose.* United States: Berrett-Koehler Publishers, 2017. See also Frankel, Carl., Bromberger, Allen. *The Art of Social Enterprise: Business as If People Mattered.* United States: New Society Publishers, 2013.

4 For cases and a more thorough examination of greenwashing even in CSR companies read Vollero, Agostino. *Greenwashing: Foundations and Emerging Research on Corporate Sustainability and Deceptive Communication.* United Kingdom: Emerald Publishing Limited, 2022.

5 Marquis, Christopher. *Better Business: How the B Corp Movement is Remaking Capitalism.* United Kingdom: Yale University Press, 2020. See also: Honeyman, Ryan., Jana, Tiffany. *The B Corp Handbook, Second Edition: How You Can Use Business as a Force for Good.* United States: Berrett-Koehler Publishers, 2019.

6 For a more in-depth look at stakeholder businesses see Schwab, Klaus., Vanham, Peter. *Stakeholder Capitalism: A Global Economy that Works for Progress, People and Planet.* United Kingdom: Wiley, 2021.

7 While Shell's decision was influenced by a mix of technical, economic, and environmental factors, the exact weight or importance of each factor in their decision-making process might not be precisely detailed in public documents. "Shell Abandons Alaska Arctic Drilling." BBC News, September 28, 2015. See here a collection of media article collected by the company: https://royaldutchshellplc.com/2015/09/

8 The effect and extent of Nike's information gathering was and still is controversial. See Wazir, Burhan. "Nike Accused of Tolerating Sweatshops." The Guardian. The Guardian, May 19, 2001. https://www.theguardian.com/world/2001/may/20/burhanwazir.theobserver#:~:text=Nike%20employees%20continue%20to%20face,the%20500%2C000%2Dstrong%20global%20workforce. For other controversies see "Nike Sweatshops." Wikimedia Foundation. Last modified August 7, 2023. https://en.wikipedia.org/wiki/Nike_sweatshops.

9 Read more about this and other Starbucks sustainability commitments here https://stories.starbucks.com/stories/2023/starbucks-furthers-commitment-to-sustainable-dairy/

SUSTAINABILITY LEADERSHIP

10 "Since 2015, adidas has partnered with the environmental organization 'Parley for the Oceans' and uses 'Parley Ocean Plastic' as a replacement for virgin polyester. Parley Ocean Plastic is plastic waste collected from remote islands, beaches, coastal communities, and shorelines, preventing it from polluting the oceans." https://www.adidas-group.com/en/sustainability/environmental-impacts/more-sustainable-materials-and-circular-services

11 Vizcarra, Hana. "Deepwater Horizon Ten Years Later: Reviewing Agency and Regulatory Reforms - Harvard Law School." Harvard Law School - Environmental & Energy Law Program, May 5, 2020. https://eelp.law.harvard.edu/2020/05/deepwater-horizon-ten-years-later-reviewing-agency-and-regulatory-reforms

12 For additional insights on ethical decision making for sustainability see may book Tavanti, Marco. *Sustainability Ethics: Common Good Values for a Better World*. Ethics International Press, Incorporated, 2023.

13 See for example the IKEA Sustainability Report FY22 https://www.ikea.com/global/en/our-business/reports/sustainability-report-fy22-230215/

14 See the 2022 sustainability report at https://www.novonordisk.com/investors/esg.html

15 See the Danone GRI reporting and SDG mapping here. https://www.danone.com/investor-relations/sustainability/reports-and-data.html

16 See L'Oréal's sustainability reporting and commitment to 2030 https://www.loreal.com/en/commitments-and-responsibilities/for-the-planet/

17 For an overview of best practices in sustainability reporting in relation to corporate values and ESG related purposes read Bini, L., Bellucci, M. *Integrated Sustainability Reporting: Linking Environmental and Social Information to Value Creation Processes*. Switzerland: Springer International Publishing, 2020. See also Gbangbola, Kye., Lawler, Nicole. *Gold Standard Sustainability Reporting: A Step-by-Step Guide to Producing Sustainability Reports*. United Kingdom: Taylor & Francis, 2020.

CHAPTER 7: SOCIAL SUSTAINABILITY PRACTICES

1 The social justice is theme frequently addressed in education and it is more recently addressed in its relation to sustainability and environmental justice. For an overview of these relations see Julie Sze. *Sustainability: Approaches to Environmental Justice and Social Power*. United States: NYU Press, 2018.

2 For a comprehensive analysis of the evolution of social sustainability combining notions such as co-evolution of cognition, demography, social organization, technology, and environmental impact see van der Leeuw, Sander. *Social Sustainability, Past and Future: Undoing Unintended Consequences for the Earth's Survival.* United Kingdom: Cambridge University Press, 2020.

3 In the pre-industrial era, organized charities like those led by St. Vincent de Paul in Paris became crucial. They addressed the urgent needs of urban migrants, war widows, and orphans affected by wartime adversities and subsequent famines from deserted farms. Anchored in religious and community values, these efforts highlighted the essential role businesses and leaders had in shaping societal well-being. For a deeper dive into St. Vincent de Paul's leadership, check the Vincentian Heritage Journal, Vol 26 (1) https://via.library.depaul.edu/vhj/vol26/iss1/

4 Jane Addams' renowned memoir sheds light on the hardships of the industrial revolution, offering vivid portrayals of the social destitution of this period. It is important to notice that Jane Addams did not limit herself to serving the community with essential human services. She also became an advocate for child labor laws, better working conditions, and supported striking workers. In 1886, a few years before Jane Addams established Hull House, the Haymarket Affair unfolded in Chicago. What began as a peaceful rally supporting workers' demands for an eight-hour workday escalated into violence, leading to the deaths of multiple police officers and civilians. This pivotal incident significantly influenced the establishment of May Day as a worldwide day of unity for workers. Addams, Jane. *Twenty Years at Hull House: History of the Settlement House and Social Reformism in Chicago's West Side.* Lulu.com, 2018. On the Haymarket see Charles River. *The Haymarket Affair: The History of the Riots in Chicago that Galvanized the Labor Movement.* CreateSpace Independent Publishing Platform, 2017.

5 For the history and evolution of CSR see Andrew Crane. *The Oxford Handbook of Corporate Social Responsibility.* OUP Oxford, 2008. See also Brejning, Jeanette. *Corporate Social Responsibility and the Welfare State: The Historical and Contemporary Role of CSR in the Mixed Economy of Welfare.* Taylor & Francis, 2016. Another good publication with numerous CSR (or lack of it) examples is Heald, Morrell. *The Social Responsibilities of Business: Company and Community, 1900-1960.* United Kingdom: Taylor & Francis, 2018.

6 For excellent overview of these emerging sustainability and CSR paradigms for corporate leadership in modern times see Gabriel Eweje, Ralph Bathurst. *CSR, Sustainability, and Leadership.* United States: Taylor & Francis, 2017. As well as Katarzyna Bachnik, et al. eds. *Corporate Social Responsibility and Sustainability: From Values to Impact.* Taylor & Francis, 2022.

7 To know more about the Salesforce model read Benioff, Marc., Langley, Monica. *Trailblazer: The Power of Business as the Greatest*

Platform for Change. United States: Crown, 2019. For other CSR approaches see Ferrell, O.C.., Thorne, Debbie M.., Ferrell, Linda. *Business & Society: A Strategic Approach to Social Responsibility & Ethics*. United States: SAGE Publications, 2023.

8 The debate over philanthropy and taxation incentives is still an open one in social policies across the Atlantic and beyond. See for example the studies edited by Giedre Lideikyte Huber, Henry Peter. *The Routledge Handbook of Taxation and Philanthropy*. United Kingdom: Taylor & Francis, 2021. Nevertheless, the systemic and policy approach to CSR should be better understood as a more mature expression of responsible leadership, or "transformative CSR 2.0" as in Visser, Wayne. *CSR 2.0: Transforming Corporate Sustainability and Responsibility*. Germany: Springer Berlin Heidelberg, 2013.

9 UNglobalcompact.org. "Poverty | UN Global Compact," September 6, 2023. https://unglobalcompact.org/what-is-gc/our-work/social/poverty

10 World. "UN Report: Global Hunger Numbers Rose to as Many as 828 Million in 2021." Who.int. World Health Organization: WHO, July 6, 2022. https://www.who.int/news/item/06-07-2022-un-report--global-hunger-numbers-rose-to-as-many-as-828-million-in-2021.

11 Feedingamerica.org. "Hunger in America | Feeding America," 2022. https://www.feedingamerica.org/hunger-in-america

12 USA for UNHCR. Refugee Statistics. https://www.unrefugees.org/refugee-facts/statistics/

13 Read more on the SDG 3 challenges due to COVID-19 and other persistent health global challenges including Maternal Mortality Rates (MMR). "Globally, approximately 800 women died every day from pregnancy or childbirth in 2020." United Nations, The Sustainable Development Goals Report 2023: Special Edition. https://unstats.un.org/sdgs/report/2023

14 UN.org. "Factsheet on Persons with Disabilities | United Nations Enable," 2022. https://www.un.org/development/desa/disabilities/resources/factsheet-on-persons-with-disabilities.html.

15 UNICEF DATA. "Child Labor Statistics - UNICEF DATA," June 28, 2023. https://data.unicef.org/topic/child-protection/child-labour/.

16 Nations, United. "Everyone Included – How to End Homelessness | United Nations." United Nations. United Nations, 2021. https://www.un.org/tr/desa/everyone-included-%E2%80%93-how-end-homelessness.

17 Johnson, Stephen. "Corruption Is Costing the Global Economy $3.6 Trillion Dollars Every Year." World Economic Forum, December 13, 2018.

https://www.weforum.org/agenda/2018/12/the-global-economy-loses-3-6-trillion-to-corruption-each-year-says-u-n.

18 UN Women – Headquarters. "Equal Pay for Work of Equal Value," 2022. https://www.unwomen.org/en/news/in-focus/csw61/equal-pay#:~:text=Worldwide%2C%20women%20only%20make%2077,every%20dollar%20earned%20by%20men

19 Unesco.org. "617 Million Children and Adolescents Not Getting the Minimum in Reading and Math," 2023. https://www.unesco.org/en/articles/617-million-children-and-adolescents-not-getting-minimum-reading-and-math.

20 The UN-DESA maintains a list of social development issues with statistics and facts on the objectives and activities in these areas. See https://social.desa.un.org/issues. To review other list of similar priorities with possible solutions also for social sustainability in the Anthropocene read Tavanti, Marco, Liz Wilp and Julie Tavanti. *Surviving the Anthropocene: A Guide to Building Resilience and Thriving.* (Planet Healing Press, 2023).

21 An excellent volume that illustrates the sustainability responsibilities of business leaders globally and according to the United Nations Global Compact is Joanne T. Lawrence, Paul W. Beamish (eds). *Globally Responsible Leadership: Managing According to the UN Global Compact.* United States: SAGE Publications, 2013.

CHAPTER 8: ENVIRONMENTAL SUSTAINABILITY PRACTICES

1 Ray, Siladitya. "2023 Will Be the Hottest Year 'Recorded in Human History,' UN Chief Confirms." *Forbes,* December 1, 2023. https://www.forbes.com/sites/siladityaray/2023/11/30/2023-will-be-the-hottest-year-recorded-in-human-history-un-chief-confirms/?sh=78eab8b95262.

2 UNglobalcompact.org. "Climate Change | UN Global Compact," September 6, 2023. https://unglobalcompact.org/what-is-gc/our-work/environment/climate.

3 Read more on the possible consequences for the climate change scenarios in the IPCC Special Report: Global Warming of 1.5°cch. Chapter 3. Impacts of 1.5°C global warming on natural and human systems https://www.ipcc.ch/sr15/chapter/chapter-3/

4 McKinsey & Company. "The Net-Zero Transition: What It Would Cost, What It Could Bring," 2022. https://www.mckinsey.com/capabilities/sustainability/our-insights/the-net-zero-transition-what-it-would-cost-what-it-could-bring

5 Deloitte. "Deloitte Research Reveals Inaction on Climate Change Could Cost the World's Economy US$178 Trillion by 2070 | Deloitte Global | Press Release."

Deloitte, May 23, 2022. https://www.deloitte.com/global/en/about/press-room/deloitte-research-reveals-inaction-on-climate-change-could-cost-the-world-economy-us-dollar-178-trillion-by-2070.html.

6 Harvard Business Review. "Climate Business | Business Climate," October 2007. https://hbr.org/2007/10/climate-business-_-business-climate

7 Strand, Robert, and Martin Mulvihill. *Levi Strauss & Co.: Driving Adoption of Green Chemistry.* The Berkeley-Haas Case Series. University of California, Berkeley. Haas School of Business, 2016.

8 Urban, Frauke. *Energy and development.* Routledge, 2019. See also: Constable, Edwin C. *Transitioning to Affordable and Clean Energy.* MDPI-Multidisciplinary Digital Publishing Institute, 2022.

9 Nieuwenhuis, Paul., Touboulic, Anne. *Sustainable Consumption, Production and Supply Chain Management: Advancing Sustainable Economic Systems.* United Kingdom: Edward Elgar Publishing, 2021.

10 Doni, Federica., Gasperini, Andrea., Torres Soares, João. *SDG13 - Climate Action: Combatting Climate Change and Its Impacts.* United Kingdom: Emerald Publishing Limited, 2020.

11 Pandey, Umesh Chandra., Nayak, Ranjan., Roka, Krishna., Kumar Jain, Trilok. *SDG14 - Life Below Water: Towards Sustainable Management of Our Oceans.* United Kingdom: Emerald Publishing Limited, 2021.

12 Ahmad Ansari, Nasim., Agus, Cahyono., Kweku Nunoo, Edward. *SDG15 – Life on Land: Towards Effective Biodiversity Management.* United Kingdom: Emerald Publishing Limited, 2021.

13 Prescott, Cindy E. "Perspectives: Regenerative forestry–Managing forests for soil life." *Forest Ecology and Management* 554 (2024): 121674.

14 Olabi, A. G., Tabbi Wilberforce, Khaled Elsaid, Enas Taha Sayed, Hussein M. Maghrabie, and Mohammad Ali Abdelkareem. "Large scale application of carbon capture to process industries–a review." *Journal of Cleaner Production* 362 (2022): 132300.

15 Benjamin W. Redekop, Deborah Rigling Gallagher, Rian Satterwhite. *Innovation in Environmental Leadership: Critical Perspectives.* United Kingdom: Taylor & Francis, 2018.

16 Some see the eco-leadership paradigm as an evolved model of leadership from the dominance "anthropocentric" model to an Earth-centered (environmental) leadership. See Manolopoulos, Mark. *A Theory of Environmental Leadership: Leading for the Earth.* United States: Taylor & Francis, 2021. See also:

Western, Simon. *Leadership: A Critical Text.* United Kingdom: SAGE Publications, 2019.

17 Isaacson, Walter. *Elon Musk.* Simon & Schuster, 2023. See other biographies like Preston, Car. *Elon Musk: Creativity and Leadership Lessons by Elon Musk:* CreateSpace Independent Publishing Platform, 2016; and Vance, Ashlee. *Elon Musk: Tesla, SpaceX, and the Quest for a Fantastic Future.* United Kingdom: HarperCollins, 2015.

18 Some studies suggest that figures like Musk go beyond the "ego" and "eco" duality and fit more in the "intuitive" category. "Leaders who have discovered the power of integrating 'eco', 'ego' and 'intuitive' intelligence drive stronger business performance." Sharon Olivier. *'Eco', 'Ego' and 'Intuitive' Leadership – A new leadership code for the 21st century.* https://www.iedp.com/articles/eco-ego-and-intuitive-leadership-a-new-leadership-code-for-the-21st-century/

CHAPTER 9: PEACE-SECURITY PRACTICES

1 Nations, United. "Global Citizenship | United Nations, Academic Impact" United Nations Website, 2023. https://www.un.org/en/academic-impact/global-citizenship.

2 Oxfam GB. "Oxfam GB | What Is Global Citizenship?" 2023. https://www.oxfam.org.uk/education/who-we-are/what-is-global-citizenship/.

3 SDSN. Indicators and a Monitoring Framework: Launching a data revolution for the Sustainable Development Goals. https://indicators.report/targets/4-7/ .

4 Schattle, Hans. *The Practices of Global Citizenship.* United States: Rowman & Littlefield, 2008.

5 Nigel Dower and John Williams. *Global Citizenship: A Critical Introduction.* Taylor & Francis, 2016.

6 To show other examples of the implications of global citizenship and human rights read Ali A. Abdi, Lynette Shultz. *Educating for Human Rights and Global Citizenship.* United States: State University of New York Press, 2009.

7 UNESCO, Global Citizenship Education. https://en.unesco.org/themes/gced

8 For a more comprehensive review of the human rights-based approach for sustainable development see Tavanti, M. and Sfeir-Younis, A. (2013). "Human Rights Based Sustainable Development: Essential Frameworks for an Integrated Approach." *The International Journal of Sustainability Policy and Practices* 8(3), 21-35. Available at http://www.marcotavanti.com/uploads/9/9/2/1/9921626/2013_tavanti_sfeir-younis-human_rights_based_sustainable_development.pdf

9 Andersen-Rodgers, David., Crawford, Kerry F. *Human Security: Theory and Action.* United Kingdom: Rowman & Littlefield Publishers, 2022.

10 For more in-depth applications and implications of the human security model in relation to capability development and the role of business leadership see Andrew Crabtree. *Sustainability, Capabilities and Human Security.* Germany: Springer International Publishing, 2020.

11 Read more about this initiative in the UNGC website of the initiative: https://unglobalcompact.org/take-action/action/peace read also this report UNCG & PRI. *Responsible Business Advancing Peace: Examples from Companies, Investors & Global Compact Local Networks* (2013). https://unglobalcompact.org/library/491

12 Read more in the UNGC, Blueprint for Business Leadership on the SDGs. 16. Peace, Justice and Strong Institutions. https://blueprint.unglobalcompact.org/sdgs/sdg16

13 UNDP. Business and Human Rights. https://www.undp.org/rolhr/business-and-human-rights

14 United Nations. Office of the High Commissioner for Human Rights. *Guiding Principles on Business and Human Rights: Implementing the United Nations "Protect, Respect and Remedy" Framework.* UN, 2011. https://www.ohchr.org/sites/default/files/documents/publications/guidingprinci plesbusinesshr_en.pdf

15 The UN Global Compact Principles, The Power of Principles – Sustainability begins with a principle-based approach to doing business. https://unglobalcompact.org/what-is-gc/mission/principles

16 View the UNGC topics and resources for human rights in https://unglobalcompact.org/what-is-gc/our-work/social/human-rights

17 Read more in UNGC, Women's Empowerment and Business: 2020 Trends and Opportunities. https://unglobalcompact.org/library/5738 ; See also World Bank. Women, Business and the Law 2023. United States: World Bank Publications.

18 Doyle, Cathal M. *Indigenous Peoples, Title to Territory, Rights and Resources: The Transformative Role of Free Prior and Informed Consent.* United Kingdom: Taylor & Francis, 2014. See also Amy Klemm Verbos, Ana Maria Peredo, Ella Henry. *Indigenous Aspirations and Rights: The Case for Responsible Business and Management.* Taylor & Francis, 2017.

19 Erdem Türkelli, Gamze. *Children's Rights and Business: Governing Obligations and Responsibility.* Cambridge University Press, 2020.

20 Riley, Charles A. *Disability and Business: Best Practices and Strategies for Inclusion.* Lebanon: University Press of New England, 2006. See also Harpur, Paul David. *Ableism at Work: Disablement and Hierarchies of Impairment.* Cambridge University Press, 2019.

CHAPTER 10: PROSPERITY-BUSINESS PRACTICES

1 To explore the role of prosperity in sustainable development, see Bartelmus, Peter L.P. *Sustaining Prosperity, Nature and Wellbeing: What Do the Indicators Tell Us?* United Kingdom: Taylor & Francis, 2018.

2 To understand the circular economy model on contrast with linear economy and its practical implications across sectors see Sillanpaa, Mika., Ncibi, Chaker. *The Circular Economy: Case Studies about the Transition from the Linear Economy.* Netherlands: Elsevier Science, 2019.

3 For a good analysis of sustainable supply chain management (SSCM) in relation to sustainable consumption and production (SCP) see Nieuwenhuis, Paul., Touboulic, Anne. *Sustainable Consumption, Production and Supply Chain Management: Advancing Sustainable Economic Systems.* United Kingdom: Edward Elgar Publishing, 2021.

4 For a good overview of sustainable and green financing, see Thompson, Simon. *Green and Sustainable Finance: Principles and Practice.* United Kingdom: Kogan Page, 2021.

5 Read the book that defined TBL: Elkington, John. *Cannibals with Forks: The Triple Bottom Line of 21st Century Business.* United Kingdom: Capstone, 1999. Read a more recent work by Prof. John Elkington in Elkington, John. *Green Swans: The Coming Boom in Regenerative Capitalism.* United States: Greenleaf Book Group Press, 2020.

6 Antonino Galati, Demetris Vrontis, Evangelos Tsoukatos, S.M.Riad Shams, Yaakov Weber. *Stakeholder Engagement and Sustainability.* United Kingdom: Taylor & Francis, 2019.

7 Christa Liedtke, Ernst Ulrich von Weizsäcker, Jan-Dirk Seiler-Hausmann. *Eco-efficiency and Beyond: Towards the Sustainable Enterprise.* United Kingdom: Taylor & Francis, 2017.

8 Xiang, Joy Y. *Climate Change, Sustainable Development and Cleantech: A Pathway for Developing Countries.* United Kingdom: Edward Elgar Publishing, 2022. See also Goldstein, Jesse. *Planetary Improvement: Cleantech Entrepreneurship and the Contradictions of Green Capitalism.* United Kingdom: Penguin Random House LLC, 2018.

9 Rahul Verma, Vannie Naidoo. *Green Marketing as a Positive Driver Toward Business Sustainability.* United States: IGI Global, 2019. See also Ottman, Jacquelyn. *The New Rules of Green Marketing: Strategies, Tools, and Inspiration for Sustainable Branding.* Taylor & Francis, 2017.

10 Larsson, Mats. *Circular Business Models: Developing a Sustainable Future.* Germany: Springer International Publishing, 2018. See also De Angelis, Roberta. *Business Models in the Circular Economy: Concepts, Examples and Theory.* Germany: Springer International Publishing, 2018.

11 Three key initiatives in integrated sustainability reporting are the Corporate Sustainability Reporting Directive (CSRD), Global Reporting Initiative (GRI), and the International Sustainability Standards Board (ISSB). The CSRD, introduced by the European Union, legally mandates companies to adhere to the European Sustainability Reporting Standards (ESRS), focusing on financial and non-financial performances to strengthen ESG commitments. Understanding the distinct features and objectives of these initiatives is vital for businesses and stakeholders as they navigate the shifting terrain of sustainability reporting. Read an overview in Sustainalize.com. "The Connection between the CSRD, GRI and ISSB Explained – Sustainalize," 2021. https://www.sustainalize.com/news/csrd-compared-to-other-reporting-initiatives/

12 Charl de Villiers, Pei-Chi Kelly Hsiao, Warren Maroun. *The Routledge Handbook of Integrated Reporting.* United Kingdom: Taylor & Francis, 2020.

13 Swedroe, Larry E. *Your Essential Guide to Sustainable Investing: How to live your values and achieve your financial goals with ESG, SRI, and Impact Investing.* United Kingdom: Harriman House Limited, 2022.

14 Anabela Marisa Azul, Luciana Brandli, Pinar Gökcin Özuyar, Tony Wall, Walter Leal Filho. *Responsible Consumption and Production.* Switzerland: Springer International Publishing, 2020. See also Moore Bernstein, Jennifer., O. Vos, Robert. *SDG12 - Sustainable Consumption and Production: A Revolutionary Challenge for the 21st Century.* United Kingdom: Emerald Publishing Limited, 2021.

15 PRME. *Responsible Management Education: The PRME Global Movement.* United Kingdom: Taylor & Francis, 2021.

16 David F. Murphy, Leda Stott. *Partnerships for the Sustainable Development Goals (SDGs).* Switzerland: Mdpi AG, 2021.

17 Haigh, Nardia. *Scenario Planning for Climate Change: A Guide for Strategists.* United Kingdom: Taylor & Francis, 2019.

18 Aarti Gupta. *Transparency in Global Environmental Governance: Critical Perspectives.* United Kingdom: MIT Press, 2014. See also Istemi Demirag. *Corporate*

Social Responsibility, Accountability and Governance: Global Perspectives. United States: Taylor & Francis, 2018.

19 Read more in Knut Johannessen Ims, Lars Jacob Tynes Pedersen. *Business and the Greater Good: Rethinking Business Ethics in an Age of Crisis.* United Kingdom: Edward Elgar Publishing, 2015.

20 Read more about the 'EESG' paradigm in my book Tavanti, Marco. *Developing Sustainability in Organizations: A Values-Based Approach.* Switzerland: Springer International Publishing, 2023.

21 We draw this definition from two connected concepts "sustainable prosperity" and "global sustainability." See Sustainable-prosperity.eu. "Sustainable Prosperity," 2019. https://sustainable-prosperity.eu/sustainable-prosperity/ and Brown, B.J., Hanson, M.E., Liverman, D.M. et al. Global sustainability: Toward definition. *Environmental Management* **11**, 713–719 (1987). https://doi.org/10.1007/BF01867238

22 United Nations. "Transforming Our World: The 2030 Agenda for Sustainable Development | Department of Economic and Social Affairs," 2015. https://sdgs.un.org/2030agenda.

23 To explore these issues, see Jackson, Tim. *Prosperity Without Growth: Foundations for the Economy of Tomorrow.* United Kingdom: Taylor & Francis, 2016.

24 Schultz, Maria, Johan Rockström, Marcus Öhman, Sarah Cornell, Åsa Persson, and Albert Norström. "Human Prosperity Requires Global Sustainability --a Contribution to the Post--2015 Agenda and the Development of Sustainable Development Goals," 2013. https://www.stockholmresilience.org/download/18.416c425f13e06f977b110f4/H uman_prosperity_requires_global_sustainability_Schultz.pdf.

25 World Bank Group. "Shared Prosperity: Monitoring Inclusive Growth." World Bank. World Bank Group, June 23, 2023. https://www.worldbank.org/en/topic/poverty/brief/global-database-of-shared-prosperity.

26 Hoek, M. (2023). *Tech For Good: Imagine Solving the World's Greatest Challenges.* Taylor & Francis.

27 Holzmeyer, C. (2021). Beyond 'AI for Social Good'(AI4SG): social transformations—not tech-fixes—for health equity. *Interdisciplinary Science Reviews, 46*(1-2), 94-125.

28 Paga, P. (2023). *Ethics in Artificial Intelligence and Its Impact on Leadership Styles* (Doctoral dissertation, Alliant International University).

29 Explore more in Daugherty, Paul., Wilson, H. James. *Radically Human: How New Technology Is Transforming Business and Shaping Our Future.* United States: Harvard Business Review Press, 2022.

30 On the "human-centered" leadership paradigm, see Flink, Cheryl., Gross, Liora., Pasmore, William. *Doing Well and Doing Good: Human-centered Digital Transformation Leadership.* Singapore: World Scientific Publishing Company, 2023; and on the paradigm of "humane leadership," read Stephen Sloan. *Humane Leadership.* Humane Leadership Institute, 2020.

CONCLUSION

1 Learn more about these principles in this article and book: Tavanti, M. (2012). Integrity for the Common Good: The Missing Link Between Neoliberalists and the Occupy Discontents. In A. Stachowicz-Stanusch and W. Amann (Eds.), *Integrity in organizations: Building the foundations for humanistic management*, (pp. 82-104). London, UK: Palgrave Macmillan Publishers.

2 Tavanti, Marco and Alfredo Sfeir-Younis. *Sustainability Beyond 2030: Trajectories and Priorities for Our Sustainable Future.* Routledge – The Principles for Responsible Management Education Series, 2024.

3 IDGs. "Inner Development Goals.", 2015. https://www.innerdevelopmentgoals.org/. See other interconnected tools for sustainability leadership development integrated in university programs like Rflect.ch. "Rflect," 2021. https://www.rflect.ch/ . See other inspiring example of tools and pedagogical frameworks that integrate leadership development with sustainability related values like the Management Exercises and the Leadership Exercises. See Stackman, Richard W. and Connor, Kimberly Rae (2016) "The Management Exercises: A Way Forward with Purpose," Jesuit Higher Education: A Journal: Vol. 5: No. 2, Article 7. Available at: https://epublications.regis.edu/jhe/vol5/iss2/7 . See also: Tavanti, Marco (2021, August 12). Leadership Exercises: Jesuit Paradigms for Cura Universalis https://usfblogs.usfca.edu/nonprofit/2021/08/12/leadership-exercises/

Printed in Great Britain
by Amazon